The Icon Programming Language

Second Edition

Ralph E. Griswold and Madge T. Griswold

Department of Computer Science
The University of Arizona
Tucson, Arizona   85721

Prentice Hall Software Series
Brian W. Kernighan, Advisor

PRENTICE HALL, Englewood Cliffs, New Jersey   07632

Library of Congress Cataloging-in-Publication Data

Griswold, Ralph E.
    The Icon programming language / Ralph E. Griswold and Madge T.
  Griswold. -- 2nd ed.
        p.   cm. -- (Prentice Hall software series)
    Includes bibliographical references.
    ISBN 0-13-447889-4
    1. Icon (Computer program language)   I. Griswold, Madge T.
  . II. Title. III. Series.
  QA76.73.I19G74 1990
  005.13'3--dc20   90-30766
                                                          CIP

Editorial/production supervision: Bayani Mendoza de Leon
Manufacturing buyer: Lori Bulwin

Macintosh is a trademark licensed to Apple Computer Inc.
MS-DOS and OS/2 are trademarks of Microsoft Corporation
ProIcon is a trademark of The ProIcon Group
UNIX is a trademark of AT&T Bell Laboratories
VAX and VMS are trademarks of Digital Equipment Corporation

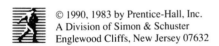

Printed in the United States of America

10 9 8 7 6 5 4 3 2 1

ISBN   0-13-447889-4

Prentice-Hall International (UK) Limited, *London*
Prentice-Hall of Australia Pty. Limited, *Sydney*
Prentice-Hall Canada Inc., *Toronto*
Prentice-Hall Hispanoamericana, S.A., *Mexico*
Prentice-Hall of India Private Limited, *New Delhi*
Prentice-Hall of Japan, Inc., *Tokyo*
Simon & Schuster Asia Pte. Ltd., *Singapore*
Editora Prentice-Hall do Brasil, Ltda., *Rio de Janeiro*

Contents

9   CO-EXPRESSIONS   107

10   DATA TYPES   120

11   INPUT AND OUTPUT   130

Appendixes

Preface

Icon is a high-level, general-purpose programming language with many features for processing symbolic data—strings of characters and structures. Icon is used in applications such as analyzing natural languages, reformatting data, generating computer programs, manipulating formulas, formatting documents, artificial intelligence, rapid prototyping, and many others. It is well suited to situations where quick solutions are needed, those that can be obtained with a minimum of time and programming effort. Icon is extremely useful for "one-shot" programs and for speculative efforts such as computer-generated poetry, in which a proposed problem solution is more heuristic than algorithmic. It also excels for very complicated problems.

Icon has been implemented for many computers and operating systems, including the Amiga, the Atari ST, the IBM 370, the Apple Macintosh, computers using MS-DOS and OS/2, VAX/VMS, and many different UNIX systems. Most of these implementations are in the public domain and are available at a nominal cost. See the ordering information at the end of this book.

Icon has several general characteristics that contribute to its "personality". It is an expression-based language with a syntax similar to Pascal and C. Although Icon programs superficially resemble programs written in these languages, Icon is much more powerful than they are.

In Icon, a string of characters is a value in its own right, as opposed to being treated as an array of characters. Strings may be arbitrarily long, limited only by the amount of available memory. Icon has neither storage declarations nor explicit allocation and deallocation operations; management of storage for strings and other values is handled automatically.

There are no type declarations in Icon. A variable may have values of different types during program execution, and structures can contain values of different types. Type conversion is automatic. For example, a numeric value read into a program as a string is converted automatically to a number if it is used in a numerical operation. Error checking is rigorous; a value that cannot be converted to a required type in a meaningful way causes termination of program execution with a diagnostic message.

Although many of Icon's control structures resemble those of other programming languages, Icon uses the concept of the success or failure of a computation, not Boolean values, to drive control structures. For example, in

if find(s1, s2) then write ("found") else write("not found")

the expression find(s1,s2) succeeds if the string s1 exists in s2 but fails otherwise. The success or failure of this expression determines which action is taken. This mechanism allows an expression to produce a meaningful value if there is one and at the same time to control program flow, as in

if i := find(s1, s2) then write(i)

The use of the natural concept of failure, as distinct from an error, allows many other computations to be phrased in natural and concise ways. For example,

while line := read() do
    process(line)

reads lines of input and processes them until an end of file is encountered, which causes read() to fail, terminating the while loop.

Many computations can have more than one result. Consider

find("th", "this thesis is the best one")

Here "th" occurs at three positions in the second argument. In most programming languages, such a situation is resolved by selecting one position for the value of the function. This interpretation discards potentially useful information. Icon generalizes the concept of expression evaluation to allow an expression to produce more than one result. Such expressions are called *generators*. The results of a generator are produced in sequence as determined by context. One context is iteration:

every *expr1* do *expr2*

which evaluates *expr2* for every result produced by *expr1*. An example is

every i := find(s1, s2) do write(i)

which writes all the positions at which s1 occurs in s2.

In many computations, several alternatives are possible. Some combinations of these alternatives may lead to successful computations, while other combinations may not. Icon uses the concepts of success and failure together with generators to perform *goal-directed* evaluation. If a computation fails, alternative values from generators are produced automatically in an attempt to produce a successful result. Consider, for example,

> if find(s1, s2) = 10 then *expr1* else *expr2*

The intuitive meaning of this expression is: "If s1 occurs in s2 at a position that is equal to 10, then evaluate *expr1*; otherwise evaluate *expr2*". This is, in fact, exactly what this expression does in Icon.

Neither generators nor goal-directed evaluation depends on any particular feature for processing strings; find() is useful pedagogically, but there are many possibilities in numerical computation. Furthermore, Icon allows programmers to write their own generators, and there is no limit to the range of their applicability.

Since Icon is oriented toward the processing of textual or symbolic data, it has a large repertoire of functions for operating on strings, of which find() is only one example. Icon also has a high-level *string scanning* facility. String scanning establishes a *subject* that is the focus for string-processing operations. Scanning operations apply to this subject. As operations on the subject take place, the *position* in the subject may be changed. A scanning expression has the form

> s ? *expr*

where s is the subject and *expr* performs scanning operations on this subject.

Matching functions change the position in the subject and produce the substring of the subject that they "match". For example, tab(i) moves the position to i and produces the substring between the previous and new positions. A simple example of string scanning is

> text ? write(tab(find("the")))

which writes the initial substring of text up to the first occurrence of "the". The function find() is the same as the one given earlier, but in string scanning its second argument need not be given explicitly. Note that any operation, such as write(), can appear in string scanning.

Icon provides several types of structures for organizing data in different ways. Lists consist of ordered sequences of values that can be referenced by position. Lists also can be used as stacks and queues. Sets are unordered collections of values that can be used to group values by attributes. Set membership can be tested and values can be inserted into and deleted from sets as needed. The usual set operators of union, intersection, and difference are available, as well. Tables provide associative lookup in which subscripting with a key produces the corresponding value. Records provide reference to values by field name. Records also provide programmer-defined data types.

These are just the highlights of Icon; there is much more to the language.

Icon, like many other programming languages, has evolved over a period of time. The first edition of this book described Version 5 of Icon. This Second Edition describes Version 8. It not only includes descriptions of features that have been added since Version 5, but it also is completely revised. It places important material earlier in the text than the first edition, and it also contains many improvements based on experience in teaching and using Icon.

The reader of this book should have a general understanding of the concepts of computer programming languages and a familiarity with the current terminology in the field. Programming experience with other programming languages, such as Pascal or C, is desirable.

This book is designed for both self-study and classroom use. There are exercises at the end of every chapter. Some exercises are comparatively simple and are useful for drill. Others are more substantial, including significant programming projects.

The first eleven chapters of this book describe the features of Icon. Chapter 12 provides information about running an Icon program. The last five chapters describe programming techniques and provide examples.

Appendix A summarizes the syntax of Icon and Appendix B lists characters and graphics. Appendix C is a reference manual that describes each Icon operation briefly. Error messages are listed in Appendix D and differences among implementations of Icon are described in Appendix E. Appendix F includes a number of larger example programs, and Appendix G contains solutions to selected exercises.

Acknowledgments

Many persons have been involved in the design and implementation of Icon. The principal contributors are Ralph Griswold, Dave Hanson, Tim Korb, Cary Coutant, Steve Wampler, Bill Mitchell, Gregg Townsend, and Ken Walker. In addition, persons too numerous to acknowledge individually, contributed ideas, assisted in parts of the implementation, and made suggestions that shaped the final result.

Several of the program examples used in this book were derived from programs written by students in computer science courses at The University of Arizona. Bob Alexander, Gregg Townsend, Ken Walker, and Steve Wampler contributed program material to Appendix F.

The authors gratefully acknowledge the assistance of the persons who read draft copies of this book and provided many helpful suggestions on its content: Mark Emmer, Bill Griswold, Clint Jeffery, Gregg Townsend, and Ken Walker.

The reference material in Appendix C is adapted from *The ProIcon Programming Language for Apple Macintosh Computers* [1] and is used here by permission of The Bright Forest Company.

The support of the National Science Foundation was instrumental in the original conception of Icon and has been invaluable in its subsequent development.

Ralph E. Griswold and Madge T. Griswold

1

Getting Started

This chapter introduces a few basic concepts of Icon — enough to get started. Subsequent chapters discuss these concepts in greater detail.

PROGRAM STRUCTURE

A good way to learn a programming language is to write programs. There is a fine tradition for beginning a new programming language by writing a program that produces a greeting. In Icon this takes the form:

```
procedure main()
   write("Hello world")
end
```

This program writes Hello world to the output file.

The reserved words procedure and end bracket a procedure declaration. The procedure name is main. Every program must have a procedure with the name main; this is where program execution begins. Most programs, except the simplest ones, consist of several procedures, each corresponding to a different computational component.

Procedure declarations contain expressions that are evaluated when the procedure is called. The call of the function write simply writes its argument, a string that is given literally in enclosing quotation marks. When execution of a procedure reaches its end, it returns. When the main procedure returns, program execution stops.

To illustrate the use of procedures, the preceding program can be divided into two procedures as follows:

```
procedure main()
  hello()
end

procedure hello()
  write("Hello world")
end
```

Note that main and hello are procedures, while write is a function that is built into the Icon language. Procedures and functions are used in the same way. The only distinction between the two is that functions are built into Icon, while procedures are declared in programs. The procedure hello writes the greeting and returns to main. The procedure main then returns, terminating program execution.

Expressions in the body of a procedure are evaluated in the order in which they appear. Therefore, the program

```
procedure main()
  write("Hello world")
  write("   this is a new beginning")
end
```

writes two lines:

```
Hello world
   this is a new beginning
```

Procedures may have parameters, which are given in a list enclosed in the parentheses that follow the procedure name in the declaration. For example, the program

```
procedure main()
  greet("Hello", "world")
end

procedure greet(what, who)
  write(what)
  write(who)
end
```

writes

```
Hello
world
```

Like most programming languages, Icon has both values and variables that have values. This is illustrated by

```
procedure main()
  line := "Hello world"
  write(line)
end
```

The operation

```
line := "Hello world"
```

assigns the value "Hello world" to the identifier line, which is a variable. The value of line is then passed to the function write.

There are 256 different characters that may occur in strings. Strings may be written literally as in the example above and they can be computed by a variety of operations. There is no limit on the length of a string except the amount of memory available. The empty string, given literally by "", contains no characters; its length is 0.

Identifiers must begin with a letter or underscore, which may be followed by other letters, digits, and underscores. Upper- and lowercase letters are distinct. Examples of identifiers are comp, Label, test10, and entry_value. There are other kinds of variables besides identifiers; these are described in later chapters.

Note that there is no declaration for the identifier line. Scope declarations, which are described in Chapter 8, are optional for local identifiers. In the absence of a scope declaration, an identifier is assumed to be local to the procedure in which it occurs, as is the case with line. Local identifiers are created when a procedure is called and are destroyed when the procedure returns. No other procedure call can access these identifiers.

Most identifiers are local. The default to local is an example of a design philosophy of Icon: Common usages usually default automatically without the need for the programmer to write them out.

Icon has no type or storage declarations. Any variable can have any type of value. The correctness of types is checked when operations are performed. Storage for values is provided automatically. The programmer need not be concerned about it.

The character # in a program signals the beginning of a comment. The # and the remaining characters on the line are ignored when the program is compiled. An example of the use of comments is

```
# This procedure illustrates the use of parameters. The
# first parameter provides the message, while the second
# parameter specifies the recipient.
#
procedure greet(what, who)
   write(what)                    # message
   write(who)                     # recipient
end
```

Note that the end of a line terminates a comment. Each line of a multiline comment must have a #.

If a # occurs in a quoted literal, it stands for itself and does not signal the beginning of a comment. Therefore,

```
write("#======#")
```

writes

```
#======#
```

SUCCESS AND FAILURE

The function read() reads a line from the input file. For example,

```
write(read())
```

reads a line and writes it out. Note that the value produced by read() is the argument of write().

The function read() is one of a number of expressions in Icon that may either *succeed* or *fail*. The term *outcome* is used to describe the result of evaluating an expression, whether it is success or failure. If an expression succeeds, it produces a value, such as a line from the input file. If an expression fails, it produces no value. In the case of read(), failure occurs when the end of the input file is reached.

Expressions that may succeed or fail are called *conditional expressions*. Comparison operations, for example, are conditional expressions. The expression

```
count > 0
```

succeeds if the value of count is greater than 0 but fails if the value of count is not greater than 0.

As a general rule, failure occurs if a relation does not hold or if an operation cannot be performed but is not actually erroneous. For example, failure occurs when an attempt is made to read but when the end of the input file has been reached. Failure is an important part of the design philosophy of Icon. It accounts for the fact that there are situations in which operations cannot be performed — but that these situations are not erroneous. It corresponds to many real-world situations and allows programs to be formulated in terms of attempts to perform computations, the recognition of failure, and the possibility of alternatives.

Two other conditional expressions are find(s1, s2) and match(s1, s2). These functions succeed if s1 is a *substring* of s2 but fail otherwise. A substring is a string that occurs in another string. The function find(s1, s2) succeeds if s1 occurs anywhere in s2, while match(s1, s2) succeeds only if s1 is an *initial* substring that occurs at the beginning of s2. For example,

    find("on", "slow motion")

succeeds, since "on" is contained in "slow motion", but

    find("on", "radio noise")

fails, since "on" is not a *substring* of "radio noise" because of the intervening blank between the "o" and the "n". Similarly,

    match("on", "slow motion")

fails, since "on" does not occur at the beginning of "slow motion". On the other hand,

    match("slo", "slow motion")

succeeds.

If an expression that fails is an argument in another expression, the other expression fails also, since there is no value for its argument. For example, in

    write(read())

if read() fails, there is nothing to write. The function write() is not called and the whole expression fails.

The context in which failure occurs is important. Consider

    line := read()
    write(line)

If read() succeeds, the value it produces is assigned to line. If read() fails, however, no new value is assigned to line, because read() is an argument of the assignment operation. There is no value to assign to line if read() fails, so no assignment is performed. In this case the value of line is left unchanged. The assignment is *conditional* on the success of read(). Since

> line := read()

and

> write(line)

are separate expressions, the failure of read() does not affect write(line); it just writes whatever value line had previously. An expression, such as write(line), that is isolated from the effects of another expression is called a *bounded expression*.

CONTROL STRUCTURES

Control structures use the success or failure of an expression to govern the evaluation of other expressions. For example,

> while line := read() do
>   write(line)

repeatedly evaluates read() in a loop. Each time read() succeeds, the value it produces is assigned to line and write(line) is evaluated to write that value. When read() fails, however, the assignment operation fails and the loop terminates. In other words, the success or failure of the expression that follows while controls evaluation of the expression that follows do.

Note that assignment is an expression. It can be used anywhere that any expression is allowed.

Words like while and do, which distinguish control structures, are reserved and cannot be used as identifiers. A complete list of reserved words is given in Appendix A.

Another frequently used control structure is if-then-else, which selects one of two expressions to evaluate, depending on the success or failure of a conditional expression. For example,

> if count > 0 then sign := 1 else sign := −1

assigns 1 to sign if the value of count is greater than 0, but assigns −1 to sign otherwise. The else clause is optional, as in

> if count > 0 then sign := 1

PROCEDURES

Procedures are the major logical units of a program. Each procedure in a program typically performs a separate logical task. Some examples follow.

The following procedure prints only the lines that contain the string s:

```
procedure locate(s)
  while line := read() do
    if find(s, line) then write(line)
end
```

For example,

```
procedure main()
  locate("fancy")
end
```

writes all the lines of the input file that contain an occurrence of the string **"fancy"**.

This procedure is more useful if it also writes the numbers of the lines that contain **s**. To do this, it is necessary to count each line as it is read:

```
procedure locate(s)
  lineno := 0
  while line := read() do {
    lineno := lineno + 1
    if find(s, line) then write(lineno, ": ", line)
    }
end
```

The braces in this procedure enclose a *compound expression*, which in this case consists of two expressions. One expression increments the line number and the other writes the line if it contains the desired substring. Compound expressions must be used wherever one expression is expected by Icon's syntax but several are needed.

Note that **write()** has three arguments in this procedure. The function **write()** can be called with many arguments; the values of the arguments are written one after another, all on the same line. In this case there is a line number, followed by a colon and a blank, followed by the line itself.

To illustrate the use of this procedure, consider an input file that consists of the following song from Shakespeare's play *The Merchant of Venice*:

Tell me, where is fancy bred,
Or in the heart or in the head?
How begot, how nourished?
    Reply, reply.
It is engender'd in the eyes,
With gazing fed; and fancy dies
In the cradle where it lies:
    Let us all ring fancy's knell;
I'll begin it, – Ding, dong, bell.

The lines written by locate("fancy") are:

> 1: Tell me, where is fancy bred,
> 6: With gazing fed; and fancy dies
> 8:   Let us all ring fancy's knell;

This example illustrates one of the more important features of Icon: the automatic conversion of values from one type to another. The first argument of write() in this example is an integer. Since write() expects to write strings, this integer is converted to a string; it is not necessary to specify conversion. This is another example of a default, which makes programs shorter and saves the need to specify routine actions where they clearly are the natural thing to do.

Like other expressions, procedure calls may produce values. The reserved word return is used to indicate a value to be returned from a procedure call. For example,

```
procedure countm(s)
  count := 0
  while line := read() do
    if match(s, line) then count := count + 1
  return count
end
```

produces a count of the number of input lines that begin with s.

A procedure call also can fail. This is indicated by the reserved word fail, which causes the procedure call to terminate but fail instead of producing a value. For example,

```
procedure countm(s)
  count := 0
  while line := read() do
    if match(s, line) then count := count + 1
  if count > 0 then return count else fail
end
```

produces a count of the number of lines that begin with s, provided that the count is greater than 0. The procedure fails, however, if no line begins with the string s.

EXPRESSION SYNTAX

Icon has several types of expressions, as illustrated in the preceding sections. A literal such as "Hello world" is an expression that designates a value literally. Identifiers, such as line, are also expressions.

Function calls, such as

write(line)

and procedure calls, such as

greet("Hello", "world")

are expressions in which parentheses separate the operation to be performed from its arguments.

Operators are used to provide a concise, easily recognizable syntax for common operations. For example, $-i$ produces the negative of i, while $i + j$ produces the sum of i and j. Operators and functions essentially are equivalent; the difference is in their syntax. The term argument is used for both operators and functions to describe the expressions on which they operate.

Infix operations, such as $i + j$ and $i * j$, have precedences that determine which operations apply to which arguments when they are used in combination. For example,

i + j * k

groups as

i + (j * k)

since multiplication has higher precedence than addition, as is conventional in numerical computation.

Associativity determines how expressions group when there are several occurrences of the same operation in combination. For example, subtraction associates from left to right so that

i − j − k

groups as

(i − j) − k

On the other hand, exponentiation associates from right to left so that

i ^ j ^ k

groups as

i ^ (j ^ k)

Assignment also associates from right to left.

The precedences and associativities of various operations are mentioned as the operations are introduced in subsequent chapters. Appendix A summarizes the precedences and associativities of all operations.

Parentheses can be used to group expressions differently from the way they would group according to their precedence and associativity, as in

```
(i + j) * k
```

Since there are many operations in Icon with various precedences and associativities, it is safest to use parentheses to assure that operations group in the desired way, especially for operations that are not used frequently.

Where the expressions in a compound expression appear on the same line, they must be separated by semicolons. For example,

```
while line := read() do {
    count := count + 1
    if find(s, line) then write(line)
    }
```

also can be written as

```
while line := read() do
    {count := count + 1; if find(s, line) then write(line)}
```

Programs usually are easier to read if the expressions in a compound expression are written on separate lines, however.

Unlike many programming languages, Icon has no statements; it just has expressions. Even control structures, such as

```
if expr1 then expr2 else expr3
```

are expressions. The outcome of such a control structure is the outcome of *expr2* or *expr3*, whichever is selected. Even though control structures are expressions, they usually are not used in such a way that the values they produce are important. That is, they usually stand alone as if they were statements, as illustrated by the examples in this chapter.

Keywords, consisting of the character & followed by one of a number of specific words, are used to designate operations that require no arguments. For example, the value of &time is the number of milliseconds that have elapsed since the beginning of program execution.

Any argument of a function, procedure, operator, or control structure may be any expression, however complicated that expression is. There are no distinctions among the kinds of expressions; any kind of expression can be used in any context where an expression is legal. However, there are limitations on the legal values of arguments.

NOTATION AND TERMINOLOGY

In describing what operators and functions do, the fact that their arguments may be syntactically complicated is not significant. It is the values produced by these expressions that are important.

Icon has several types of data: strings, integers, real numbers, and so forth. Many functions and operations require specific types of data for their arguments. Single letters, sometimes followed by numbers, are used in this book to indicate the arguments of operations and functions. The letters are chosen to indicate the types that operations and functions expect. These letters usually are taken from the first character of the type name. For example, i indicates an argument that is expected to be an integer, while s indicates an argument that is expected to be a string. For example, −i indicates the operation of computing the negative of the integer i, while i1 + i2 indicates the operation of adding the integers i1 and i2. This notation is extended following usual mathematical conventions, so that j and k also are used to indicate integers. Other types are indicated in a similar fashion. Finally, x and y are used for arguments that are of unknown type or may have one of several types. Chapter 10 discusses types in more detail.

This notation does not mean that arguments of operations and functions must be written as identifiers. As mentioned previously, any argument of any operation or function can be an expression, no matter how complicated that expression is. The use of letters to stand for expressions is just a device that is used in this book for conciseness and to emphasize the required data types of arguments. These are only conventions. The letters in identifiers have no meaning to Icon. For example, the value of s in a program could be an integer. In situations where the type produced by an expression is not important, the notation *expr, expr1, expr2,* ... is used. Therefore,

> while *expr1* do *expr2*

emphasizes that the control structure is concerned with the evaluation of its arguments, not with their values or their types.

In describing functions, phrases such as "the function match(s1, s2) ... " are used to indicate the name of a function and the number and types of its arguments. Strictly speaking, match(s1, s2) is not a function but rather a *call* of the function match. The shorter phraseology is used when there can be no confusion about its meaning. In describing function calls in places where the specific arguments are not relevant, the arguments are omitted, as in write(). Similarly, other readily understood abbreviations are used. For example, "an integer between 1 and i" sometimes is used in place of "an integer between 1 and the value of i".

As illustrated by examples in this chapter, different typefaces are used to distinguish program material and terminology. The sans-serif typeface denotes literal program text, such as **procedure** and **read**(). Italics are used for expressions in general, such as *expr*.

EXERCISES

1.1*   Modify the procedure **locate**(s) so that it produces a count of the number of lines that are written but fails if no lines are written.

1.2   Why does subtraction associate from left to right? Why is it more useful for assignment to associate from right to left than from left to right?

* Appendix G contains solutions for exercises that are marked by asterisks.

2

Expressions

The evaluation of expressions causes the computations that are performed during program execution. Roughly speaking, anything that has a computational outcome is an expression. To program in Icon, it is not necessary to know what computations its expressions perform. Some expressions, like arithmetic operations, are obvious. Icon also has a large repertoire of functions, each of which performs a different kind of computation.

The most important aspect of expression evaluation in Icon is that the outcome of evaluating an expression may be a single result, no result at all (failure), or a sequence of results (generation). The possibilities of failure and generation distinguish Icon from most other programming languages and give it its unusual expressive capability. These possibilities also make expression evaluation a more important topic than it is in most other programming languages.

The possibilities of failure and generation are not just important for specific operators and functions. There are several control structures that are specifically concerned with failure and generation. This chapter introduces the basic concepts of expression evaluation in Icon and describes the control structures that are used most frequently. Chapter 7 contains additional information about expression evaluation.

SEQUENTIAL EVALUATION

In the absence of control structures, expressions in an Icon procedure are evaluated in the order they appear; this is called sequential evaluation. Where expressions are nested, inner expressions are evaluated first to provide values for outer ones. For example, in

```
i := k + j
write(i)
```

the values of k and j are added to provide the value assigned to i. That is,

```
i := k + j
```

groups as

```
i := (k + j)
```

Next, the value of i is written. The two lines also could be written

```
write(i := k + j)
```

although the former version is more readable and generally better style.

The sequential nature of expression evaluation is familiar and natural. It is mentioned here because of the possibilities of failure and generation. Consider, for example

```
i := find(s1, s2)
write(i)
```

As shown in Chapter 1, find(s1, s2) may produce a single result or it may fail. It may also generate a sequence of results.

The single-result case is easy — it is just like

```
i := k + j
```

(Addition always produces a single result.) In

```
i := find(s1, s2)
```

suppose that find(s1, s2) fails. There is no value to assign to i and the assignment is not performed. The effect is as if the assignment failed because one of its arguments failed. In fact, the failure in evaluation of an argument just prevents computation from proceeding in the enclosing expression. Consequently, in

```
i := find(s1, s2)
write(i)
```

if find(s1, s2) fails, i is not changed, and execution continues with write(i), which writes the value i had prior to the evaluation of these two lines. It generally is not good programming practice to let possible failure go undetected. This subject is discussed in more detail later.

Since a substring can occur in a string at more than one place, find(s1, s2) can have more than one possible result. The results are generated, as needed, in order from left to right.

In the example above, assignment needs only one result, so the first result is assigned to i and sequential execution continues (writing the newly assigned value of i). The other possible results of find(s1, s2) are not produced.

The next section illustrates situations in which a generator may produce more than one result.

GOAL-DIRECTED EVALUATION

Failure during the evaluation of an expression causes previously evaluated generators to produce more results. This is called *goal-directed evaluation*, since failure of a part of an expression does not necessarily cause the entire expressions to fail; instead other possibilities (additional values from generators) are tried in an attempt to find a combination of values that makes the entire expression succeed.

Goal-directed evaluation is illustrated by the following expression

if find(s1, s2) > 10 then write("good location")

Suppose s1 occurs in s2 at positions 2, 8, 12, 20, and 30. The first value produced by find(s1, s2) is 2, and the comparison is:

2 > 10

This comparison fails, which causes find(s1, s2) to produce its next value, 8. The comparison again fails, and find(s1, s2) produces 12. The comparison now succeeds and good location is written. Note that find(s1, s2) does not produce the values 20 or 30. As in assignment, once the comparison succeeds, no more values are needed.

Observe how natural the formulation

find(s1, s2) > 10

is. It embodies in a concise way a conceptually simple computation. Try formulating this computation in Pascal or C for comparison. This method of expression evaluation is used very frequently in Icon programs. It is a large part of what makes Icon programs short and easy to write. It is not necessary to think about all the details of what is going on.

Failure may cause expression evaluation to go back to a previously evaluated expression. For example, in the preceding example, failure of a comparison operation caused evaluation to return to a function that had already produced a value. This is called *control backtracking*. Control backtracking only happens in the presence of generators. An expression that produces a value and may be capable of producing another *suspends*. Instead of just producing a value and "going away", it keeps track of what it was doing and remains "in the background" in case it is needed again. Failure causes a suspended generator to be *resumed* so that it may produce another value. If a generator is resumed but has no more values, it is as if it had failed. While the term *failure* is used to describe an expression that produces no value at all, a resumed generator that does not produce a value (*failed resumption*) has the same effect on expression evaluation — there is no value to use in an outer expression.

Note that when an outer computation succeeds there may be suspended generators. When this happens, they are discarded, since there is no longer any need for them.

ITERATION

It is not necessary to rely on failure and goal-directed evaluation to produce several values from a generator. In fact, there are many situations in which all (or most) of the values of a generator are needed, but without any natural concept of failure. The *iteration* control structure

> every *expr1* do *expr2*

is provided for these situations. In this control structure, *expr1* is first evaluated and then repeatedly resumed to produce all its values. For every value produced by *expr1*, *expr2* is evaluated.

For example,

> every i := find(s1, s2) do
>   write(i)

writes all the values produced by find(s1, s2). Note that the repeated resumption of find(s1, s2) provides a sequence of values for assignment. Thus, as many assignments are performed as there are values for find(s1, s2).

The do clause is optional. This expression can be written more compactly as

> every write(find(s1, s2))

INTEGER SEQUENCES

Icon has several expressions that generate sequences of values. One of the most useful is

> i to j by k

which generates the integers from i to j in increments of k. The by clause is optional; if it is omitted, the increment is 1. For example,

> every i := 1 to 10 do
>   write(i ^ 2)

writes the squares 1, 4, 9, 16, 25, 36, 49, 64, 81, and 100.

Note that iteration in combination with integer generation corresponds to the for control structure found in many programming languages. There are, however, many other ways iteration and integer generation can be used in combination. For example, the expression above can be written more compactly as

   every write((1 to 10) ^ 2)

The function seq(i, j) generates a sequence of integers starting at i with increments of j, but with no upper bound (except the maximum size that an integer may have).

ALTERNATION

Since a generator may produce a sequence of values and those values may be used in goal-directed evaluation and iteration, it is natural to extend the concept of a sequence of values to apply to more than one expression. The *alternation* control structure,

   expr1 | *expr2*

does this by first producing the values for *expr1* and then the values for *expr2*. For example,

   0 | 1

generates 0 and 1. Thus, in

   if i = (0 | 1) then write("okay")

okay is written if the value of i is either 0 or 1. The arguments in an alternation expression may themselves be generators. For example,

   (1 to 3) | (3 to 1 by −1)

generates 1, 2, 3, 3, 2, 1.

When alternation is used in goal-directed evaluation, such as

   if i = (0 | 1) then write(i)

it reads naturally as "if i equals 0 *or* 1, then …". On the other hand, if alternation is used in iteration, as in

   every i := (0 | 1) do
      write(i)

it reads more naturally as "i is assigned 0 *then* 1".

The *or/then* distinction reflects the usual purpose of alternation in the two different contexts and suggests how to use alternation to formulate computations.

CONJUNCTION

As explained earlier, an expression succeeds only if all of its component subexpressions succeed. For example, in

find(s1, s2) = find(s1, s3)

the comparison expression fails if either of its arguments fails. The same is true of

find(s1, s2) + find(s1, s3)

and, in fact, of all operations and functions. Often it is useful to know if two or more expressions succeed, although their values may be irrelevant. This operation is provided by *conjunction*,

expr1 & *expr2*

which succeeds (and produces the value of *expr2*) only if both *expr1* and *expr2* succeed. For example,

if find(s1, s2) & find(s1, s3) then write ("okay")

writes okay only if s1 is a substring of both s2 and s3.

Note that conjunction is just an operation that performs no computation (other than returning the value of its second argument). It simply binds two expressions together into a compound expression in which the components are mutually involved in goal-directed evaluation. Conjunction normally is read as *and*. For example,

if (i > 100) & (i = j) then write(i)

might be read as "if i is greater than 100 *and* i equals j ..."

Note also that in goal-directed contexts,

expr1 | *expr2* | ... | *exprn*

and

expr1 & *expr2* & ... & *exprn*

correspond closely to logical disjunction and conjunction, respectively. Thus, *and/or* conditions can be easily composed using conjunction and alternation.

LOOPS

There are two control structures that evaluate an expression repeatedly, depending on the success or failure of a control expression:

> while *expr1* do *expr2*

described earlier, and

> until *expr1* do *expr2*

which repeatedly evaluates *expr2* until *expr1* succeeds. In both cases *expr1* is evaluated before *expr2*. The do clauses are optional in while and until expressions. For example,

> while write(read())

copies the input file to the output file.

A related control structure is

> not *expr*

which fails if *expr* succeeds, but succeeds if *expr* fails. Therefore,

> until *expr1* do *expr2*

and

> while not *expr1* do *expr2*

are equivalent. The form that is used should be the one that is most natural to the situation in which it occurs.

The while and until control structures are loops. Loops normally are terminated only by the failure or success of their control expressions. Sometimes it is necessary to exit from a loop, independent of the evaluation of its control expression.

The break expression causes immediate termination of the loop in which it occurs. The following program illustrates the use of the break expression:

```
procedure main()
  count := 0
  while line := read() do
    if match("stop", line) then break
    else count := count + 1
  write(count)
end
```

This program counts the number of lines in the input file up to a line beginning with the substring "stop".

Sometimes it is useful to skip to the beginning of the control expression of a loop. This can be accomplished by the next expression. Although the next expression is rarely needed in simple cases, the following example illustrates its use:

```
procedure main()
   while line := read() do
      if match("comment", line) then next
      else write(line)
end
```

This program copies the input file to the output file, omitting lines that begin with the substring "comment".

The break and next expressions may appear anywhere in a loop but apply only to the innermost loop in which they occur. For example, if loops are nested, a break expression exits only from the loop in which it appears, not from any outer loops. The use of a break expression to exit from an inner loop is illustrated by the following program, which copies the input file to the output file, omitting lines between those that begin with "skip" and "end", inclusive.

```
procedure main()
   while line := read() do
      if match("skip", line) then {        # check for lines to skip
         while line := read() do           # skip loop
            if match("end", line) then break
         }
      else write(line)                     # write line in main loop
end
```

Another way to exit from a loop (or any expression) is by exit(), which terminates program execution.

There is one other looping control structure:

```
repeat expr
```

This control structure evaluates *expr* repeatedly, regardless of whether it succeeds or fails. It is useful when the controlling expression cannot be placed conveniently at the beginning of a loop. A repeat loop can be terminated by a break expression.

Consider an input file that is organized into several sections, each of which is terminated by a line beginning with "end". The following program writes the number of lines in each section and then the number of sections.

```
procedure main()
  setcount := 0
  repeat {
    setcount := setcount + 1
    linecount := 0
    while line := read() do {
      linecount := linecount + 1
      if match("end", line) then {
        write(linecount)
        break
        }
      }
    if linecount = 0 then break        # end of file
    }
  write(setcount, "sections")
end
```

The outcome of a loop, once it is complete, is failure. That is, a loop itself produces no value. In most cases, this failure is not important, since loops usually are not part of larger expressions.

SELECTION EXPRESSIONS

The commonest form of selection occurs when one or another expression is evaluated, depending on the success or failure of a control expression. As described in Chapter 1, this is performed by

> if *expr1* then *expr2* else *expr3*

which evaluates *expr2* if *expr1* succeeds but evaluates *expr3* if *expr1* fails.

If there are several possibilities, if-then-else expressions can be chained together, as in

```
if match("begin", line) then depth := depth + 1
else if match("end", line) then depth := depth − 1
else other := other + 1
```

The else portion of this control structure is optional:

> if *expr1* then *expr2*

evaluates *expr2* only if *expr1* succeeds. The not expression is useful in this abbreviated if-then form:

if not *expr1* then *expr2*

which evaluates *expr2* only if *expr1* fails.

While if-then-else selects an expression to evaluate, depending on the success or failure of the control expression, it is often useful to select an expression to evaluate, depending on the *value* of a control expression. The case control structure provides selection that is based on a value and has the form

```
case expr of {
    case-clause
        .
        .
        .
}
```

The expression after case is a control expression whose value controls the selection. There can be several case clauses. Each has the form

expr1 : *expr2*

The value of the control expression is compared with the value of *expr1* in each case clause in the order in which the case clauses appear. If the values are the same, the corresponding *expr2* is evaluated, and its outcome becomes the outcome of the entire case expression. If the values of the control expression and *expr1* are different, or if *expr1* fails, the next case clause is tried.

There is also an optional default clause that has the form

default : *expr2*

If no comparison of the value of the control expression with *expr1* is successful, *expr2* in the default clause is evaluated, and its outcome becomes the outcome of the case expression. The default clause may appear anywhere in the list of case clauses, but it is evaluated last. Since the default clause is evaluated last, it is good programming style to place it last in the list of case clauses.

Once an expression is selected, its outcome becomes the value of the case expression. Subsequent case clauses are not processed, even if the selected expression fails. A case expression itself fails if (1) its control expression fails, (2) if the selected expression fails, or (3) if no expression is selected.

Any kind of value can be used in the control expression. For example,

```
case s of {
    "begin"    : depth := depth + 1
    "end"      : depth := depth − 1
    }
```

increments depth if the value of s is the string **"begin"** but decrements depth if the value of s is the string "end". Since there is no default clause, this case expression fails if the value of s is neither "begin" nor "end". In this case, the value of depth is not changed.

The expression in a case clause does not have to be a constant. For example,

```
case i of {
    j + 1       : write("high")
    j – 1       : write("low")
    j           : write("even")
    default     : write("out of range")
    }
```

writes one of four strings, depending on the relative values of i and j.

The expression in a case clause can be a generator. If the value it produces is not the same as the value of the control expression, it is resumed for other possible values. Consequently, alternation provides a useful way of combining case clauses. An example is:

```
case i of {
    0           : write("at origin")
    1 | –1      : write("near origin")
    default     : write("not near origin")
    }
```

Since the outcome of a case expression is the outcome of the selected expression, it sometimes is possible to "factor out" common components in case clauses. For example, the case expression above can be written as

```
write(case i of {
    0           : "at origin"
    1 | –1      : "near origin"
    default     : "not near origin"
    })
```

Such constructions can be difficult to read and should be used with restraint.

COMPARISON OPERATIONS

A comparison operation such as

```
i = j
```

produces the value of its right argument if it succeeds. For example

```
write(find(s1, s2) = find(s3, s4))
```

writes the common position if there is one.

Comparison operations are left associative, so an expression such as

i < j < k

groups as

(i < j) < k

Since a comparison operation produces the value of its left argument if it succeeds, the expression above succeeds if and only if the value j is between the values of i and k.

ASSIGNMENT

One of the most commonly used operations in Icon is assignment, which has the form

x := y

and assigns the value of y to the variable x.

Assignment associates to the right, so that

x := y := z

groups as

x := (y := z)

Consequently, the value of z is assigned to both y and x.

Augmented Assignment

One of the most common operations in programming is incrementing the numerical value of a variable, as in

i := i + 1

In order to make such operations more concise and to avoid two references to the same variable, Icon has *augmented assignment* operations that combine assignment with the computation to be performed. For example,

i +:= 1

adds one to the value of i.

There are augmented assignment operations corresponding to all infix operations (except the assignment operations themselves); the := is simply appended to the operator symbol. For example,

    i *:= 10

is equivalent to

    i := i *10

Similarly,

    i >:= j

assigns the value of j to i if the value of i is greater than the value of j. This may seem a bit strange at first sight, since most programming languages do not treat comparison operations as numerical computations, but this feature of Icon sometimes can be used to advantage.

Exchanging Values

The operation

    x :=: y

exchanges the values of x and y. For example, after evaluating

    s1 := "begin"
    s2 := "end"
    s1 :=: s2

the value of s1 is "end" and the value of s2 is "begin".

The exchange operation associates from right to left and returns its left argument as a variable. Consequently,

    x :=: y :=: z

groups as

    x :=: (y :=: z)

VALUES, VARIABLES, AND RESULTS

Some expressions produce values, while others (such as assignment) produce variables, which in turn have values. For example, the string literal "hello" is a value, while the identifier line is a variable. It is always possible to get the value of a variable. This is done automatically by operations such as i + j, in which the values of i and j are used in the computation.

On the other hand, values are not obtained from variables unless they are needed. For example, the expression x | y generates the variables x and y, so that

> every (x | y) := 0

assigns 0 to both x and y. The if-then-else and case control expressions also produce variables if the selected expression does.

The term *result* is used collectively to include both values and variables. Consequently, it is best to describe

> *expr1* | *expr2*

as generating the results of *expr1* followed by the results of *expr2*.

Note that the term *outcome* includes results (values and variables) as well as failure.

The keyword &fail does not produce a result. It can be used to indicate failure explicitly.

ARGUMENT EVALUATION

The arguments of function and procedure calls are evaluated from left to right. If more arguments are given in a call than are expected, the extra arguments are evaluated, but their values are not used. If the evaluation of an extra argument fails, the function is not called, just as in the case of the evaluation of any other argument.

If an argument is omitted, as in write(), the value of that argument is *null*. Many functions have defaults that are used if an argument is null. For example, in write(), the null value defaults to an empty string and an empty (blank) line is written. Another example is the function seq(i, j), which was described earlier. If its arguments are omitted, and hence null, they default to 1. Consequently, seq() generates 1, 2, 3, ...

The keyword &null produces the null value. Consequently, write() and write(&null) are equivalent.

PROCEDURE RETURNS

As shown in Chapter 1, a procedure call may return a value, as in

> return count

or it may fail and not return a value by using fail. A procedure call also may fail by flowing off the end of the procedure body without an explicit return.

A procedure also may generate a sequence of values by using suspend, as in the following example:

```
procedure To(i, j)
  while i <= j do {
    suspend i
    i +:= 1
    }
  fail
end
```

The suspend expression produces a value from the procedure call in the same manner as return, but the call is suspended and can be resumed. If it is resumed, evaluation continues following the point of suspension. In the example above, the first result produced is the value of i, provided it is less than or equal to j. If the call is resumed, i is incremented. If i is still less than or equal to j, the call suspends again with the new value of i. If i is greater than j, the loop terminates and fail is evaluated, which causes the resumption of the call to fail. The fail expression is not necessary, since flowing off the end of the procedure body has the same effect. Consequently,

```
every write(To(1, 10))
```

is equivalent to

```
every write(1 to 10)
```

The suspend expression is like the every expression; if its argument is a generator, the generator is resumed when the procedure call is resumed. Thus,

```
suspend (1 | 3 | 5 | 7 | 11)
```

suspends with the values 1, 3, 5, 7, 11 as the call in which it appears is successively resumed.

SYNTACTIC CONSIDERATIONS

The way that the Icon compiler groups expressions in the absence of braces or parentheses is determined by the precedence and associativity of the syntactic tokens that comprise expressions. Appendix A contains detailed information on these matters.

Ideally, precedence and associativity leads to natural groupings of expressions and produces the expected results. In some cases, however, what is natural in one context is not natural in another, and Icon's precedence and associativity rules may cause expressions to group differently than expected. Such potential problems are noted at the ends of subsequent chapters.

The grouping of conjunction and alternation with other operations is a frequent source of problems. Conjunction has the lowest precedence of all operations. Alternation, on the other hand, has medium precedence. Consequently,

   expr1 **&** *expr2* | *expr3*

groups as

   expr1 **&** (*expr2* | *expr3*)

Since, in the absence of parentheses, such expressions are easily misinterpreted, it is good practice to use parentheses even if they are not necessary. There are many other cases where this rule applies. For example,

   1 to 10 | 20

groups as

   (1 to 10) | 20

The moral is clear: Parenthesize for readability as well as correctness.

   When control structures are nested, braces can be used for grouping as shown in examples earlier in this chapter. Even if braces are not necessary, using them helps avoid errors that may result from unexpected groupings in complicated expressions. Using braces to delimit expressions also can make programs easier to read — it is difficult for human beings to parse nested expressions.

   Consistent and appropriate indentation ("paragraphing") also makes programs easier to read. There are several styles of indentation. The one to use is largely a matter of taste, but it should be consistent and should accurately reflect the grouping of expressions.

   There are a few common syntactic problems that arise in control structures. One is that the **do** clause in **every, which,** and **until** is optional. If a **do** clause is intended but omitted by accident, the results can be unexpected. Consider for example,

   while line := read()
      process(line)

This is syntactically correct, but since there is no **do**, all input lines are read and then **process(line)** is evaluated once. Because of the omitted **do**, only the last input line is processed.

   The precedence of **not** is higher than that of any infix operation. For example,

   not find(s1, s2) = 10

groups as

```
(not find(s1, s2)) = 10
```

As a general rule, it is advisable to use parentheses for grouping in expressions containing not to avoid such unexpected results.

If there is a "dangling" else in nested if-then-else expressions, the else clause is grouped with the nearest preceding if. Consider, for example, the following section of a program for analyzing mailing lists:

```
if find("Mr.", line) then
if find("Mrs.", line)
then mm := mm + 1
else mr := mr + 1
```

These lines group as

```
if find("Mr.", line) then {
    if find("Mrs.", line) then mm := mm + 1
    else mr := mr + 1
    }
```

The precedence of then and else is lower than the precedence of any infix operation, so

```
if i > j then k := i else k := j
```

groups as

```
if i > j then (k := i) else (k := j)
```

which usually is what is intended.

In Icon, unlike many other programming languages, control structures also are expressions. For example, the outcome of

```
if expr1 then expr2 else expr3
```

is the outcome of *expr2* or *expr3* depending on whether *expr1* succeeds or fails. Consequently, it is possible to write expressions such as

```
(if i > j then i else j) := 0
```

to assign 0 to either i or j, depending on the relative magnitudes of their values. Although Icon allows such constructions, they tend to make programs difficult to read. It usually is better style to write such an expression as

```
if i > j then i := 0 else j := 0
```

The assignment and numerical comparison operators are easily confused. Thus,

i = (1 | 2)

compares the value of i to 1 and then 2, while

i := (1 | 2)

assigns 1 to i. (The second argument of alternation is not used, since assignment only needs one value.)

EXERCISES

2.1*   Write a program that writes only the last line of the input file.

2.2*   Write a program that copies the input file to the output file, but omitting the even-numbered lines.

2.3*   Write a procedure first(i) that copies the first i lines of the input file to the output file.

2.4   Write a procedure omit(s) that copies the input file to the output file, omitting lines that contain the string s.

2.5   Write a procedure skipto(s) that reads and discards input lines until a line beginning with the string s is found, returning this line but failing if no such line is found.

2.6   Write a procedure both(s1, s2) that generates those input lines that contain both strings s1 and s2.

2.7*   Write a procedure exor(s1, s2) that generates those input lines that contain either of the strings s1 or s2 but not both.

2.8   Write a procedure nest() that succeeds if the input file contains only properly nested occurrences of braces but fails otherwise. For example,

```
while line := read() do {
  if fine(s, line) then {
    write(line)
    scount := scount + 1
    }
  }
```

is properly nested, but

```
while line := read() do {
  if find(s, line) then
    write(line)
    scount := scount + 1
    }
  }
```

is not properly nested. For simplicity, assume that there is at most one occurrence of a brace on any one line.

2.9   Characterize the consequences of a compound exchange such as

$$x1 :=: x2 :=: \ldots :=: xn$$

3

String Scanning

Icon has many facilities for manipulating strings of characters (text). Its most powerful facility is high-level scanning for analyzing and synthesizing strings in a general way. This chapter is devoted to string scanning. Other string-processing facilities are described in Chapter 4.

THE CONCEPT OF SCANNING

Icon's string scanning facility is based on the observation that many operations on strings can be cast in terms of a succession of operations on one string at a time. By making this string, called the *subject*, the focus of attention of this succession of operations, it need not be mentioned in each operation. Furthermore, operations on a string often involve finding a position of interest in the string and working from there. Thus, the position serves as a focus of attention in the subject. The term *scanning* refers to changing the position in the subject. String scanning therefore involves operations that examine a subject string at a specific position and possibly change the position.

The form of a string-scanning expression is

expr1 ? *expr2*

where *expr1* provides the subject to be scanned and *expr2* does the scanning. The outcome of the scanning expression is the outcome of *expr2*. String scanning is illustrated by the function move(i), which increments the position by i characters if that is possible but fails if it is not. This function also produces the portion of the subject between the old and new positions. A function that produces a portion of the subject while changing the position is called a *matching function*.

Scanning starts at the beginning of the subject, so that

```
text ? {
    while move(1) do
       write(move(1))
    }
```

writes the even-numbered characters of text on separate lines.

STRING POSITIONS

Positions in strings in Icon are between characters and are numbered starting with 1, which is the position to the left of the first character:

```
   l    i    z    a    r    d
   ↑    ↑    ↑    ↑    ↑    ↑    ↑
   1    2    3    4    5    6    7
```

For convenience in referring to characters with respect to the right end of the string, there are corresponding nonpositive position specifications:

```
   l    i    z    a    r    d
   ↑    ↑    ↑    ↑    ↑    ↑    ↑
  −6   −5   −4   −3   −2   −1    0
```

The matching function tab(i) sets the position in the subject to i. For example,

```
text ? {
    if tab(3) then
       while move(1) do
          write(move(1))
    }
```

writes the even-numbered characters of text starting at 4, provided text is that long. The argument of tab() can be given by a nonpositive specification, and a negative argument to move() decreases the position in the subject. Consequently,

```
text ? {
    tab(0)
    while write(move(−1))
    }
```

writes the characters of **text** from right to left. Notice that it is not necessary to know how long **text** is.

The function **pos**(i) succeeds if the position in the subject is i but fails otherwise. For example,

expr & **pos**(0)

succeeds if the position is at the right end of the string after *expr* is evaluated.

STRING ANALYSIS

String analysis often involves finding a particular substring. The string-analysis function **find**(s1, s2), used earlier to illustrate failure and generation, performs this operation. When **find**() is used in string scanning, its second argument is omitted, and the subject is used in its place. For example,

write(text ? find("the"))

writes the position of the first occurrence of **"the"** in **text**, provided there is one. Similarly,

every write(text ? find("the"))

writes all the positions of **"the"** in **text**. Note that the scanning expression generates all the values generated by **find**("the").

In string analysis, the actual value of the position of a substring usually is not as interesting as the context in which the substring occurs — for example, what precedes or follows it. Since a string-analysis function produces a position and the matching function **tab**() moves to a position and produces the matched substring, the two can be used in combination. For example,

write(text ? tab(find(",")))

writes the initial portion of **text** prior to the first comma in it (if any). Similarly,

```
text ? {
  if tab(find(",") + 1) then
    write(tab(0))
  }
```

writes the portion of **text** after the first comma in it (if any).

Alternation may be used in the argument of **find**() to look for any one of several strings. For example,

```
text ? {
  if tab(find("a" | "e" | "i" | "o" | "u") + 1) then
    write(tab(0))
}
```

writes the portion of text after a lowercase vowel. Since alternatives are tried only if they are needed, if there is an "a" in text, the string after it is written, even if there is another vowel before the "a".

CSETS

In the example above, the alternative arguments of find() are ordered; what happens depends on the order in which the alternatives are written. On the other hand, in this kind of string analysis, order often is not important or even appropriate. For example, alternation does not determine which lowercase vowel comes first in the example in the preceding section.

Csets (character sets) are provided for this purpose. A cset is just what it sounds like — a set of characters. There is no concept of order in a cset; all the characters in it are on a par. A cset is therefore very different from a string, which is a sequence of characters in which order is very important.

A cset can be given literally by using single quotes to enclose the characters (as opposed to double quotes for string literals). Thus,

```
vowel := 'aeiouAEIOU'
```

is a cset that contains the ten "vowels". There also are built-in csets. For example, the value of the keyword &letters is a cset containing the upper- and lowercase letters.

Icon has several string-analysis functions that use csets instead of strings. One of these is upto(c), which generates the positions in the subject in which any character in the cset c occurs. For example,

```
every write(text ? upto(vowel))
```

writes the positions of every vowel in text, and

```
text ? {
  if tab(upto(vowel) + 1) then
    write(tab(0))
}
```

writes the portion of text after the first instance of a vowel (if any).

Another string-analysis function that uses csets is many(c), which produces the position after a sequence of characters in c. For example,

```
text ? {
  while write(tab(upto(' '))) do
    tab(many(' '))
  write(tab(0))
  }
```

writes the strings of characters between strings of blanks. The expression tab(many(' '))
matches strings of blanks, skipping over them in scanning. Note that tab(0) is used to match
the remainder of the subject after the last blank (if any).

Similarly, the following scanning expression writes all the "words" in text:

```
text ? {
  while tab(upto(&letters)) do
    write(tab(many(&letters)))
  }
```

Of course, treating a "word" as simply a string of letters is somewhat naive. In fact, there
really is no simple definition of "word" that is satisfactory in all situations. However, this
naive one is easy to express and suffices in many situations.

STRING-ANALYSIS FUNCTIONS

There are three string-analysis functions in addition to find(), many(), and upto().

Matching Substrings

If s occurs at the current position in the subject, the function match(s) produces the
position in the subject at the end of s. It fails if s does not occur at the current position in the
subject. For example,

```
"The theory is fallacious" ? match("The")
```

produces 4, while

```
"The theory is fallacious" ? match(" theory")
```

fails.

The operation =s is equivalent to tab(match(s)). For example, if line begins with the
substring "checkpoint", then

```
line ? {
  if ="checkpoint" then
    base := tab(0)
  }
```

assigns the remainder of line to base.

Matching a Character

If the character at the current position in the subject is in the cset c, any(c) produces the position after that character. It fails otherwise. For example,

write("Our conjecture has support" ? tab(any('aeiouAEIOU')))

writes O, while

write("Our conjecture has support" ? tab(any('aeiou')))

fails and does not write anything.

Note that any() resembles match(), except that any() depends on the initial character, not an initial substring, and that any one of several of initial characters may be specified.

Matching Balanced Strings

The function bal(c1, c2, c3) generates the positions of characters in c1, provided the preceding substring is balanced with respect to characters in c2 and c3. This function is useful in applications that involve the analysis of formulas, expressions, and other strings that have balanced bracketing characters.

The function bal() is like upto(), except that c2 and c3 specify sets of characters that must be balanced in the usual algebraic sense up to a character in c1. If c2 and c3 are omitted, '(' and ')' are assumed. For example,

"–35" ? bal('–')

produces 1 (the string preceding the minus is empty) but

write("((2∗x)+3)+(5∗y)" ? tab(bal('+')))

writes ((2∗x)+3). Note that the position of the first "+" is not preceded by a string that is balanced with respect to parentheses.

Other bracketing characters can be specified. The expression

write("[+, [2, 3]], [∗, [5, 10]]" ? tab(bal(',', '[', ']')))

writes [+, [2, 3]].

In determining whether or not a string is balanced, a count is kept starting at zero as characters in the subject are examined. If a character in c1 is encountered and the count is zero, bal() produces that position. Otherwise, if a character in c2 is encountered, the count is incremented, while the count is decremented if a character in c3 is encountered. Other characters leave the count unchanged.

If the counter ever becomes negative, or if the count is positive after examining the last character of the subject, bal() fails.

All characters in c2 and c3 have equal status; bal() cannot be used to determine proper nesting of different bracketing characters. For example, the value produced by

```
"([a+b))+c]" ? bal('+', '([', ')]')
```

is 8.

If c2 and c3 both contain the same character, its presence in c2 counts; it has no effect as a character in c3.

Since bal() is a generator, it may produce more than one result. For example,

```
every write(formula ? bal('*'))
```

writes the positions of all asterisks in formula that are preceded by parenthesis-balanced substrings.

SCANNING ENVIRONMENTS

The subject and position in string scanning, taken together, constitute an "environment" in which matching and string-analysis functions operate.

A scanning expression,

expr1 ? *expr2*

starts a new scanning environment. It first saves the current scanning environment, then starts a new environment with the subject set to the string produced by *expr1* and the position set to 1 (the beginning of the subject). Next, *expr2* is evaluated. When the evaluation of *expr2* is complete (whether it produces a result or fails), the former scanning environment is restored.

Since scanning environments are saved and restored in this fashion, string-scanning expressions can be nested. An example is:

```
text ? {
  while tab(upto(&letters)) do {
    word := tab(many(&letters))
    word ? {
      if upto('aeiou') then write(move(1))
      }
    }
  }
```

This expression writes the first letter of those words that contain a lowercase vowel.

SCANNING KEYWORDS

The subject and position in scanning environments are maintained automatically by scanning expressions and matching functions. There usually is no need to refer to the subject and position explicitly — in fact, the whole purpose of string scanning is to treat these values implicitly so that they do not have to be mentioned during string scanning.

In some situations, however, it may be useful, or even necessary, to refer to the subject or position explicitly. Two keywords are provided for this purpose: &subject and &pos.

For example, the following line writes the subject and position for diagnostic purposes:

```
write("subject=", &subject, ", position =", &pos)
```

If a value is assigned to &subject, it becomes the subject in the current scanning environment and the position is automatically set to 1. If a value is assigned to &pos, the position in the current scanning environment is changed accordingly, provided the value is in the range of the subject. If it is not in range, the assignment to &pos fails.

AUGMENTED STRING SCANNING

Augmented assignment,

```
s ?:= expr
```

can be used to scan s and assign a new value to it as a result. The value assigned is the value produced by *expr*. For example,

```
line ?:= {
   tab(many(' ')) & tab(0)
   }
```

removes any initial blanks from line. If line does not begin with a blank, the scanning expression fails and the value of line is not changed.

Since scanning expressions can be complicated, it is important to be careful that the outcome of scanning is the intended one. Consider the following expression:

```
line ?:= {
   while tab(upto(&letters)) do
      tab(many(&letters))
   }
```

The scanning expression eventually fails, regardless of the value of line, since the while loop itself fails. Consequently, no value is assigned to line.

SYNTACTIC CONSIDERATIONS

The second argument of ? often is fairly complicated, since it contains the expressions that perform scanning. Consequently, the precedence of ? is low, and

text ? i := find(s)

groups as

text ? (i := find(s))

However, the precedence of ? is greater than & (conjunction), so that

text ? i := find(s1) & j := find(s2)

groups as

(text ? i := find(s1)) & (j := find(s2))

This probably is not what is intended, and the source of the problem may be hard to locate. The difficulty is that j := find(s2) is not evaluated with text as the subject, since the completion of the scanning expression at the left of the conjunction restores the subject and position to their former values. Consequently, find(s2) does not operate on text but on some other subject. (In the absence of any scanning expression, the subject is a zero-length, empty string.) Whether find(s2) succeeds or fails, its outcome has nothing to do with text. However, it looks like it does, which may make debugging difficult.

Because of the likelihood of conjunction in scanning expressions, it is good practice to clearly delimit the second argument of the scanning expression. One such form, which is used in most of the examples of string scanning in this book, is

s ? {

.
.
.

}

EXERCISES

3.1 Write a procedure genchar(s, c) that generates the characters from s that are in c in order from left to right in s. For example, genchar("abracadabra", 'ab') should generate "a", "b", "a", "a", "a", "b", and "a".

3.2* Write a procedure swords(s) that generates only those words in the input file that contain the substring s.

3.3 Write a procedure cwords(c) that generates only those words in the input file that contain a character in the cset c.

3.4   Write a procedure selwords(n, c) that generates all *n*-letter words in the input file that contain at least one character in the cset c.

3.5*   Write a procedure pre(s, c) that generates all the initial substrings of s that are followed by a character in c.

3.6*   Write a procedure strip(s) that strips off any outer parentheses in a parenthesis-balanced string. For example, strip("((a+b))") should produce "a+b".

4

Csets and Strings

Icon has no character data type, but it has two data types that are composed of characters. *Csets* are sets of characters, while *strings* are sequences of characters. These two organizations of characters, described briefly in previous chapters, are useful for representing various kinds of information and for operating on textual data in different ways.

CHARACTERS

Since strings are of major importance in Icon, and csets only somewhat less so, it is important to understand the significance of the characters from which they are composed.

Icon uses eight-bit characters and allows all 256 of them to be used; no characters are excluded from use in strings or csets. Although most computer systems do not allow all 256 characters to be entered from input devices, they all can be represented in Icon programs by escape sequences in string and cset literals and any character can be computed directly during program execution.

Most files are composed of characters, and most input and output consists of characters. Some characters are "printable" and have graphics associated with them. Other characters are used for control purposes, such as indicating the end of a line on a display device or printer. The printable characters, control characters, and their uses vary from one computer system to another. The association between the numeric value of the bits (codes) for a character and its graphic also depend on the "character set" the system uses. For example, the letter A is associated with the bit pattern 01000001 (decimal code 65) in the ASCII character set, but with the bit pattern 11000001 (decimal code 193) in the EBCDIC character set.

Most text processing involves printable characters that have graphics and, for the most part, it does not matter which codes correspond to which characters. For example, programs that analyze text files usually work the same way, regardless of whether the character set is ASCII or EBCDIC. Such programs usually are written in terms of the graphics for the characters (such as A) and the associated codes are irrelevant.

There are exceptions, however. Comparison of characters and sorting depend on the numeric codes associated with graphics. In ASCII, the digits are associated with codes near the beginning of the character set, while in EBCDIC they are near the end. In both cases, the digits are in the order of their character codes, so strings of digits compare the same way in both ASCII and EBCDIC. However, the digits occur before the letters in ASCII but after the letters in EBCDIC, so strings containing both letters and digits may compare differently in ASCII and EBCDIC. While these differences cannot be helped, they usually do not cause problems because an Icon program running on an ASCII system produces the results that the user of an ASCII system expects, and similarly on an EBCDIC system.

CSETS

Cset Literals

A cset can be written literally by using single quotes to enclose the characters.

Characters that cannot be keyboarded directly can be represented using escape sequences that start with the character \ (backslash). For example, ' \ t' is a cset consisting of a tab and ' \ n' is a cset consisting of a newline character. Similarly, ' \' ' is a cset representing a single quote and ' \\' is a cset consisting of a single backslash. A listing of escape sequences is given in Appendix A.

The order of the characters in a cset literal is not important, and duplicate characters are ignored. Consequently, 'aeiou', 'uoiea', and 'aeiouaeiou' all produce the same cset.

Built-in Csets

Csets cannot be very large — there are only 256 different characters. However, having to write out even 26 letters in a literal is annoying. Icon provides keywords for commonly needed csets, such as the uppercase letters, lowercase letters, all the letters, and digits: &ucase, &lcase, &letters, and &digits, respectively.

For example,

```
text ? {
  while tab(upto(&digits)) do
    write(move(1))
  }
```

writes out all the digits in text, one per line.

Other built-in csets are &cset, the set of all 256 characters, and &ascii, the set of the first 128 characters in ASCII.

Operations on Csets

Icon has four operations on csets:

    c1 ++ c2   union

    c1 ** c2   intersection

    c1 − − c2   difference

    ~c   complement

The union of two csets is a cset that contains all the characters in either of the two. For example, &letters ++ &digits contains all the letters and digits. The intersection of two csets is a cset that contains all the characters that appear in both csets. The difference of two csets is a cset that contains all the characters in the first that are not in the second. For example, &cset − − &digits contains all the characters that are not digits. The complement of a cset contains all the characters that are not in it. For example, ~&digits is equivalent to &cset − − &digits. The operation *c produces the number of characters in c.

STRINGS

Strings are used more frequently than csets because the sequential organization of strings allows the representation of complex relationships among characters. Written text, such as this book, is just a sequence of characters. Most of the information processed by computers consists of sequences of characters, especially when it is read in, written out, and stored in files.

String Literals

As described earlier, strings are represented literally with surrounding double quotation marks (as opposed to single quotation marks for csets). For example,

    vowel := "aeiou"

assigns the string "aeiou" to vowel. Unlike csets, the order of characters in a string is significant, as are duplicate characters. For example,

    vowel := "uoieaou"

assigns a different value to vowel than the previous expression; it is longer, and "u" and "o" occur twice.

The escape sequences used in cset literals can also be used in string literals. A double quotation mark can be represented by "\"". Therefore, write("What I want to say is\n\"Hello world\"")

writes

What I want to say is
"Hello world"

Character Codes

The function char(i) produces the one-character string corresponding to the integer i. For example, the internal integer representation for A is 65 in ASCII, so char(65) produces the one-character string "A" in ASCII.

The inverse function ord(s) produces the integer (ordinal) corresponding to the one-character string s.

String Length

The length of a string is the number of characters in it. The operation *s produces the length of s. For example,

*"Hello world"

produces the integer 11.

There is no practical limit to the length of a string, although very large strings are awkward and expensive to manipulate. The smallest string is the *empty string*, which contains no characters and has zero length. The empty string is represented literally by "".

Concatenation

One of the more commonly used operations on strings is *concatenation*,

s1 || s2

which produces a string consisting of the characters in s1 followed by those in s2. For example,

"Hello " || "world"

produces the string "Hello world".

The empty string is the identity with respect to concatenation; concatenating the empty string with another string just produces the other string. The empty string therefore is a natural initial value for building up a string value by successive concatenations. For example, suppose that the input file consists of a number of lines, each of which contains a single word. Then the following procedure produces a list of these words with each followed by a comma.

```
procedure wordlist()
   wlist := ""                                      # initialize wlist
   while word := read() do
      wlist := wlist || word || ","
   return wlist
end
```

The augmented assignment operation for concatenation is particularly useful for appending strings onto an evolving value. For example,

   wlist ||:= word || ","

is equivalent to

   wlist := wlist || word || ","

The do clause in the while loop above is not necessary. The expression can be written more compactly as

   while wlist ||:= read() || ","

SUBSTRINGS

Since a string is a sequence of characters, any subsequence or *substring* is also a string. A substring is simply a portion of another string. For example, "Cl" is a substring of "Cleo", as are "leo" and "e". "Co", however, is not a substring of "Cleo", since "C" and "o" do not occur consecutively in "Cleo". Any string is a substring of itself. The empty string is a substring of every string.

A substring is produced by a subscripting expression, in which a *range specification* enclosed in brackets gives the positions that bound the desired substring. One form of range specification is i:j, where i and j are the bounding positions. For example,

   "Cleo"[1:3]

produces "Cl". Note that this is a substring of two characters, not three, because the characters are between the specified positions. Range specifications usually are applied to strings that are the values of identifiers, as in

   text[1:4]

which produces the first three characters of text, those between positions 1 and 4. If the value of text is less than three characters long, the subscripting expression fails. This is another example of the design philosophy of Icon: If an operation cannot be performed, it does not produce a result. In this case the failure occurs because the specified substring does not exist.

Expressions can be used to provide the bounds in range specifications. For example,

    text[2:*s]

produces the substring of text between 2 and the size of s. Similarly, any expression whose value is a string can be subscripted, as in

    s := read()[2:10]

which assigns a substring of a line of input to s. Note that this expression may fail for two reasons: if read() fails because there is no more input, or if read() produces a line that is not long enough. Expressions containing such *ambiguous failure* should be avoided, since they can be the source of subtle programming errors.

The following program illustrates the use of substrings to copy the input file to the output file, truncating long output lines to 60 characters.

```
procedure main()
  while line := read() do {
    line := line[1:61]                    # truncate
    write(line)
    }
  end
```

Note that

    write(line[1:61])

does not work properly in place of the two lines in the previous procedure, since the subscripting expression fails if a line is less than 60 characters long. There is no output for such lines.

Nonpositive position specifications, described in Chapter 3, also can be used in range specifications. For example, line[−1:0] is the last character of line. Positive and nonpositive specifications can be mixed.

The two positions in a range specification can be given in either order. The leftmost position need not be given first; only the bounding positions are significant. Therefore, line[1:4] and line[4:1] are equivalent.

Range specifications also can be given by a position and an offset from that position. The range specification i+:j specifies a substring starting at i of size j. The offset can be negative: i −:j specifies a substring starting at i but consisting of the j characters to the left of i, rather than to the right. For example,

```
write(line[1+:60])
```

writes the first 60 characters of line, as does

```
write(line[61−:60])
```

If a substring consists of only a single character, it can be specified by the position before it. Therefore,

```
write(line[2])
```

writes the second character of line and is equivalent to

```
write(line[2+:1])
```

Similarly,

```
last := line[−1]
```

assigns the last character of line to last.

Assignment can be made to a subscripted variable to change the substring corresponding to the range specification. For example, if the value of word is "two",

```
word[2] := "o"
```

changes the value of word to "too". Similarly,

```
word[−1] := ""
```

deletes the last character of word so that its value becomes "to". Note that assignment to change a substring may change the length of a string. Assignment to change a substring only is a shorthand notation for concatenation. For example,

```
word[2] := "o"
```

is shorthand for

```
word := word[1] || "o" || word[3:0]
```

If two variables have the same string value, changing a substring in one does not change the value of the other. Therefore, in

```
line := read()
old := line
line[2+:3] := ""
```

the value of old is not changed by the assignment to line[2+:3]. A new value is assigned to line, but not to old.

Assignment can be made to a subscripting expression to change the value of a string only if the range specification is applied to a variable. For example,

"Cleo"[1] := "K"

is erroneous.

Randomly Selected Characters

The operation ?s produces a randomly selected one-character substring of s provided that s is not empty. If s is empty, ?s fails. For example,

?"HT"

produces the string "H" or "T" with approximately equal probability.

If s is a string-valued variable, assignment can be made to ?s to replace a randomly selected character of s. For example,

?s := ""

deletes a randomly selected character of s.

Character Generation

The expression !s generates the one-character substrings of s in order from first to last, left to right. For example,

every write(!s)

writes the characters of s, one per line. This expression is equivalent to

every write(s[1 to *s])

If s is a string-valued variable, the expression !s produces a variable, just as s[i] does. For example,

!s := ""

is equivalent to

s[1] := ""

and deletes the first character in the value of s.

In an expression such as

every !s := *expr*

the value of s is changed with each assignment, but the position in s is incremented repeatedly until the end of the string is reached. If the assignment changes the size of the value of s, the result can be confusing.

LEXICAL COMPARISON

Strings can be compared for their relative magnitude in a manner similar to the comparison of numbers. The comparison of strings is based on lexical (alphabetical) order rather than numerical value. Lexical order is based on the codes for the characters. The character c1 is lexically less than c2 if the code for c1 is less than the code for c2. For example, in ASCII the code for "A" is 65, while the code for "R" is 82, so "A" is lexically less than "R".

Although the relative values of letters and digits are the same in ASCII and EBCDIC and produce the expected results in lexical comparisons, there are important differences between the ordering in the two character sets. As mentioned earlier, the ASCII codes for the digits are smaller than the codes for letters, while the opposite is true in EBCDIC. In addition, uppercase letters in ASCII have smaller codes than lowercase letters, while the opposite is true in EBCDIC. Furthermore, there is relatively little relationship between the codes for other characters, such as punctuation, in the two character sets.

For longer strings, lexical order is determined by the lexical order of their characters, from left to right. Therefore, in ASCII "AB" is less than "aA" and "aB" is less than "ab". If one string is an initial substring of another, the shorter string is lexically less than the longer. For example, "Aba" is lexically less than "Abaa" in both ASCII and EBCDIC. The empty string is lexically less than any other string. Two strings are lexically equal if and only if they have the same length and are identical, character by character. There are six lexical comparison operations:

s1 << s2	lexically less than
s1 <<= s2	lexically less than or equal
s1 >> s2	lexically greater than
s1 >>= s2	lexically greater than or equal
s1 == s2	lexically equal
s1 ~== s2	lexically not equal

The use of lexical comparison is illustrated by the following program, which determines the lexically largest and smallest lines in the input file.

```
procedure main()
  min := max := read()              # initial min and max
  while line := read() do
    if line >> max then max := line
    else if line << min then min := line
  write("lexically largest line is: ", max)
  write("lexically smallest line is: ", min)
end
```

This program can be rephrased in a way that is more idiomatic to Icon by using augmented assignment operations:

```
procedure main()
  min := max := read()              # initial min and max
  while line := read() do
    (max <<:= line) | (min >>:= line)
  write("lexically largest line is: ", max)
  write("lexically smallest line is: ", min)
end
```

STRING-VALUED FUNCTIONS

When producing formatted output, it often is useful to have "fields" of a specific width that line up in columns. There are three functions that position a string in a field of a specified width, aligning the string in the field at the right, left, or in the center.

Positioning Strings

The function right(s1, i, s2) produces a string of length i in which s1 is positioned at the right and s2 is used to pad out the remaining characters to the left. For example,

    right("Detroit", 10, "+")

produces "+++Detroit". Enough copies of s2 are concatenated on the left to make up the specified length. If s2 is omitted, blanks are used for padding.

If the length of s1 is greater than i, it is truncated at the left so that the value has length i. Therefore,

    right("Detroit", 6)

produces "etroit".

The value of s2 usually is a one-character string, but it may be of any length. The resulting string is always of size i, however; any extra characters that might result from prepending copies of s2 are discarded. For example, right("Detroit", 10, "+*")

produces "+*+Detroit". Note that the padding string is truncated at the right.

A common use of right() is to position data in columns. The following program, which prints out a table of the first four powers of the integers from 1 to 10, illustrates such an application:

```
procedure main()
  every i := 1 to 10 do {
    write(right(i, 5), right(i ^ 2, 8), right(i ^ 3, 8),  right(i ^ 4, 8))
    }
end
```

The output written by this program is:

```
        1        1        1        1
        2        4        8       16
        3        9       27       81
        4       16       64      256
        5       25      125      625
        6       36      216     1296
        7       49      343     2401
        8       64      512     4096
        9       81      729     6561
       10      100     1000    10000
```

The function left(s1, i, s2) is similar to right(s1, i, s2) except that the position is reversed: s1 is placed at the left, padding is done on the right, and truncation (if necessary) is done at the right. Therefore,

left("Detroit", 10, "+")

produces "Detroit+++" and

left("Detroit", 6)

produces "Detroi". The padding string is truncated at the left if necessary.

The function center(s1, i, s2) centers s1 in a string of length i, padding on the left and right, if necessary, with s2. If s1 cannot be centered exactly, it is placed to the left of center. Truncation is then done at the left and right if necessary. Therefore,

center("Detroit", 10, "+")

produces "+Detroit++", while

center("Detroit", 6)

produces "etroit" and center("Detroit, 9, "+ –") produces "+Detroit–".

Tabular Data

Tab characters are useful for separating fields and displaying them in an aligned fashion on devices such as computer terminals.

The function entab(s, i1, i2, ..., in) produces a string obtained by replacing runs of consecutive blanks in s by tab characters. There is an implicit tab stop at 1 to establish the interval between tab stops. The remaining tab stops are at i1, i2, ..., in. Additional tab stops, if necessary, are obtained by repeating the last interval. If no tab stops are specified, the interval is 8 with the first tab stop at 9.

For the purposes of determining positions, printable characters have a width of 1, the backspace character has a width of −1, and a linefeed character restarts the counting of positions. Other nonprintable characters have zero width.

A lone blank is never replaced by a tab character, but a tab character may replace a single blank that is part of longer run.

The function detab(s, i1, i2, ..., in) produces a string obtained by replacing each tab character in s by one or more blanks. Tab stops are specified in the same way as for entab().

Replicating Strings

When several copies of the same string are to be concatenated, it is more convenient (and more efficient) to use repl(s, i), a function that produces the concatenation of i copies of s. For example,

repl("+*+", 3)

produces "+*++*++*+". The expression repl(s, 0) produces the empty string.

Reversing Strings

The function reverse(s) produces a string consisting of the characters of s in reversed order. For example,

reverse("string")

produces "gnirts".

Mapping Characters

The function map(s1, s2, s3) produces a string resulting from a character mapping of s1 in which each character of s1 that appears in s2 is replaced by the corresponding character in s3. Characters of s1 that do not appear in s2 are not changed. For example,

map("mad hatter", "a", "+")

produces "m+d h+tter" and

map("mad hatter", "aeiou", "12345")

produces "m1d h1tt2r".

Several characters in s2 may have the same corresponding character in s3. For example,

map("mad hatter", "aeiou", "+++++")

produces "m+d h+tt+r".

If a character appears more than once in s2, the rightmost correspondence with s3 applies. Duplicate characters in s2 provide a way to mask out unwanted characters. For example, marking the positions of vowels in a string can be accomplished by mapping every vowel into an asterisk and mapping all other characters into a blank. An easy way to do this is to set up a correspondence between every character and a blank and then append the correspondences for the vowels:

```
s2 := &cset || "AEIOUaeiou"
s3 := repl(" ", *&cset) || "**********"
```

In this correspondence, s2 is a string consisting of all characters followed by the vowels, 266 characters in all, since each vowel appears twice. The value of s3 is 256 blanks followed by 10 asterisks. The last 10 characters in s2 and s3 override the previous correspondences between the vowels and blanks. Consequently,

map(line, s2, s3)

produces a string with asterisks in the positions of the vowels and blanks in all the other positions.

Trimming Strings

The function trim(s, c) produces a string consisting of the initial substring of s with the omission of any trailing characters contained in c. That is, it trims off characters in c. If c is omitted, blanks are trimmed. For example,

trim("Betelgeuse   ")

produces "Betelgeuse", while

trim("Betelgeuse", &lcase)

produces just "B".

STRING ANALYSIS

String analysis functions are not restricted to string scanning. The analysis functions can be applied to a specific string by adding that string as a trailing argument. For example, find(s1, s2) generates the positions where s1 occurs as a substring of s2, and upto(c, s) generates the position at which characters in c occur in s. In such usages, the subject and the position in it are irrelevant.

All the string analysis functions also may have two additional arguments that restrict the range in which the analysis is done. For example, upto(c, s, i, j) restricts the value to positions between i and j in s. Therefore,

upto('aeiou', "The theory is fallacious", 5, 11)

produces 7. Note that this is a position in s; the value produced by

upto('aeiou', "The theory is fallacious"[5:11])

is 3.

An omitted value of i defaults to 1, the beginning of s. An omitted value of j defaults to 0 and restricts the value to positions between i and the end of the string.

Like range specifications, the range-restriction arguments can be given either as positive or nonpositive position specifications and can be given in either order. For example,

find(s1, s2, 0, −10)

restricts the range in s2 to the last 10 characters. Substrings are always found to the right, regardless of the form of the specification.

CONVERSION BETWEEN CSETS AND STRINGS

As described in Chapter 1, Icon automatically converts values from one type to another according to context. This conversion applies to csets and strings. For example, the following procedure produces a cset of all the characters that occur in the input file.

```
procedure inset()
  chars := ' '                          # empty to start
  while line := read() do
    chars := chars ++ line
  return chars
end
```

The cset chars originally starts out empty, given literally by enclosing no characters in single quotes. Then the characters in each line of the input file are added to chars. In the union operation, the value of line is a string that is automatically converted to a cset.

This procedure can be written more compactly using augmented assignment:

```
procedure inset()
  chars := ' '                          # empty to start
  while chars ++:= read()
  return chars
end
```

STRING IMAGES

If x is a string or cset, image(x) produces its string image with surrounding quotes and escape sequences, if necessary, as for string literals. For example,

```
write(image("Hello world"))
```

writes "Hello world" (with the quotes), while

```
write(image(char(0)))
```

writes "\x00". Similarly,

```
write(image('Hello world'))
```

writes ' Hdelorw'. Note that the characters in the image of a cset are in lexical order.

SYNTACTIC CONSIDERATIONS

Concatenation associates from left to right and its precedence is higher than that of the numerical comparison operations, but lower than that of addition. Concatenation usually does not occur in combination with numerical computation, however.

All the lexical comparison operations associate from left to right and have the same precedence as the numerical comparison operations. A lexical comparison operation produces the value of its right argument, provided that the comparison succeeds. Therefore, the expression

> s1 << s2 << s3

succeeds and produces s3, provided s2 is strictly between s1 and s3 in lexical order.

EXERCISES

4.1* Write a program that determines the number of different characters that occur in the input file.

4.2 Write a procedure that determines whether a program is running on an ASCII or EBCDIC system.

4.3* Write a procedure space(s) that produces a string consisting of the characters in s interspersed with blanks. For example,

> space("Hello world")

should produce "H e l l o   w o r l d".

4.4* Write a procedure rotate(s, i) that produces the result of rotating the value of s left by i characters. For example,

> rotate("abcde", 3)

should produce "deabc".

4.5 Write a procedure that does what the function image() does for strings and csets.

4.6 Write a program that produces a weight conversion table consisting of the equivalent values of pounds, ounces, kilograms, and grams for weights from 1 to 10 pounds in increments of one-tenth of a pound.

4.7 Write a procedure that enciphers the input file by using a simple substitution cipher. Write a corresponding procedure that deciphers the results.

4.8*   Write a procedure delete(s, c) that produces a string in which all characters in c that occur in s are deleted. For example,

delete("becomes", 'aeiou')

should produce "bcms".

4.9   Write a procedure replace(s1, s2, s3) that produces the result of replacing all occurrences of s2 in s1 by s3.

4.10   A palindrome is a string, such as "madam", that reads the same forward and backward. In palindromic sentences, upper- and lowercase letters are considered to be equivalent, and nonletters are ignored, as in "A man, a plan, a canal – Panama!". Write a procedure palin(s) that succeeds and produces s if s is a palindromic sentence, but fails otherwise.

4.11   Write a procedure anagram(s) that produces a string containing the characters in s in lexical order, but without the deletion of duplicates. For example, anagram("hello") should produce "ehllo".

4.12   Write a program that counts the number of lines, words, and characters in the input file.

4.13   Write a program that writes the lines of the input file with dashes under each word.

4.14*   Write a procedure enrepl(s) that abbreviates strings of repeated characters by replacing the repeated characters by one instance of the character followed by the number of times it occurs enclosed in parentheses. Assume that s does not contain parentheses. Do not replace a repeated string of characters that has a size of less than five. For example,

enrepl("aaaaaabbbbbbbbccccccdd")

should produce "a(6)b(8)c(6)dd".

4.15*   Write a corresponding procedure derepl(s) that restores strings produced by enrepl(s) to their original form.

4.16*   Write a procedure allbal(s, c) that generates all the strings of s up to a character in c that are balanced with respect to parentheses. Omit empty strings.

4.17   Write a program that counts the number of times each character occurs in the input file. Produce the output in a form in which every character can be easily identified.

4.18   Write a procedure printable(s) that succeeds and returns s if s contains only printable characters but fails otherwise. The procedure should work on both ASCII and EBCDIC systems.

5

Arithmetic and Bit Operations

Icon integers usually are represented by 32-bit quantities and arithmetic is performed in two's-complement mode. Thus, Icon integers usually have values in the range -2^{31} to $2^{31}-1$. The range may be larger on some computers, but it is never smaller. Some implementations of Icon support large-integer arithmetic for which these limitations do not apply.

Real (floating-point) numbers vary in range and precision from computer to computer. They normally are represented by the double-precision floating-point values native to the computer on which Icon runs.

Numerical computation in Icon is similar to that in most programming languages. The usual operations on integers and real numbers are provided. Integers are converted to real numbers automatically in mixed-mode operations that involve both integers and real numbers. There are also bit operations on integer values.

NUMERIC LITERALS

Integers are represented literally in the usual way. For example, 36 represents the integer 36 and 1024 represents the integer 1,024. Real numbers can be represented literally using either decimal or exponent notation. For example, 27e2 and 2700.0 are equivalent and represent the real number 2,700.0.

Bases other than 10 can be used for integer literals. Such *radix literals* have the form *i* r *j*, where *i* is a base-10 integer that specifies the base for *j*. For example, 2r11 represents the integer 3, while 8r10 represents 8. The base can be any value from 2 through 36; the letters a, b, ..., z are used to specify "digits" in *j* that are larger than 9. For example, 16ra represents 10, while 36rcat represents 15,941. See Appendix A for additional details of the syntax of numeric literals.

NUMERICAL COMPUTATION

Icon has two prefix operations for numerical computation. The operation +N produces the numeric value of N, while –N produces the negative of N. The infix operations for numerical computation are as follows:

expression	operation	relative precedence	associativity
N1 ^ N2	exponentiation	3	right to left
N1 % N2	remaindering	2	left to right
N1 / N2	division	2	left to right
N1 * N2	multiplication	2	left to right
N1 − N2	subtraction	1	left to right
N1 + N2	addition	1	left to right

In integer division the remainder is discarded; that is, the value is truncated toward 0. For example,

    −7 / 2

produces −3.

The operation

    N1 % N2

produces the remainder of N1 divided by N2 with the sign of N1. For example,

    −10 % 3

produces −1, but

    10 % −3

produces 1.

Division by zero and raising a negative real number to a real power are erroneous. Such errors cause program execution to terminate with a diagnostic message.

The function abs(N) produces the absolute value of N. For example,

    abs(−7 / 2)

produces 3.

Any numerical computation that involves a real number is performed using floating-point arithmetic and produces a real number. For example, the result of

10 + 3.14159

is 13.14159 and the result of

−7 / 2.0

is −3.5.

NUMERICAL COMPARISON

Icon's numerical comparison operations are

N1 < N2	less than
N1 <= N2	less than or equal to
N1 = N2	equal to
N1 >= N2	greater than or equal to
N1 > N2	greater than
N1 ~= N2	not equal to

MATHEMATICAL COMPUTATIONS

Icon provides the standard trigonometric functions:

sin(r)	sine of r
cos(r)	cosine of r
tan(r)	tangent of r
asin(r)	arc sine of r
acos(r)	arc cosine of r
atan(r1, r2)	arc tangent of r1 / r2

In all cases, angles are given in radians. The default for r2 in atan() is 1.0.

The following functions convert between radians and degrees:

dtor(r)	the radian equivalent of r given in degrees
rtod(r)	the degree equivalent of r given in radians

Icon also provides the following functions for mathematical calculations:

sqrt(r)	square root of r
exp(r)	*e* raised to the power r
log(r1, r2)	logarithm of r1 to the base r2

The default for r2 is *e*.

RANDOM NUMBERS

The operation ?i produces a number from a pseudo-random sequence. If the value of i is a positive integer *i*, the value produced by ?i is an integer *j* in the range $1 \le j \le i$. If the value of i is 0, the value produced by ?i is a real number *r* in the range $0.0 \le r < 1.0$.

For example, the expression

if ?2 = 1 then "H" else "T"

produces the string "H" or "T" with approximately equal probability.

The pseudo-random sequence is produced by a linear congruence relation starting with an initial seed value of 0. This sequence is the same from one program execution to another, allowing programs to be tested in a reproducible environment. The seed can be changed by assigning an integer value to &random. For example,

&random := 0

resets the seed to its initial value.

The same pseudo-random sequence is used for all random operations. For example, the operation ?s described in Chapter 4 uses the same sequences as ?i.

BIT OPERATIONS

Icon has five functions that operate on integers at the bit level. All these operations produce integers.

The function iand(i, j) produces the bitwise *and* of i and j. For example,

iand(4, 5)

produces 4.

The functions ior(i, j) and ixor(i, j) produce the bitwise inclusive and exclusive *or* of i and j, respectively. For example,

ior(4, 6)

produces 6, while

ixor(4, 6)

produces 2.

The function icom(i) produces the bit-wise complement of i. For a computer with 32-bit Icon integers and two's complement arithmetic,

icom(1)

produces −2.

The function ishift(i, j) shifts i by j positions. If j is positive, the shift is left, while if j is negative, the shift is right. Vacated bit positions are filled with zeros. For example,

ishift(2, 3)

produces 16, while

ishift(2, −3)

produces 0.

SYNTACTIC CONSIDERATIONS

Real literals must begin with a digit, not a period. For example, 0.25 is a real literal, but .25 is not. See Chapter 8.

All arithmetic infix operations have precedence higher than that of assignment. Consequently,

N := N + 1

groups as

N := (N + 1)

Prefix operations have higher precedence than infix operations. For example,

−N + 3

groups as

(−N) + 3

The comparison operations all have the same precedence, which is lower than that of any numerical computation operation, but higher than that of assignment. Therefore,

N1 > N2 + 1

groups as

N1 > (N2 + 1)

while

N1 := N2 > 10

groups as

N1 := (N2 > 10)

Note that this expression assigns the value 10 to N1 if the comparison succeeds.

Comparison operations associate from left to right, which allows compound comparisons to be written in a natural way. For example,

1 <= N <= 10

groups as

(1 <= N) <= 10

and succeeds if the value of N is between 1 and 10, inclusive.

EXERCISES

✓ **5.1*** Assuming that the input file consists of lines each of which contains a single number, write programs that

      (a) compute the sum of the numbers,

      (b) compute the average of the numbers, and

      (c) determine the largest and smallest numbers.

5.2 Write a procedure that computes the greatest common divisor of two positive integers.

✓ **5.3*** Write a procedure that computes factorials.

5.4 Write a procedure that generates the factorials, starting at 1.

✓ **5.5** Write a procedure that computes binomial coefficients.

6

Structures

Structures are aggregates of values. Icon has three kinds of built-in structures: lists, sets, and tables. Records also can be declared. Different kinds of structures have different access methods and organizations. Structures are created during program execution.

LISTS

Lists in Icon have two roles. In one role, they are one-dimensional arrays that can be subscripted by position. In the other role, they can be manipulated by stack and queue access functions and grow and shrink automatically. The two ways of manipulating lists can be used in combination.

List Creation

One way to create a list is to place brackets around a list of expressions:

[*expr1*, *expr2*, ..., *exprn*]

This expression produces a list of the *n* values produced by *expr1*, *expr2*, ..., *exprn*. For example,

oracles := ["Delphi", "Heracles", "Claros"]

assigns a list of three strings to oracles. Similarly,

powers := [i, i ^ 2, i ^ 3, i ^ 4]

assigns a list of four integers to **powers**.

The values in a list do not have to be of the same type. For example,

city := ["Tucson", 550000, "Arizona", "Pima"]

assigns a list of four values to **city**: three strings and one integer.

The values in a list may be of any type. For example,

expression := ["+", ["a"], ["/", ["c"], ["d"]]]

assigns a list of three values to **expression**. The first value is a string, while the second and third values are other lists, and so on. Such a list can be thought of as representing a tree in which the first value in the list is associated with the contents of a node and subsequent values represent subtrees. The tree for **expression** can be visualized as:

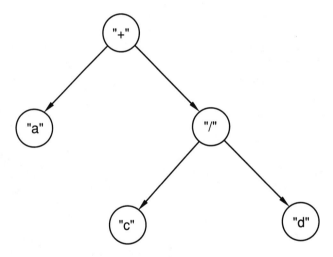

The function

list(i, x)

creates a list of i values, each of which has the value of x. For example,

vector := list(100, 0.0)

assigns to **vector** a list of 100 values, each of which is 0.0.

An *empty list*, which contains no values, can be created by [ ] or list(0). The size of a list is produced by the same operation that is used for strings. For example, ∗**vector** produces 100, while ∗[ ] produces 0.

List Referencing

The values in a list are referenced, or *subscripted*, by position much as are the characters in a string. For example,

    write(oracles[2])

writes Heracles. Similarly,

    every i := 1 to *L do
       write(L[i])

writes all the values in the list L. Since the position can be computed in the subscripting expression, this loop can be written more compactly as

    every write(L[1 to *L])

A value in a list can be changed by assignment to its position, which may be specified positively or nonpositively. For example,

    oracles[−1] := "Branchidae"

changes the last value of oracles, so that the list becomes

    ["Delphi", "Heracles", "Branchidae"]

Similarly,

    city[2] +:= 1000

changes the second value in city to 551,000.

As for string subscripting, list subscripting fails if the position specified does not correspond to a value in the list; that is, if the subscript is out of range.

The operation !L generates the elements of L in order from beginning to end. For example, the values in the list L can be written without reference to an index:

    every write(!L)

Assignment can be made to !L to change the values of the elements. For example

    every !L := 0

assigns 0 to every element of L.

The following program, which tabulates word lengths, illustrates a typical use of lists.

```
procedure main()
  wordlen := list(20, 0)          # initial zero counts
  while line := read() do
    line ? {
      while tab(upto(&letters)) do {
        word := tab(many(&letters))
        wordlen[*word] +:= 1
      }
  every i := 1 to *wordlen do
    write(right(i, 2), right(wordlen[i], 5))
end
```

The values in **wordlen** accumulate counts of word lengths from 1 to 20. After the input file has been processed, the results are written out. Note that any word that is longer than 20 characters is not tabulated; the expression

```
wordlen[*word] +:= 1
```

fails, since the subscript is out of range for word lengths greater than 20.

Lists are one dimensional, but a list of lists can be used to simulate a multidimensional array. The following procedure constructs an i-by-j array in which each value is x:

```
procedure array(i, j, x)
  L := list(i)
  every !L := list(j, x)
  return L
end
```

For example,

```
board := array(8, 8, 0)
```

assigns to **board** an 8-by-8 array in which each value is 0. A list reference can be subscripted so that

```
board[2][4]
```

references the value in "row" 4 of "column" 2 of **board**.

The operation ?L produces a randomly selected reference to the list L. If L is empty, ?L fails. Assignment can be made to ?L to change the subscripted value. For example,

```
?L := 0
```

assigns 0 to a randomly selected element of L.

List Concatenation

Lists can be concatenated in a manner similar to the concatenation of strings. The list concatenation operation has three vertical bars to distinguish it from string concatenation. An example is

city := city ||| [1883]

which assigns the list

["Tucson", 550000, "Arizona", "Pima", 1883]

to city. An empty list is an identity with respect to list concatenation.

As for other infix operations, there is an augmented assignment operation for list concatenation operation, as in

city |||:= [1883]

Note that both arguments in list concatenation must be lists;

city |||:= 1883

is erroneous.

List Sections

A list section is a list composed of a sequence of values from another list. List sections are like substrings, except that they are distinct from the list from which they are obtained, instead of being a part of it. List sections are produced by range specifications applied to lists, much as substrings are produced by range specifications applied to strings. For the value of city given in the preceding section, the value of

city[3:5]

is the list

["Arizona", "Pima"]

There is one other important distinction between subscripting lists and strings: If L is a list, L[i] refers to the ith *value* in the list, while L[i : j] is a *list* consisting of the values between positions i and j in L. In particular, L[i : j] is a list that is distinct from L, and assignment cannot be made to it to change L.

Queue and Stack Access to Lists

Queue and stack access functions provide ways to add and to remove values from the ends of lists. L[1] is the left end of a list and L[*L] is the right end of a list.

The function put(L, x) adds the value of x to the right end of the list L, increasing the size of L by 1. One use of put() is to build a list whose size cannot be determined when the list is created. For example, the following procedure produces a list of all words in the input file.

```
procedure words()
  wordlist := [ ]
  while line := read() do
    line ? {
      while tab(upto(&letters)) do
        put(wordlist, tab(many(&letters)))
    }
  return wordlist
end
```

Since put() adds values at the right end, the words in the list are in the order that they appear in the input file. That is, the first value in the list is the first word, the second value is the second word, and so on.

Values are removed from a list by the converse operation, get(L). Each time get(L) is evaluated, it removes a value from the left end of L and produces this value. If L is empty, get(L) fails.

For example, the following program uses the procedure words() to produce a list of words and then writes out only those words that begin with an uppercase letter:

```
procedure main()
  wlist := words()
  while word := get(wlist) do
    if any(&ucase, word) then write(word)
end
```

When the execution of this program is complete, the list wlist is empty, since each call of get() removes a value from it.

The functions put() and get() provide a queue access method for lists; put(L, x) adds x to the right end of L, and get(L) removes a value from the left end of L.

Two functions provide a corresponding stack access method for lists. The function push(L, x) adds x to the left end of L and pop(L) removes a value from the left end of L. For example, if the expression

```
put(wordlist, tab(many(&letters)))
```

in the procedure **words**() given previously is replaced by

    push(wordlist, tab(many(&letters)))

the list that is produced has the words in the opposite order from their order in the input file: the first word in the list is the last in the input file, and so on.

    Note that **get**(L) and **pop**(L) both remove a value from the left end of L. The two names for the same function are provided to accommodate the usual terminology for queue and stack access methods. The function **pull**(L) removes a value from the right end of L, so **push**() and **pull**() also provide a queue access method. The four functions together provide an access method for double-ended queues, or *deques*.

    The functions **put**(L, x) and **push**(L, x) produce L.

    Since the queue and stack access functions add and remove elements from lists, they affect subsequent subscripting. For example, after **push**(L, x), the former element L[1] is L[2]. The effects of the queue and stack access function on subscripting generally are not a problem, since queue and stack access usually are not used in combination with positional access.

SETS

A set is an unordered collection of values. Sets have many of the properties normally associated with sets in the mathematical sense. The function

    set(L)

creates a set that contains the distinct elements of the list L. For example,

    set(["abc", 3])

creates a set with two members, **"abc"** and 3. If the argument to **set**() is omitted, an empty set is created.

    Any specific value can occur only once in a set. For example,

    set([1, 2, 3, 3, 1])

creates a set with the three members 1, 2, and 3.

    There are several operations on sets. The function

    member(S, x)

succeeds and produces x if x is a member of the set S, but fails otherwise. Note that

```
member(S1, member(S2, x))
```

succeeds if x is a member of both S1 and S2.

The function

```
insert(S, x)
```

inserts x into the set S and returns S. For example, the following procedure produces a set containing all the different words in the input file:

```
procedure diffwords()
  wordset := set()
  while line := read() do
    line ? {
      while tab(upto(&letters)) do
        insert(wordset, tab(many(&letters)))
      }
  return wordset
end
```

The function

```
delete(S, x)
```

deletes the member x from the set S and produces S.

The functions insert(S, x) and delete(S, x) always succeed, whether or not x is in S. This allows their use in loops in which failure may occur for other reasons. For example,

```
S := set()
while insert(S, read())
```

builds a set that consists of the (distinct) lines from the input file.

The operations

```
S1 ++ S2
S1 ** S2
S1 −− S2
```

create the union, intersection, and difference of S1 and S2, respectively. In each case, the result is a new set.

Note that these operations apply both to sets and csets. There is no automatic type conversion between csets and sets; the result of the operation depends on the types of the arguments. For example, 'aeiou' ++ 'abcde'

produces the cset 'abcdeiou', while

set([1, 2, 3]) ++ set([2, 3, 4])

produces a set that contains 1, 2, 3, and 4.

Several operations that apply to lists apply to sets also. *S produces the size of S, and ?S produces a randomly selected member of S. The operation !S generates the members of S but in no predictable order.

TABLES

A table is a collection of pairs, where a pair consists of a key and a corresponding value. These pairs are called elements. Tables resemble lists, except that the keys, or "subscripts", need not be integers but can be values of any type. Tables are much like the symbol tables found in typical compilers, but lookup and insertion are taken care of automatically.

Table Creation and Referencing

A table is created by the function

table(x)

where x is the default value for new elements in the table. Table references are similar to list references in appearance. For example, if words is a table created by

words := table(0)

then

words["The"] := 1

assigns the value 1 to the key "The" in words. Subsequently,

write(words["The"])

writes 1.

The value associated with a key can be changed, as in

words["The"] := words["The"] + 1

Augmented assignment is particularly useful for tables. The expression

```
words["The"] +:= 1
```

performs the same operation as the preceding expression, but "The" is looked up only once, not twice.

When a table is first created, it is empty and has a size of zero. Every time a value is assigned to a new key, the size of the table increases by 1. The operation *T produces the size of T.

An element is added to a table only when an assignment is made to a new key. Therefore, if "way" has not been assigned a value in words, the expression

```
words["way"]
```

produces the default value of 0, but "way" is not added to the table and the size of the table does not change. On the other hand,

```
words["way"] +:= 1
```

adds "way" to words and increases the size of words by 1.

Since tables often are used to count values, a typical default value is 0. For example, the following procedure produces a table of the number of times each different word occurs in the input file.

```
procedure countwords()
  wordcount := table(0)
  while line := read() do
    line ? {
      while tab(upto(&letters)) do
        wordcount[tab(many(&letters))] +:= 1
    }
  return wordcount
end
```

The operation ?T produces a randomly selected reference to the table T. If T is empty, ?T fails. Assignment can be made to ?T to change the value of the element. For example,

```
?T +:= 1
```

increments the value of a randomly selected element in T.

The operation !T generates the values of elements in T, while key(T) generates the keys in T. For example, the following expression writes all the keys and their corresponding values in the table T:

```
every x := key(T) do
  write(x, ":", T[x])
```

Note that it is always possible to get from a key to its corresponding value. Consequently, key(T) usually is more useful than !T.

Testing and Changing Table Elements

The functions member(), insert(), and delete() apply to tables as well as sets. The function member(T, x) succeeds if x is a key in the table T but fails otherwise.

The function insert(T, x, y), which is equivalent to T[x] := y, inserts an element with key x and value y into table T. If there already is a key x in T, its corresponding value is changed. An omitted third argument defaults to the null value. Note that insert() has three arguments when used with tables but only two when used with sets.

The function delete(T, x) removes the element with key value x from T. If x is not a key in T, no operation is performed; delete() succeeds in either case.

RECORDS

Records are similar to lists, except that records are fixed in size and their values are referenced by field names. Records, like procedures, are declared and are global to the entire program. A record declaration cannot appear within a procedure declaration. The declaration of a record with *n* fields has the form

record *name*(*field1*, *field2*, ..., *fieldn*)

where *name* is the name of the record and *field1*, *field2*, ..., *fieldn* are the field names associated with the record. The syntax of record names and field names is the same as the syntax for identifiers (see Appendix A). An example of a record declaration is

record complex(rpart, ipart)

Such a record declaration could be used to represent complex numbers with real and imaginary parts. Similarly, the record declaration

record employee(name, age, ssn, salary)

could be used to represent an employee whose name, age, social security number, and salary are attributes of interest.

An instance of a record is created by a *record constructor* function corresponding to the record name and with values as specified in the record declaration. For example,

origin := complex(0.0, 0.0)

assigns a complex record with zero real and imaginary parts to origin, while

clerk := employee("John Doe", 36, "123–45–6789", 35000.00)

assigns an employee record to clerk.

Fields of records are referenced by expressions of the form *name. field*. For example, the value of

origin.rpart

is 0.0. Field references, like list and table references, are variables, and values can be assigned to the corresponding fields. Therefore,

origin.ipart := 6.0

changes the imaginary part of origin to 6.0.

Several operations that apply to lists also apply to records. For example, records can be subscripted by position, as in

origin[2] +:= 2.5

which adds 2.5 to the ipart field of origin. The operation ?R produces a randomly selected reference to a field of R. The size of a record is produced as for other kinds of structures. For example, *origin produces 2. The operation !R generates the fields of R from first to last. For example,

every !R := 0

assigns 0 to every field of R.

PROPERTIES OF STRUCTURES

Structures are created during program execution. A structure value is a reference (pointer) to an aggregate of values. Furthermore, assignment copies the reference (pointer) but not the aggregate of values to which it points. There are several consequences of these properties of structures that may not be immediately obvious. Consider

```
index := list(50, 0)
temp := index
temp[1] := 1
```

The assignment of the value of index to temp does not copy the 50 values pointed to by the value of index. Instead, index and temp both point to the *same* aggregate of values. Therefore, the assignment of 1 to temp[1] changes the contents of the list that temp and index share as their value. The effect is as if

index[1] := 1

had been evaluated. Consider also

```
cycle := ["x"]
put(cycle, cycle)
```

These expressions construct a loop in which cycle contains its own value. This can be visualized as follows:

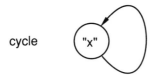

Since assignment does not copy structures, the result of an expression such as

```
L1 := L2 := list(i, 0)
```

is to assign the *same* list to both L1 and L2. Subsequently, assignment to a position in L2 changes the value of that position in L1, and conversely. Similarly, the effect of

```
L := list(3, list(5, 0))
```

is to assign the *same* list of five values to each of the three values in L. Compare this to the procedure for constructing two-dimensional arrays that is given earlier in this chapter.

The remarks above apply to all types of structures. For example, a set can be a member of (point to) itself, as in

```
S := set()
insert(S, S)
```

SORTING STRUCTURES

The values in lists, sets, and tables can be sorted to produce lists with the values in order.

Lists and Sets

If X is a list or set, the function sort(X) produces a list with the values in sorted order. If the list or set contains various types of values, the values are first sorted by type. (See Chapter 10 for more information about types.) The order of types in sorting is:

> null
> integer
> real
> string
> cset
> file
> co-expression
> procedure
> list
> set
> table
> record types

For example,

> sort([[ ], &letters, 1, 2.0])

produces a new list with the values in the following order:

> [1, 2.0, &letters, [ ]]

Integers and real numbers are sorted in nondecreasing numerical order, while strings and csets are sorted in nondecreasing lexical order. For example,

> sort(["bcd", 3, 2, 'abc', "abc", 'bcd'])

produces

> [2, 3, "abc", "bcd", 'abc', 'bcd']

Within values of one structure type, values are sorted in order of the time of their creation, with the oldest first. There is no sorting among records of different types; all records are treated as one (structure) type in sorting. The order for values of other types is unpredictable.

Tables

The function sort(T, i) produces a sorted list from the table T. The form of the result produced and the sorting order depends on the value of i.

If i is 1 or 2, the size of the sorted list is the same as the size of the table. Each value in the list is itself a list of two values: a key and the corresponding value. If i is 1, these lists are in the sorted order of the keys. If i is 2, the lists are in the sorted order of the corresponding values. If i is omitted, 1 is assumed.

If i is 3 or 4, the size of the sorted list is twice the size of the table and the values in the list are alternating keys and corresponding values for the elements in the table. If i is 3, the values are in the sorted order of the keys. If i is 4, the values are in the sorted order of the corresponding values. For example, the following program prints a count of word occurrences in the input file, using the procedure countwords() given previously:

```
procedure main()
    wlist := sort(countwords(), 3)
    while write(left(get(wlist), 12), right(get(wlist), 4))
end
```

Note that get() obtains a key first and then its corresponding value. The list is consumed in the process, but it is not needed for anything else.

SYNTACTIC CONSIDERATIONS

The field reference operation associates from left to right. Consequently,

x.y.z

groups as

(x.y).z

where y and z are field names. The field reference operation has higher precedence than any other operation, including the prefix operations. This is an exception to the general rule that prefix operations have higher precedence than infix operations. As a result,

−x.y

groups as

−(x.y)

E X E R C I S E S

6.1   Modify the program that tabulates word lengths so that there is no output for counts of zero.

6.2*   Write a program that copies the input file to the output file with the order of the lines reversed, so that the first line written is the last line read, and so on.

6.3   Modify the procedure that counts word occurrences so that the output is written in order of increasing count.

6.4   Write a program that tabulates word lengths without restriction on the length that a word may have.

6.5   Write a procedure setexor(S, x) that inserts x into the set S if it is not in S but deletes it if it is.

6.6*   Write a procedure Default(T) that produces the default value for the table T.

6.7   An *n*-gram is a sequence of *n* characters. For example, the 2-grams (digrams) in the word "ngram" are "ng", "gr", "ra", and "am". Write a procedure ngrams(i) that produces a table of the i-grams and their counts from the words in the input file. Map the words to lowercase.

6.8*   Write a set of procedures for performing complex arithmetic.

6.9   Write a set of procedures for performing rational arithmetic.

6.10   Write a procedure lmap(L1, L2, L3) that maps list elements in a manner anaolgous to map(s1, s2, s3).

7

Expression Evaluation

The way that Icon evaluates expressions is one of the most important aspects of the language. It gives Icon much of its power and provides many interesting ways of programming that are not available in most other programming languages.

Most aspects of expression evaluation are described in Chapter 2 and are illustrated by examples in subsequent chapters. This chapter describes a few more advanced aspects of expression evaluation and explores in more depth the interaction between generators and goal-directed evaluation.

BACKTRACKING

Control Backtracking

In function calls and operations (as opposed to control structures), arguments are evaluated from left to right. For example, in

   expr1 < *expr2*

the order of evaluation is *expr1* then *expr2*. If these expressions produce results, the comparison operation is performed. It is easier to follow the order of evaluation if such expressions are written in postfix form with the operator following its arguments:

$(expr1, expr2) <$

This is not Icon syntax and is used here only to explain the order of evaluation.

In this form, evaluation is strictly left to right: *expr1*, *expr2*, and then the comparison. Consider the following example:

!x < !y

written in postfix form, this becomes

(x!, y!) <

Suppose both expressions produce results and suspend. This can be depicted as follows:

g1 ← *g2*   ← last suspended generator

↑   ↑

(x!,   y!) <

The arrow from the suspended generator for !y, *g2*, back to the suspended generator for !x, *g1*, shows the order for resumption. If the comparison fails, *g2* is resumed. If it produces another result, the situation is as it was before and the comparison is performed again. However, if *g2* does not produce a result, it is removed from the chain of suspended generators and *g1* is resumed:

g1 ← last suspended generator

↑

(x!,   y!) <

If *g1* produces another result, !y is evaluated again, just as it was when !x produced its first result. On the other hand, if *g1* does not produce another result, the entire expression fails.

The left-to-right expression evaluation and last-in/first-out resumption of suspended generators results in what is called "cross-product evaluation with depth-first search". Note that it may be advisable to compose expressions in ways that take advantage of this form of search. For example, since find() produces values in increasing magnitude, it is better to use

if find(s1) < find(s2) then write("condition satisfied")

than to use

if find(s2) > find(s1) then write("condition satisfied")

since if a value for find(s1) is less than a value for find(s2), any subsequent values for find(s2) are also.

Cross-product evaluation of several generators potentially tries all possible combinations of values from the generators. This allows complex searches to be expressed very simply. Of course it is possible for such searches to be very time consuming. Three things diminish this potential problem: (1) the search is done internally and hence more efficiently than if it had to be written at the source-language level with loops and local variables, (2) most situations in which cross-product evaluation is used do not involve large "search spaces" (the problem is rarely seen in practice), and (3) generation can be limited as shown later.

Data Backtracking

Although the matching functions tab() and move() are not generators, they suspend when they produce a result. If they are resumed because of subsequent failure, they restore the former position in the subject before themselves failing. That is, they undo the change they made to the position. This is called *data backtracking*.

Only a few Icon expressions perform data backtracking. Most changes in values caused by expression evaluation are not undone during control backtracking. For example, in

```
text ? {
  (i := 10) &
  (j := (i < find(s)))
}
```

the assignment of 10 to i is not undone even if i < find(s) fails, despite the conjunction and resulting control backtracking.

The reason that matching functions perform data backtracking on the position in the subject is so that alternative matches can be specified without the failure of one interfering with another. For example, in

```
text ? {
  (tab(upto(',') +1) & write(move(1))) | write(tab(upto('.')))
}
```

if text contains a comma, the character after it is written, while otherwise the initial position of text up to a period is written (if any). If text contains only one comma as its last character, the move(1) fails, and nothing is written. Since

```
tab(upto(',') + 1)
```

is evaluated in conjunction with write(move(1)), the suspended generator from tab() is resumed and it restores the position to the beginning of the subject. Consequently the alternative tab(upto('.')) starts at the beginning of the subject. If tab() had not performed data backtracking, the position would have been left at the end of the subject, so the alternative tab(upto('.')) would have inevitably failed.

As mentioned earlier, an assignment expression such as i := 10 does not perform data backtracking; its effect is irreversible. There is, however, a reversible form of assignment, indicated by <– instead of := . For example, in

```
text ? {
  (i <– 10) &
  (j := (i < find(s)))
}
```

the assignment of 10 to i is reversed if i < find(s) fails, and it is restored to the value it had prior to the scanning expression.

There is also a reversible exchange operation, <–>, which is like :=: except that the assignments are reversed if it is resumed.

BOUNDED EXPRESSIONS

Failure within an expression causes the resumption of suspended generators, resulting in backtracking to previously evaluated portions of the expression. If there were no limits on backtracking, failure would cause control to backtrack further and further toward the first expression in a program.

Such unlimited backtracking has several undesirable effects. The most serious is that there usually are places in a program beyond which backtracking is inappropriate. For example, in

if find(s) then *expr1* else *expr2*

If find(s) produces a result, *expr1* is evaluated. However, if *expr1* fails, find(s) should not be resumed. While there might be a use for such behavior, it would not be what is meant by if-then-else.

Another problem with unlimited backtracking is that suspended generators must be kept until program execution terminates. This obviously requires space that in most cases is unneeded.

Icon handles the problem of limiting backtracking by using *bounded expressions*. If an expression is bounded and it produces a result, all suspended generators in it are discarded.

It is therefore impossible to backtrack into a bounded expression. Put another way, a bounded expression cannot generate a sequence of results.

Expressions are bounded in specific syntactic contexts. For example, the control clause in if-then-else is bounded. Consequently, in

> if find(s) then *expr1* else *expr2*

if find(s) produces a result but *expr1* fails, find(s) is not resumed. The places that bounded expressions occur are the natural ones for control flow. These are shown below, enclosed in ovals:

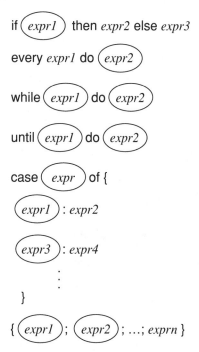

All the expressions in a compound expression are bounded except the last one.

A few consequences of bounding (and the lack of it) deserve attention. Since *expr2* and *expr3* in if-then-else are not bounded, they can generate sequences of results. An example of the usefulness of this is

> if i < j then (i to j) else (j to i)

In most cases of sequential execution, when an expression is evaluated, it is logically complete and backtracking into it is neither intended nor desired. Since all expressions in a compound expression except the last one are bounded, compound expressions provide the primary means of avoiding backtracking in sequential execution.

The composition of sequential portions of a program when backtracking is not desired is facilitated by the fact that the Icon compiler automatically inserts a semicolon at the end of a line, provided the expression on the line is complete and a new expression begins on the next line. Consequently,

```
i := find(s1); write(i); j := find(s2);
```

can be written as

```
i := find(s1)
write(i)
j := find(s2)
```

which the Icon compiler interprets as

```
i := find(s1);
write(i);
j := find(s2);
```

Thus, it is natural to write separate (bounded) expressions on separate lines. As execution goes from one line to the next, suspended generators are discarded and backtracking to preceding lines is impossible.

On the other hand, conjunction can be used to bind several lines together without bounding the expressions. For example, in

```
i := find(s1) &
write(i) &
j := find(s2)
```

semicolons are not inserted by the Icon compiler at the ends of the first two lines, since the expressions on those lines are not complete. Consequently, if find(s1) produces a result but find(s2) fails, find(s1) is resumed.

Note that bounded expressions prevent data backtracking in string scanning by preventing control backtracking.

For example, in

```
if tab(upto(',') + 1) then write(move(1))
```

the tab() expression is bounded, so that if the move() fails, tab() is not resumed and the former position is not restored.

MUTUAL EVALUATION

If the mutual success of several expressions is needed, conjunction can be compounded, as in

expr1 & *expr2* & ... & *exprn*

This notation is cumbersome, especially if the expressions are themselves complex. An alternative is *mutual evaluation*, denoted by

(*expr1*, *expr2*, ..., *exprn*)

which evaluates *expr1*, *expr2*, ..., *exprn* just like the evaluation of the arguments in a function call. If all the expressions produce results, the result of mutual evaluation is the result of *exprn*. Otherwise, the mutual-evaluation expression fails. The effect is exactly the same as in a compound conjunction. For example,

i := (upto(' ', line1), upto(' ', line2))

assigns to i the position of the first blank in line2, provided both line1 and line2 contain a blank.

Sometimes a number of expressions need to be mutually evaluated, but a result other than the last one is desired. The expression

expr (*expr1*, *expr2*, ..., *exprn*)

produces the result of *expri*, where the value of *expr* is the integer *i*, provided that all the expressions produce a result. If any of the expressions fails, however, the mutual evaluation expression fails. For example, the value of

i := 1(upto(' ', line1), upto(' ', line2))

assigns to i the position of the first space in line1, provided both line1 and line2 contain a space.

The value of e*xpr* can be negative, in which case the result is selected from right to left in the manner of nonpositive position specifications.

If the value of *expr* is out of range, the mutual-evaluation expression fails. For example,

3(*expr1, expr2*)

always fails, regardless of whether or not *expr1* and *expr2* produce results.

Although mutual evaluation has the same syntax as a function call, there is no ambiguity. If the value of *expr* is an integer *i*, the result is the result of *expri*. If the value of *expr* is a function or procedure, however, the function or procedure is called with the arguments, and the outcome of the expression is the outcome of the call.

LIMITING GENERATION

While a bounded expression is limited to at most one result, it sometimes is useful to explicitly limit an expression to a specific number of results. This can be done by the *limitation* control structure,

expr \ i

which limits *expr* to at most i results (the value of i is computed before *expr* is evaluated, an exception to the left-to-right evaluation of expressions). For example,

```
every write(upto(&lcase, line) \ 3)
```

writes at most the first three positions at which lowercase letters occur in line.

Note that limitation to one result corresponds to a bounded expression. This form of limitation is particularly useful in preventing unwanted backtracking. Consider the following procedure, which is intended to generate the words in its argument

```
procedure words(text)
  text ? {
    while tab(upto(&letters)) do
      suspend tab(many(&letters))
  }
end
```

The problem in this formulation is that when the procedure is resumed after generating one word, suspend resumes its argument. Since tab() suspended to allow for data backtracking, it is resumed and restores the scanning position to its former value. The while loop continues, but since the position is now back to where it was (at a letter), upto() produces this same position again. This procedure just generates the first word in text endlessly!

In order to prevent the unwanted data backtracking, the suspend expression can be limited as follows:

> suspend tab(many(&letters)) \ 1

In this case, tab() is not resumed, and the loop continues to the next word.

REPEATED ALTERNATION

Sometimes it is useful to generate a sequence of results repeatedly. The *repeated alternation* control structure,

> |*expr*

repeatedly generates the sequence of results for *expr*. A simple example is

> |1

which generates the sequence 1, 1, ... Another example is

> |(1 to 3)

which generates the (endless) sequence 1, 2, 3, 1, 2, 3, ...

Such sequences never terminate of their own accord and normally are used in situations where outside intervention prevents endless generation. For example,

> every write(|(0 to 7) \ 128)

writes the octal digits 16 times.

If the sequence for *expr* is empty, then the sequence for |*expr* is empty; it fails. Furthermore, if *expr* has a non-empty sequence initially, but its sequence subsequently becomes empty during the evaluation of |*expr*, the sequence for |*expr* terminates at that point. For example, the sequence for

> |read()

consists of the lines of the input file, terminating when the end of the input file is reached.

EXERCISES

7.1   Write a procedure that determines whether or not two strings have a blank in the same position. Do not use generators.

7.2   Write a procedure findi(s1, s2, i) that produces the ith position at which s1 occurs
as a substring of s2 but fails if there are less than i occurrences of s1 in s2.

7.3   Write an expression that generates the positive even integers without using seq().

7.4*   Write a procedure genpos(L, x) that generates the positions in the list L at which the
value of x occurs.

7.5*   Write a procedure geneq(L1, L2) that generates all the values in the lists L1 and L2
that are the same.

7.6   Write a procedure ranseq(i) that generates an infinite sequence of pseudo-random
integers between 1 and i, inclusive.

8

Procedures and Variables

Procedures contain expressions that are evaluated when the program is run. The arrangement of the expressions in a program into procedures specifies the organization of the program. Icon has no block structure; procedures cannot be nested.

Functions and procedures are very similar in Icon. Functions are essentially procedures that are built into the Icon system. Both procedures and functions are "first-class" values that can be assigned to variables, passed as arguments in procedure calls, and so forth.

Most values are accessed via identifiers. Scope determines how procedures can access identifiers. Icon uses lexical scoping. Global identifiers are available to all procedure calls and last until the end of program execution. Local identifiers come into existence when a procedure is called, are accessible only within that call, and cease to exist when the procedure returns. Static identifiers are accessible to all calls of the procedure in which they are declared, and last until the end of program execution.

PROCEDURE DECLARATIONS

A procedure declaration has the form

> **procedure** *name (parameter-list)*
>   *local-declarations*
>   *initial-clause*
>   *procedure-body*
> **end**

The procedure name is a global identifier. The procedure itself is a value. It is assigned to the identifier that is the name of the procedure prior to program execution.

The parameter list, which is optional, consists of identifiers separated by commas:

identifier, identifier, ...

These identifiers are local to the procedure and are not accessible elsewhere in the program. Different procedure declarations can have parameters with the same names, but parameters with the same names in different procedures have no connection with each other.

Other identifiers can be declared to be local to a procedure in optional local declarations, which have the form

local *identifier-list*

There may be more than one local declaration at the beginning of a procedure.

The initial clause, which also is optional, has the form

initial *expr*

where *expr* is an expression that is evaluated the first time the procedure is called. Uses of the initial clause are discussed later.

The body of the procedure consists of a sequence of expressions. These expressions are evaluated when the procedure is called.

Representative procedure declarations appear in preceding chapters but without declarations for local identifiers. A typical procedure with local declarations is

```
procedure exor(s1, s2)
  local count, line

  count := 0
  while line := read() do
    line ? {
      if find(s1) then {
        if not find(s2) then count +:= 1
        }
      else if find(s2) then count +:= 1
      }
  return count
end
```

A procedure can be declared to have a variable number of arguments by appending [ ] to the last (or only) parameter in the parameter list. In this form of declaration, the arguments are passed to the last parameter in a list. An example is:

```
procedure cat(s1, s2, L[ ])
   result := s1 || s2
   every result ||:= !L
   return result
end
```

If called as cat("a", "b", "c", "d", "e"), the parameters have the following values:

    s1   "a"
    s2   "b"
    L   ["c", "d", "e"]

and the result returned is "abcde".

The last parameter always is a list. This list consists of the arguments not assigned to previous parameters. If the previous parameters consume all the arguments, the list is empty. If there are not enough arguments for the previous parameters, the null value is used for the remaining ones, but the last parameter still is an empty list.

SCOPE

The identifiers in the parameter list and the identifiers in the local declarations of a procedure are local to calls of that procedure and are accessible only to expressions in the body of that procedure. Such identifiers are called *dynamic local identifiers*.

Identifiers can be made global and accessible to all procedures in a program by global declarations, which have the form

    global *identifier-list*

Global declarations are on a par with procedure declarations and they may not appear inside procedure declarations. If an identifier that is declared global also appears in a parameter list or local declaration, it is local to the procedure, not global. A declaration of a global identifier need not appear before the appearance of the identifier in a procedure.

Global identifiers are used to share values among procedures. Suppose, for example, procedures p1() and p2() both must increment the same counter. Then the following format could be used:

    global counter

    procedure p1()
            .
            .
            .
        counter +:= 1
            .
            .
            .
    end
```
```

```
procedure p2()
        .
        .
        .
    counter +:= 1
        .
        .
        .

end
```

Procedures names are global, as are the names of record types. Record field names are not identifiers; they apply to the entire program and are not affected by scope declarations.

Identifiers that are not declared to be global are local to the procedure in which they occur, whether or not they are actually declared local in that procedure. This default scope interpretation saves writing but may lead to errors. For example, a global declaration, perhaps unrelated to the procedure containing an undeclared local identifier, can cause an undeclared identifier that otherwise would be local to be interpreted as global. It, therefore, is good practice to declare all local identifiers explicitly.

Variables for dynamic local identifiers come into existence when a procedure is called and cease to exist when the procedure returns; they are only accessible during the duration of the procedure call. Local identifiers can be made *static* by using the declaration

```
static identifier-list
```

A static local identifier does not cease to exist when the procedure in which it is declared returns. Such an identifier retains its value for subsequent calls of that procedure. Therefore, a static identifier can provide "memory" for a procedure.

Static identifiers are useful when a procedure that is called many times uses a value that must be computed but is always the same. Consider a program that writes the first string of letters and digits of each line of the input file. This program can be adapted to other uses more easily if it is divided into two procedures: one that generates the strings and another that writes them. In this way, the string can be used in different ways without changing the procedure that produces them. An example is:

```
procedure main()
  every write(alphan())
end

procedure alphan()
  local line, chars

  chars := &letters ++ &digits
  while line := read() do
    line ? {
      if tab(upto(chars)) then suspend tab(many(chars))
      }
end
```

Note that the value assigned to chars is computed every time alphan() is called. This unnecessary computation can be avoided by making chars a static identifier and computing its value only once the first time that alphan() is called:

```
procedure alphan()
    local line
    static chars

    initial chars := &letters ++ &digits

    while line := read() do
        line ? {
            if tab(upto(chars)) then suspend tab(many(chars))
            }
end
```

One programming error that is difficult to locate is the failure to declare an identifier to be static, even though it is assigned a value in an initial clause. In this case, the procedure works properly the first time it is called, but the value of the identifier is lost when the procedure returns. When the procedure is called again, the new version of the identifier then has the null value.

Keywords have global scope and are not affected by procedure calls.

PROCEDURE INVOCATION

Procedure Calls

Procedures are invoked by procedure calls, which have the form

expr (*expr1*, *expr2*, ..., *exprn*)

where the value of *expr* is the procedure to be called and *expr1*, *expr2*, ..., *exprn* are expressions that provide the arguments.

Normally, there are as many arguments as there are parameters in the procedure declaration. For example,

exor("Mr.", "Mrs.")

is a call of the procedure exor() given previously. The values of the expressions are assigned to the identifiers in the parameter list (s1 and s2 in this case). Evaluation then starts at the beginning of the body of the procedure for exor().

Arguments are transmitted by value; there is no call-by-reference or other method of argument transmission.

A procedure or function also can be called with a list that contains its arguments. This form of call is

> *expr1* ! *expr2*

where the value of *expr1* is the procedure or function to be called and *expr2* is a list of arguments. For example,

> cat ! ["a", "b", "c", "d", "e"]

is equivalent to

> cat("a", "b", "c", "d", "e")

Returning from a Procedure

Evaluation of the expression

> return *expr*

causes a return from the procedure call in which it occurs. The outcome of *expr* becomes the outcome of the procedure call, and evaluation continues at the place where the call was made. A return expression *always* returns. If *expr* fails, the procedure call fails. If *expr* is omitted, the null value is returned.

The fail expression, which is equivalent to return &fail, causes a procedure to return and fail explicitly, as illustrated in previous examples. An implicit fail expression is provided at the end of the procedure body. Consequently, a procedure call that returns by flowing off the end of the procedure body fails. It is important to provide an explicit return expression at the end of such a procedure body unless failure is intended.

The return and fail expressions cause return from a procedure call and destruction of all dynamic local identifiers for that call. On the other hand,

> suspend *expr1* do *expr2*

returns from the procedure call and produces the value of *expr1* but leaves the call in suspension with the values of dynamic local variables intact. In this case, the procedure call can be resumed to continue evaluation.

The do clause is optional. If it is present, *expr2* is evaluated when the suspending procedure is resumed. Next, *expr1* is resumed again. If it produces another result, the procedure suspends again. In this sense, suspend is very similar to every; the difference is that suspend causes the procedure in which it occurs to generate a value for each value generated by *expr1*.

Recursive Calls

It is common in mathematics to define functions recursively in terms of themselves. The Fibonacci numbers provide a classic example:

$$f(i) = 1 \qquad\qquad i = 1, 2$$
$$f(i) = f(i-1) + f(i-2) \qquad i > 2$$
$$f(i) \qquad\qquad\qquad\qquad \text{undefined otherwise}$$

The sequence of Fibonacci numbers for $i = 1, 2, 3, \ldots$ is $1, 1, 2, 3, 5, 8, 13, \ldots$.

Since a procedure can call itself, this mathematical definition can be transcribed mechanically into a procedure that computes the Fibonacci numbers:

```
procedure fib(i)
   if i = (1 | 2) then return 1
   else return fib(i – 1) + fib(i – 2)
end
```

Recursive calls rely on the fact that the identifier for the procedure name is global. For example, within the procedure body for fib(), fib is a global identifier whose value is the procedure itself.

While a recursive definition may be elegant and concise, the use of recursion for computation can be very inefficient, especially when it depends on the computation of previous values. For example, to compute fib(5), it is necessary to compute fib(4) and fib(3). The computation of fib(4) also requires the computation of fib(3), and so on. Redundant computations often can be avoided by finding an alternative iterative solution (see the exercises at the end of this chapter). In some cases, however, iterative solutions can be difficult or cumbersome to formulate. The classic example is Ackermann's function [2]:

$$a(i,j) = j + 1 \qquad\qquad\qquad\qquad i = 0, \ j \geq 0$$
$$a(i,j) = a(i-1, 1) \qquad\qquad\qquad i > 0, \ j = 0$$
$$a(i,j) = a(i-1, a(i, j-1)) \qquad i > 0, \ j > 0$$
$$a(i,j) \qquad\qquad\qquad\qquad\qquad \text{undefined otherwise}$$

One method for avoiding redundant computation in recursive procedures is to provide a tabulation mechanism whereby the values of previous computations are remembered [3]. These values then can be looked up instead of being recomputed. A static identifier can be used to provide the necessary memory. Consider the following reformulation of fib(i):

```
procedure fib(i)
  static fibmem
  local j

  initial {
    fibmem := table(0)
    fibmem[1] := fibmem[2] := 1
    }

  if (j := fibmem[i]) > 0 then return j
  else return fibmem[i] := fib(i − 1) + fib(i − 2)
end
```

A table with default value 0 is assigned to the static identifier fibmem when the procedure is called the first time. Note that 0 is not a possible value in the Fibonacci sequence. The values for 1 and 2 are placed in this table. In general, if the desired value has already been computed, fibmem[i] is greater than zero and is returned. Otherwise the desired value is computed and stored in the table before returning. Note that the computation still is recursive, but no value is computed recursively more than once.

VARIABLES

Roughly speaking, a variable is anything to which a value can be assigned. There are several kinds of variables: Identifiers (global, local, and static), the elements of lists and tables, the fields of records, subscripted string-valued variables, and certain keywords.

Dereferencing

When an expression produces a variable, but a value is needed, the value of the variable is obtained automatically. This process is called *dereferencing*. Dereferencing, like type conversion, occurs implicitly. For example, in

        write(line)

the variable line is dereferenced to produce its value, which then is written.

Variables are dereferenced only when a value is needed. For example, in

        (if i > j then i else j) := 0

the variable in the selected clause is not dereferenced and 0 is assigned to i or j, depending on which has the larger prior value.

If the argument of a return expression is a local variable, it is dereferenced and the value is returned, since local variables are accessible only to the procedure in which they are declared. For example, in

```
procedure max(i, j)
   return (if i > j then i else j)
end
```

the result returned is the value of i or j, not the variable.

Non-local variables are not dereferenced. These are global identifiers, structure references, subscripted global string-valued identifiers, and those keywords that are variables. If such a variable is returned from a procedure call, it may be assigned to a value. Consider the following procedure, which produces the largest value in the list L:

```
procedure maxel(L)
   local i, j, max

   j := 1
   max := L[1]
   every i := 2  to *L do
      if max <:= L[i] then j := i
   return L[j]
end
```

Since the result that is returned is a list element, it is not dereferenced and a value can be assigned to it. For example,

```
maxel(L) := 0
```

replaces the maximum value in L by 0.

The possibility of such an assignment can be prevented by use of the explicit dereferencing operation .*expr*, which produces the value of *expr*. For example, if the return expression in the previous procedure is changed to

```
return .L[j]
```

the result returned is the value of the list element and an attempt to assign to it is erroneous.

The dereferencing operation can be applied to any expression, not just one that produces a variable. Consequently, it is not necessary to know whether or not an expression produces a variable in order to apply the dereferencing operation to it.

In a function or procedure call, dereferencing is done after all arguments have been evaluated. Consider

```
write(line, line := read())
```

In this expression a new value is assigned to line when the second argument,

```
line := read()
```

is evaluated. The first argument is not dereferenced until the value of line is changed by the evaluation of the second argument. At this time, both arguments have the same value, and two copies of the newly read line are written, not the former value of line followed by the newly read value.

Argument expressions with such side effects as this one generally should be avoided, but explicit dereferencing can be used, if necessary, to prevent unexpected results from side effects, as in

```
write(.line, line := read())
```

Variables and Names

Since references to variables usually are explicit in a program, they are obvious when reading a program. Sometimes, however, especially when debugging a program, it is handy to know the *name* of a variable. This is provided by name(v), which produces a string name for the variable v.

The names of identifiers are obvious. For example, name(main) produces "main". Similarly, keyword variables have obvious names: name(&subject) produces "&subject". In general, there is no unique string name for an element of a list. Consider, for example

```
count := list(100)
backup := count
```

Here both count and backup have the same list as value (as described in Chapter 6, they point to the same aggregate of values). Thus, the same list may be the value of many different variables. In fact, a list may not be the value of any identifier, as in

```
count[1] := list(10)
```

in which the list of 10 elements is merely the element of another list. For these reasons, the name of a list is given by its type. For example, name(count[10]) produces "list[10]". Table elements are treated similarly. For example, if the value of constants is a table, name(constants[0]) produces "table[0]".

For subscripted string-valued variables, the variable name is given, followed by the subscript range. For example, if the value of noun is "piano", name(noun[2]) produces "noun[2:3]".

In the name of a field reference, the record type and field name are used. For example, in

```
record complex(r, i)
           .
           .
           .
z := complex(2.0, 3.5)
```

name(z.r) produces "complex.r".

For identifiers and keywords that are variables, it is possible to go the other way — to get a variable from its name. The function variable(s) produces the variable whose name is s, provided s is an identifier or a keyword that is a variable. It fails otherwise. For example, if summary is a global identifier, then

        variable("summary") := 1

assigns 1 to the global identifier summary.

Local variables are accessible only in the current procedure call. For example, if summary is a local identifier in the current procedure call, variable("summary") refers to this local variable, not to the global one or any local variable in other calls.

The use of name() and variable() is illustrated by writing out the names and values of the local identifiers in a procedure. Consider the following procedure declaration:

        procedure encapsulate(term, value)
          local i, j
              .
              .
              .

Diagnostic lines such as

        write("The value of term is: ", term)

could be provided in this procedure for each local identifier of interest. This is tedious and not suited to the interaction that is needed in debugging. An interactive interface, such a

        while var := read() do
          write("The value of ", var, " is: ", image(variable(var))) |
            write(var, " is not a variable")

allows the user to specify variables of interest.

Some kinds of diagnostic output can be simplified by taking advantage of the fact that name() and variable() are inverses for identifiers. For example,

        every x := name(x1 | x2 | x3 | x4 | x5) do
          write(x, ":", image(variable(x)))

writes the name and values of x1, x2, x3, x4, and x5. It also is easy to change the identifiers in such an expression.

PROCEDURES AND OPERATORS AS VALUES

As mentioned earlier, functions are built-in procedures. The term procedure is used here for both declared procedures and built-in procedures. Procedures are the initial values of global identifiers. Procedures are known and accessed by these global identifiers — their "names". For example, the value of the global identifier write is the function that writes strings. Consequently, in write(s), the value of write is the function that is applied to s.

Since procedures are values, they may be assigned to variables, passed as arguments, and so forth. Therefore,

    print := write

assigns the procedure for write to print, and print(s) subsequently performs the same operations as write(s).

Similarly, if a procedure is declared with the name write, the declared procedure value replaces the built-in one, which is then inaccessible. It is good practice to avoid using names for declared procedures that have the same names as built-in ones.

Although the procedure that is applied in a procedure call usually is produced by an identifier, it can be the value of an expression. Therefore,

    plist := [upto, any, many]

constructs a list of procedures and

    plist[2](c, s)

is equivalent to

    any(c, s)

The procedure that is applied in a call is just the "zeroth" argument; it is evaluated before the other arguments.

Operators, unlike procedures, are not the values of global identifiers. Every operator, instead, has a special syntactic form. Except for their syntactic representation, operators are the same as built-in procedures. Although operators are not the values of global identifiers, operators have string names. For example, "!" is the name of the element generation operator. The string "*" is the name of both the unary "size" operator and the binary multiplication operator.

Procedure values, including those for operators, can be obtained from their names. The function proc(s, i) produces the procedure or operator named s but fails if s is not the name of a procedure or operator. The value of i is used to specify the number of arguments for operators. The default for i is 1. This second argument is not used for the names of procedures. For example, proc("repl") produces the function repl and proc("main") produces the main procedure. Similarly, proc("*", 1) produces the unary size operation, while proc(*, 2) produces the value for the multiplication operation.

Since the value of an operator can be obtained in this way, it can be assigned to an identifier and the operator subsequently can be called like a function. For example, in

> mult := proc("*", 2)
> :
> :
> write(mult(i, j))

the product of i and j is written.

Although assignment operations are values, their arguments are dereferenced if used in this way, resulting in an error rather than an assignment.

The string names of prefix operators and infix operators consist of the operator symbols as illustrated previously. Some operators have special forms. These operators and their string names are:

operator	string name
s[i]	"[ ]"
s[i:j]	"[:]"
i to j by k	"..."

The value of i in proc(s, i) must be correct for the name of an operator. For example, proc("...", 3) produces the operator for to-by, but proc("...") fails, since the default value of the second argument is 1.

Control structures are not operators, although some, such as alternation, are represented by an infix syntax as for operations. Field references and conjunction also are not operators.

The function args(p) produces the number of arguments expected by the procedure p. args() produces –1 for a function, like write(), that accepts a variable number of arguments. For a declared procedure with a variable number of arguments, args() produces the negative of the number of formal parameters. While proc() accepts a string argument, args() requires a procedure argument.

For example, the name of a one-argument procedure can be read in and invoked as follows:

```
while fnc := read() do
  if (fnc := proc(fnc)) & (args(fnc) = 1) then fnc(x)
  else write("invalid input")
```

STRING INVOCATION

Procedures and operators also can be invoked directly by their string names. For example,

"write"(s)

has the same effect as

write(s)

Similarly, operators can be invoked like procedures by using their string names. For example,

"−"(i1, i2)

produces the difference of i1 and i2.

In string invocation, unary operators (which have operator symbols in prefix position) are distinguished from binary operators (which have operator symbols in infix position) by the number of arguments given. Thus,

"−"(i)

computes the negative of i.

In string invocation, all arguments are dereferenced. Consequently, string invocation of an assignment operation results in an error. That is

":="(x, y)

is equivalent to

.x := .y

so that the variable to which the assignment is to be made is lost. Similarly,

"[ ]"(s1, i) := s2

is erroneous.

SYNTACTIC CONSIDERATIONS

The precedence of return is lower than that of any infix operation, so

> return i + j

groups as

> return (i + j)

Since the *expr* following return is optional, if *expr* is omitted, the null value is returned. This is useful in procedures that do not have any other value to return and corresponds to the initial null value of identifiers. Since *expr* is optional, if the value of an expression is to be returned, the expression must begin on the same line as the return. For example,

> return
>> *expr*

returns the null value and *expr* is never evaluated.

The dereferencing operation can be applied to any expression. Consequently, an expression such as .25 is not a real literal, but instead produces the integer 25.

EXERCISES

8.1   Write a procedure that produces a "snapshot" of the state of string scanning showing the value of the subject with a vertical bar underneath the character that follows the current position.

8.2   The procedure fib(i) does not check that the Fibonacci sequence is defined for the given value of i. Modify the procedure so that it fails if i is less than 1. What might be done if the value of i is not an integer?

8.3   Write an iterative procedure fib(i) that computes the ith Fibonacci number without using tabulation.

8.4*   Write a procedure acker(i, j) that computes Ackermann's function. *Warning:* The value of Ackermann's function and the time required to compute it increase *very* rapidly as the values of its arguments increase.

8.5   The "chaotic sequence" [4] is defined as follows:

$$
\begin{array}{ll}
q(i) = 1 & i = 1,\ 2 \\
q(i) = q(i - q(i-1)) + q(i - q(i-2)) & i > 2 \\
q(i) & \text{undefined otherwise}
\end{array}
$$

Write a procedure that computes $q(i)$. Compute $q(i)$ for $i = 1, 2, \ldots, 17$.

8.6   Provide tabulation for the computation of the chaotic sequence in Exercise 8.5 and compute $q(i)$ for $i = 1, 2, \ldots, 500$.

8.7*   Provide tabulation for acker(i, j) in Exercise 8.4 and compute acker(3,3).

8.8*   Write a procedure that generates the chaotic sequence.

8.9   Write a procedure comb(s, i) that generates all combinations of characters from s taken i at a time. For example, comb("abcd", 3) should generate

```
"abc"
"abd"
"acd"
"bcd"
```

8.10   Write procedures to compute the values in the sequences for the following two mutually recursive functions [4]:

$$
\begin{aligned}
f(0) &= 1 \\
m(0) &= 0 \\
f(i) &= i - m(f(i-1)) & i > 0 \\
m(i) &= i - f(m(i-1)) & i > 0 \\
f(i), m(i) & & \text{undefined otherwise}
\end{aligned}
$$

8.11   Write an interface that allows the user to set the values of variables in a running program.

8.12   Write a reverse Polish (stacking) "desk calculator" for performing Icon computations. Accept Icon numeric, cset, and string literals as values, and perform Icon operations and functions. For example, the input

```
"abc"
3
repl
```

should leave "abcabcabc" on the top of the stack. Include other operations as necessary for printing the top value of the stack, clearing the stack, and so forth.

9

Co-Expressions

In normal expression evaluation, the results produced by an expression are limited to the place where that expression appears in the program. Furthermore, the results of an expression can be produced only by iteration or by goal-directed evaluation; there is no mechanism for explicitly resuming an expression to get a result. Consequently, the results produced by an expression are strictly constrained, both in location and in the sequence of program evaluation.

Co-expressions overcome these limitations. A co-expression "captures" an expression so that it can be explicitly resumed at any time and place.

CO-EXPRESSION OPERATIONS

Co-Expression Creation

A co-expression is a data object that contains a reference to an expression and an environment for the evaluation of that expression. A co-expression is created by the control structure

　　　create *expr*

The **create** expression does not evaluate *expr*. Instead, it produces a co-expression that references *expr*. This co-expression can be assigned to a variable, passed as an argument to a procedure, returned from a procedure, and in general handled like any other value. A co-expression contains not only a reference to its argument expression, but also a copy of the dynamic local variables for the procedure in which the create appears. These copied variables have the same values as the corresponding dynamic local variables have at the time the create expression is evaluated. This frees *expr* from the place in the program where it appears and provides it with an environment of its own.

An example is

```
procedure writepos(s1, s2)
   locs1 := create find(s1)
   locs2 := create find(s2)
                  .
                  .
                  .
end
```

Here the values assigned to locs1 and locs2 are co-expressions corresponding to the expressions find(s1) and find(s2), respectively.

Activating Co-Expressions

Control is transferred to a co-expression by *activating* it with the operation @C. At this point, execution continues in the expression referenced by C. When this expression produces a result, control is returned to the activating expression and the result that is produced becomes the result of the activation expression. For example, if

```
articles := create("a" | "an" | "the")
```

then

```
write(@articles)
```

transfers control to the expression

```
"a" | "an" | "the"
```

which produces "a", and returns control to the activation expression, which writes out that result.

If the co-expression is activated again, control is transferred to the place in its expression where it last produced a result, and execution continues there. Thus, subsequent to the activation above,

```
second := @articles
```

assigns "an" to second and

third := @articles

assigns "the" to third. If article is activated again, the activation fails because there are no more results for the expression that is resumed. The activation operation produces at most one result and fails when all results of the co-expression have been produced. Consequently,

while write(@locs1)

writes out all the positions at which s1 occurs in the subject and the loop terminates when find(s1) has no more results and @locs1 fails. Note that this expression produces the same results as

every write(find(s1))

In general, in the absence of side effects

|@C

generates the same results as the expression referenced by C. Activation may occur at any time and place, however, while producing results by iteration is confined to the site at which the expression occurs.

An important aspect of activation is that it produces at most one result. Therefore, the results of a generator can be produced one at a time, where and when they are needed. For example, the results of generators can be intermingled, as in

while write(@locs1, " ", @locs2)

which writes the locations of s1 and s2 in the subject, side-by-side in columns. Since activation fails when there are no more results, the loop terminates when either generator runs out of results.

The results produced by a co-expression are dereferenced according to the same rules that apply to procedures. Specifically, if the result is a local variable, it is dereferenced.

Refreshing Co-Expressions

Since activation produces a result for a co-expression, it has the side effect of changing the "state" of the co-expression, and effectively consumes a result, much in the way that reading a line of a file consumes that line. Sometimes it is useful to "start a co-expression over". Although there is no way to reset the state of a co-expression to its initial value at the time of its creation, the operation ^C produces a "refreshed" *copy* of a co-expression C. The term "refresh" is somewhat of a misnomer, since it sounds like C is refreshed; in fact, it does not change C, but instead produces a new co-expression. Typical usage is

C := ^C

Number of Values Produced

The "size" of a co-expression, given by $*C$, is the number of results it has produced. Each successful activation of a co-expression increments its size (which starts at 0). For example,

```
if *C = 0 then write(@C)
```

writes a result for C, provided it has not yet produced a result. Of course, $@C$ fails if there are no results at all. Similarly,

```
while @C
write(*C)
```

writes the number of results for the expression referenced by C. Such usage obviously is risky, since an expression may have an infinite number of results.

Co-Expression Environments

As mentioned earlier, a co-expression is created with *copies* of the dynamic local variables for the procedure in which the **create** expression occurs. These copies have the values of the corresponding local variables at the time the **create** expression is evaluated. This aspect of co-expression creation has several implications.

Since every co-expression has its own copies of dynamic local variables, two co-expressions can share a variable only if it is global or static. Failure to recognize that every co-expression has its own copy of its local variables can lead to programming mistakes, since the names of the variables in different co-expressions created in the same procedure are the same, making the variables appear to be the same.

When a new co-expression is created by ^{C}, new copies of the dynamic local variables are made, but with the values they had at the time that C was originally created. Consider, for example,

```
local i
i := 1
seq1 := create |(i *:= 2)
i := 3
seq2 := create |(i *:= 2)
```

The results produced by successive activations of **seq1** are 2, 4, 8, 16, ... , while the results produced by **seq2** are 6, 12, 24, ... Then, for

```
seq3 := ^seq1
```

the results produced by **seq3** are 2, 4, 8, 16, ... , since the initial value of i in **seq1** is 1 and it is not affected by the subsequent assignment of 3 to i — the two variables are distinct.

USING CO-EXPRESSIONS

As mentioned earlier, co-expressions are useful in situations in which the production of the results of a generator needs to be controlled, instead of occurring automatically as the result of goal-directed evaluation or iteration. Since most of the utility of co-expressions comes from generators, most co-expression applications depend on the use of generators.

Labels and Tags

In some situations, a sequence of labels or tags is needed. For example, an assembler may need a source of unique labels for referencing the code it produces, while a procedure that traverses a graph may need tags to name nodes.

A generator, such as

```
"L" || seq()
```

is a convenient way of formulating a sequence of labels. However, the need for a new label may occur at different times and places in the program and a single generator such as the one above cannot be used. One solution to this problem is to avoid generators and use a procedure such as

```
procedure label()
  static i
  initial i := 0
  return "L" || (i +:= 1)
end
```

Thus, label() produces the next label.

The use of such a procedure gives up much of the power of expression evaluation in Icon, since it encodes, at the source level, the computation that a generator does internally and automatically. To use a generator, a co-expression such as

```
label := create ("L" || seq())
```

suffices. Here, @label produces the next label.

Parallel Evaluation

One of the common paradigms that motivates co-expression usage is the generation of results from generators in parallel. Consider, for example, producing a tabulation showing the decimal, hexadecimal, and octal values for all characters, along with their images. The values for each column are easily produced by generators:

0 to 255

!"0123456789ABCDEF" || !"0123456789ABCDEF"

(0 to 3) || (0 to 7) || (0 to 7)

image(!&cset)

In order to produce a tabulation, however, the results of these generators are needed in parallel. This cannot be done by simple expression evaluation. The solution is to create a co-expression for each generator and to activate these co-expressions in parallel:

```
decimal := create (0 to 255)
hex := create (!"0123456789ABCDEF" || !"0123456789ABCDEF")
octal := create ((0 to 3) || (0 to 7) || (0 to 7))
character := create image(!&cset)
```

Then an expression such as

```
while write(right(@decimal, 3), " \t ", right(@hex, 3), " \t ", @octal, " \t ",
   right(@character, 4))
```

can be used to produce the tabulation:

0	00	000	"\x00"
1	01	001	"\x01"
2	02	002	"\x02"
3	03	003	"\x03"
4	04	004	"\x04"
		.	
		.	
		.	
97	61	141	"a"
98	62	142	"b"
99	63	143	"c"
100	64	144	"d"
		.	
		.	
		.	
251	FB	373	"\xfb"
252	FC	374	"\xfc"
253	FD	375	"\xfd"
254	FE	376	"\xfe"
255	FF	377	"\xff"

Another example of parallel evaluation occurs when the results produced by a generator are to be assigned to a sequence of variables. Suppose the first three results for find(s) are to be assigned to i, j, and k, respectively. This can be done as follows:

```
loc := create find(s)
every (i | j | k) := @loc
```

Of course, if find(s) has fewer than three results, not all of the assignments are made.

PROGRAMMER-DEFINED CONTROL OPERATIONS

Control structures are provided so that the flow of control during program execution can be modified depending on the results produced by expressions. In Icon, most control structures depend on success or failure. For example, the outcome of

if *expr1* then *expr2* else *expr3*

depends on whether or not *expr1* succeeds or fails.

Icon's built-in control structures are designed to handle the situations that arise most often in programming. There are many possible control structures in addition to the ones that Icon provides (parallel evaluation is perhaps the most obvious).

Co-expressions make it possible to extend Icon's built-in repertoire of control structures. Consider a simple example of parallel evaluation:

```
procedure parallel(C1, C2)
  local x

  repeat {
    if x := @C1 then suspend x else fail
    if x := @C2 then suspend x else fail
    }
end
```

where C1 and C2 are co-expressions. For example, the results for

parallel(create !&lcase, create !&ucase)

are "a", "A", "b", "B", ... "z", and "Z". In this case, both co-expressions have the same number of results. In general, parallel(C1, C2) terminates when either C1 or C2 runs out of results.

This formulation of parallel evaluation is cumbersome, since the user must explicitly create co-expressions for each invocation of parallel(). Icon provides a form of procedure invocation in which arguments are passed as a list of co-expressions. This form of invocation is denoted by braces instead of parentheses, so that

p{*expr1*, *expr2*, ..., *exprn*}

is equivalent to

p([create *expr1*, create *expr2*, ..., create *exprn*])

Thus, p() is called with a single argument, so that of an arbitrary number of co-expressions can be given.

Using this facility, parallel evaluation can be formulated as follows:

```
procedure Parallel(L)        # called as Parallel{expr1, expr2}
   local x

   repeat {
      if x := @L[1] then suspend x else fail
      if x := @L[2] then suspend x else fail
      }
end
```

For example, the results for Parallel{!&lcase, !&ucase} are "a", "A", "b", "B" ... "z", and "Z".

It is easy to extend parallel evaluation to an arbitrary number of arguments:

```
procedure Parallel(L)        # called as Parallel{expr1, expr2, ..., exprn}
   local x, C

   repeat
      every C := !L do
         if x := @C then suspend x else fail
end
```

Another example of the use of programmer-defined control operations is a procedure that generalizes alternation to an arbitrary number of expressions:

```
procedure Alt(L)             # called as Alt{expr1, expr2, ..., exprn}
   local C

   every C := !L do
      suspend |@C
end
```

Some operations on sequences of results are more useful if applied in parallel, rather than on the cross product of results. An example is

```
procedure Add(L)             # called as Add{expr1, expr2}
   suspend |(@L[1] + @L[2])
end
```

String invocation often is useful in programmer-defined control operations. An example is a procedure that "reduces" a sequence by applying a binary operation to successive results:

```
procedure Reduce(L)           # called as Reduce{op, expr}
   local op, opnds, result

   op := @L[1] | fail          # get the operator
   opnds := L[2]               # get the co-expression for the arguments
   result := @opnds | fail
   while result := op(result, @opnds)
   return result
end
```

For example, the result of Reduce{"+", 1 to 10} is 55.

Another application for programmer-defined control operations is in the production of a string representation of a sequence of results:

```
procedure Seqimage(L)         # called as Seqimage{expr, i}
   local seq, result, i

   seq := ""
   i := @L[2] | 10                    # limit on number of results
   while result := image(@L[1]) do {
      if *L[1] > i then {
         seq ||:= ", ..."
         break
         }
      else seq ||:= ", " || result
      }
   return "{" || seq[3:0] || "}" | "{}"
end
```

For example, the result produced by Seqimage{1 to 8} is "{1, 2, 3, 4, 5, 6, 7, 8 }".

ADVANCED USES OF CO-EXPRESSIONS

Although co-expressions are motivated by the need to control the results produced by generators, they also can be used as coroutines. A general description of coroutine programming is beyond the scope of this book; see [.knuth coroutines, marlin coroutines, scoexp.].

Transfer of Control Among Co-Expressions

As illustrated earlier, a co-expression can transfer control to another co-expression by two means: Activating it explicitly, as in @C or returning control to it implicitly by producing a result. Despite the appearance of dissimilarity between these two methods for transferring control, they really are symmetric.

It is important to understand that transferring control from one co-expression to another co-expression by either method changes the place in the program where execution is taking place and changes the environment in which expressions are evaluated. Unlike procedure calls, however, transfer of control among co-expressions is not hierarchical.

This is illustrated by the use of co-expressions as coroutines. Consider, for example, the following program:

```
global C1, C2

procedure main()
  C1 := create note(C2, "co–expression C2")
  C2 := create note(C1, "co–expression C1")
  @C1

end

procedure note(C, tag)
  local i

  i := 0
  repeat {
    write("activation ", i +:= 1, " of ", tag)
    @C
  }

end
```

When C1 is activated, the procedure note() is called with two arguments: the co-expression C2 and a string used for identification. Execution continues in note(). A line of output is produced, and C2 is activated. As a result, there is another call of note(). It writes a line of output and activates C1. At this point, control is transferred to the first call of note() at the point it activated C2. Control then transfers back and forth between the two procedure calls, and the output produced is

```
activation 1 of co–expression C2
activation 1 of co–expression C1
activation 2 of co–expression C2
activation 2 of co–expression C1
activation 3 of co–expression C2
activation 3 of co–expression C1
activation 4 of co–expression C2
activation 4 of co–expression C1
activation 5 of co–expression C2
activation 5 of co–expression C1
activation 6 of co–expression C2
activation 6 of co–expression C1
          :
          :
```

This continues endlessly and neither procedure call ever returns.

Built-In Co-Expressions

There are three built-in co-expressions that facilitate transfer of control: &source, &current, and &main.

The value of &source is the co-expression that activated the currently active co-expression. Thus,

    @&source

"returns" to the activating co-expression.

The value of &current is the co-expression in which execution is currently taking place. For example,

    process(&current)

passes the current co-expression to the procedure process(). This co-expression could be used to assure return of control to the co-expression that was current when process() was called.

The value of &main is the co-expression for the invocation of the main procedure. This co-expression corresponds to the invocation of the main procedure that initiates program execution, which can be viewed as

    @(create main())

The co-expression &main is the first co-expression that is created in every program.

If program execution is taking place in any co-expression,

    @&main

returns control to the co-expression for the procedure main() at the point it activated a co-expression. Note that this location need not be in the procedure main() itself, since main() may have called another procedure from which the activation of a co-expression took place.

Transmission

A result can be transmitted to a co-expression when it is activated. Transmission is done by the operation

    expr @ C

where C is activated and the result of *expr* is transmitted to it. In fact, @C is just an abbreviation for

&null @ C

so that every activation actually transmits a result to the co-expression that is being activated.

On the first activation of a co-expression, the transmitted result is discarded, since there is nothing to receive it. On subsequent activations, the transmitted result becomes the result of the expression that activated the current co-expression.

The use of transmission is illustrated by the following program, which reads in lines from standard input, breaks them up into words, and writes out these words on separate lines. Co-expressions are used to isolate the tasks: reading lines, producing the words from the lines, and writing out the words.

```
global words, lines, writer

procedure main()
  words := create word()
  lines := create reader()
  writer := create output()
  @writer
end

procedure word()
  while line := @lines do
    line ? while tab(upto(&letters)) do
      tab(many(&letters)) @ writer
end

procedure reader()
  while read() @ words
end

procedure output()
  while write(@words)
  @&main
end
```

Note that output() activates main() to terminate program execution.

This example is designed to illustrate transmission, not as a recommended programming technique. The problem above can be solved more simply by using generators and procedure calls, since there is nothing in the problem that requires coroutine control flow or the generation of results at arbitrary times or places. Coroutine programming generally is appropriate only in large programs that benefit from the organization that coroutines allow. Knuth [5] says "It is rather difficult to find short, simple examples of coroutines which illustrate the importance of the idea; the most useful coroutine applications generally are quite lengthy", and Marlin [6] remarks " ... the choice of an example program is ... difficult ... . The programming methodology is intended for programming-in-the-large".

SYNTACTIC CONSIDERATIONS

The reserved word create has lower precedence than any operator symbol. For example,

> articles := create "a" | "an" | "the"

groups as

> articles := create ("a" | "an" | "the")

Although parentheses usually are unnecessary, they improve the readability of create expressions.

E X E R C I S E S

9.1   Write a procedure labgen(s) that produces a co-expression for a label sequence with the prefix s.

9.2   Write a procedure eqlseq(C1, C2) that succeeds if C1 and C2 have sequences of equal length but fails otherwise.

9.3*   Write a programmer-defined control operation Odd{*expr*} that generates the odd-numbered values in the sequence generated by *expr*.

9.4*   Write a programmer-defined control operation Repalt{*expr*} that models |*expr*.

9.5*   Write a programmer-defined control operation Limit{*expr1, expr2*} that models *expr1* \ *expr2*.

9.6   Write a programmer-defined control operation

> Amplify{*expr1, expr2, expr3, ..., exprn*}

that generates the first result from its first argument, then the first two results from its second argument, then the first three results from its third argument, and so on, starting all over again after generating the first *n* results from its *n*th argument. However, it should stop generating results if any argument does not produce the required number of results. For example, Amplify{1 to 10, !&lcase} should generate 1, "a", "b", 1, "a", "b", ..., but Amplify{1 to 10, !&lcase, 3} should generate 1, "a", "b", 3.

10

Data Types

As illustrated in the previous chapters, Icon has a large repertoire of types, eleven in all:

co–expression	list	set
cset	null	string
file	procedure	table
integer	real	

Record declarations add new "programmer-defined" types.

TYPE DETERMINATION

Sometimes it is useful, especially in program debugging, to be able to determine the type of a value. The function type(x) produces a string that is the name of the type of x. For example, the value of

        type("Hello world")

is "string". Similarly,

        if type(i) == "integer" then write("okay")

writes okay if the value of i is an integer.

Functions, which are simply built-in procedures, have type procedure. For example, the value of

    type(write)

is "procedure".

A record declaration adds a type to the built-in repertoire of Icon. For example, the declaration

    record complex(rpart, ipart)

adds the type complex. If a complex record is assigned to origin, as in

    origin := complex(0.0, 0.0)

then the value of

    type(origin)

is "complex".

TYPE CONVERSION

Values of four types can be converted to values of other types. The possible type conversions are given in the following table.

type in	*type out*			
	cset	integer	real	string
cset	=	?	?	√
integer	√	=	?	√
real	√	?	=	√
string	√	?	?	=

The symbol √ indicates a conversion that is always possible, while ? indicates a conversion that may or may not be possible, depending on the value. The = indicates that nothing needs to be done to convert a value to its own type.

A string can be converted to a numeric type only if it "looks like a number". For example, "1500" can be converted to the integer 1,500, but "a1500" and "1,500" cannot be converted to integers. Signs and radix literals are allowed in conversion of strings to numeric types. For example, "–2.5" can be converted to –2.5 and "16ra" can be converted to 10. Blanks are ignored in strings that are converted to numeric types. The empty string is not convertible to zero. On implementations of Icon that do not support large integers, the conversion of strings to integers is limited by the allowable size of integers (see Chapter 5).

Since numbers are limited in size, the strings that can be converted to numbers are correspondingly limited. A real number can be converted to an integer provided the real number is not too large. Any fractional part is discarded in the conversion; no rounding occurs.

When csets are converted to strings, the characters are put in lexical order. For example, conversion of &lcase to a string produces "abcdefghijklmnopqrstuvwxyz".

When a cset is converted to a numeric type, it is first converted to a string, and then string-to-numeric conversion is performed.

Type conversions take two forms: *implicit* and *explicit*.

Implicit Type Conversion

Implicit conversion occurs in contexts where the type of a value that is expected by an operation is different from the type that is given. For example, in

    write(*line)

the integer produced by *line is converted to a string in order to be written. Similarly, in

    i := upto("aeiou", line)

the string "aeiou" is automatically converted to a cset.

In some situations, implicit conversion can be used to explicitly convert a value to a desired type. For example,

    N := +s

is a way of converting a string that looks like a number to an actual number. Note that the converted value is assigned to N, but the value of s remains unchanged.

Implicit type conversion sometimes can occur unexpectedly. For example, a comparison operation produces the value of its right argument, converted to the type expected by the comparison. Therefore,

    i := (j > "20")

assigns the integer 20, not the string "20" to i, provided the comparison succeeds.

Unnecessary type conversion can be a significant source of program inefficiency. Since there is no direct evidence of implicit type conversion, this problem can go unnoticed. For example, in an expression such as

upto("aeiou")

the argument is converted from a string to a cset every time the expression is evaluated. If this expression occurs in a loop that is evaluated frequently, program execution speed may suffer considerably. Where a cset is expected, it is important to use a cset literal or some other cset-valued expression that does not require conversion.

An implicit type conversion that cannot be performed is an error and causes program execution to terminate with a diagnostic message. For example,

N +:= "a"

is erroneous.

Implicit type conversion is not performed for comparing values in case clauses or for the keys in tables. For example, T[1] and T["1"] reference different elements in T.

Explicit Type Conversion

Explicit conversion is performed by functions whose names correspond to the desired types. For example,

s := string(x)

converts x to a string and assigns that string value to s. The other explicit type-conversion functions are cset(x), integer(x), and real(x). The function numeric(x) converts strings to their corresponding numeric values if possible. This function is useful for converting a value that may represent either an integer or a real number. For example,

numeric("10.0")

produces 10.0, but

integer("10.0")

produces 10.

Explicit conversion sometimes can be used as a way of performing a computation that otherwise would be difficult. For example,

s := string(cset(s))

eliminates duplicate characters of s and puts the remaining characters in lexical order.

If an explicit type conversion cannot be performed, the type conversion function fails. For example,

    numeric("a")

fails. Explicit type conversion therefore can be used to test the convertibility of a value without risking program termination.

THE NULL VALUE

The null value is a single, unique value of type null. All identifiers have the null value initially.

The null value, usually provided as the result of an omitted argument, is also used to specify default values in many functions. Most other uses of the null value are erroneous. This prevents the accidental use of an uninitialized identifier in a computation. For example, if no value has been assigned to i, evaluation of the expression

    j := i + 10

causes program termination with a diagnostic message.

Since the null value cannot be used in most computations, care should be taken to specify appropriate initial values for structures. Similarly,

    words := table()

creates a table in which the default value is null. Consequently,

    words["The"] +:= 1

is erroneous, since this expression attempts to add 1 to the null value.

Assignment is indifferent to the null value. Therefore,

    x := &null

assigns the null value to x.

There are two operations that succeed or fail, depending on whether or not an expression has the null value. The operation

    /x

succeeds and produces the null value if x produces the null value, but it fails if x produces any other value.

The operation

    \x

succeeds and produces the value of x if that value is any value except the null value, but fails if x produces the null value. This operation is useful for determining whether or not a variable has been assigned a value.

If the argument of one of these operations is a variable and the operation succeeds, the operation produces the variable. Therefore, assignment can be made to the result of such an operation, so that

/x := 0

assigns 0 to x if x has the null value, while

\x := 0

assigns 0 to x if x does not have the null value.

As in all operations, the arguments of these operations can be expressions. For example, if a table is created with the null default value, as in

T := table()

then

\T["the"]

succeeds if the key "the" in T has been assigned a nonnull value; otherwise, this expression fails.

The control structure not *expr* produces the null value if *expr* fails.

COMPARING VALUES

Five of the eleven built-in data types in Icon: cset, integer, null, real, and string, have the property of having "unique" values. This means that equivalent values of these types are indistinguishable, regardless of how they are computed. For example, there is just one distinguishable integer 0. This value is the same, regardless of how it is computed.

Whether or not two numbers are the same is determined by a numerical comparison operation. Therefore,

$$(1 - 1) = (2 - 2)$$

succeeds, because the two arguments have the same value (by definition).

The property of uniqueness is natural for numbers and is essential for numerical computation. The uniqueness of csets and strings is not a necessary consequence of their inherent properties, but it plays an important role in Icon. For example, ("ab" || "cd") == ("a" || "bcd")

succeeds because both arguments have the same value, even though the value is computed in different ways.

Numerical and string comparisons are restricted to specific data types, although type conversions are performed automatically. For example, csets are converted to strings in string comparison operations.

There is also a general value-comparison operation

x === y

which compares arbitrary values x and y, as well as the converse operation

x ~=== y

Unlike string comparison, value comparison fails if x and y do not have the same type: No implicit type conversion is performed. For the types that have unique values, value comparison succeeds if the values are the same, regardless of how they are computed. For other types, value comparison succeeds only if the values are *identical*.

Lists can be equivalent without being identical. For example,

[1] === [1]

fails because the two lists are not identical, even though they are equivalent in size and contents. However, in

L := [1]
L === L

the comparison succeeds, because assignment does not copy structures, and the two arguments have identical values.

Value comparison is used implicitly in case expressions and table references. For example, if the value of x is the integer 1, in

case x of {
  "1": *expr*
       .
       .
       .
}

the first case clause is not selected, since the types of the values compared are different. Similarly,

T["abcdefghijklmnopqrstuvwxyz"]

and

T[&lcase]

reference different values in the table T, but

T["abcdefghijklmnopqrstuvwxyz"]

and

T[string(&lcase)]

reference the same value, since string values are unique.

COPYING VALUES

Any value can be copied by copy(x). For lists, sets, tables, and records, a new copy of x is made. This copy is distinct from x. For example, in

```
L := [1]
L === copy(L)
```

the comparison fails. Only the list itself is copied; values in the copy are the same as in the original list (copying is "one level"). For example, in

```
L1 := [ ]
L2 := [L1]
L3 := copy(L2)
L3[1] === L2[1]
```

the comparison succeeds, since both L2[1] and L3[1] are the same list, L1.

For values other than lists, sets, tables, and records, copy(x) simply produces the value of x; no actual copy is made. Therefore,

```
write === copy(write)
```

succeeds. Copying a co-expression does not produce a refreshed copy of it.

STRING IMAGES

When debugging a program it is often useful to know what a value is. Its type can be determined by type(x), but this is not helpful if the actual value is of interest. Its value can be written, provided it is of a type that can be converted to a string, although there is no way to differentiate different types whose written values are the same, such as the integer 1 and the string "1".

The function image(x), described for strings and csets in Chapter 4, provides a string representation of x for all types. The data type, current size, and a serial number are given for lists, sets, tables, and records. For example,

    image([1, 4, 9, 16])

produces a result such as "list_10(4)". The number after the underscore is the serial number, which starts at 1 for the first list created during program execution and increases with each newly created list. Lists, sets, tables, and each record type have separate serial-number sequences.

Although functions and procedures have the same type, they are distinguished in string images. For example,

    image(main)

produces "procedure main", while

    image(trim)

produces "function trim".

In the case of a record declaration such as

    record complex(rpart, ipart)

the record constructor is distinguished from functions, so

    image(complex)

produces "record constructor complex". On the other hand, complex values have the same kind of string image that other structures have:

    image(complex(0.0, 0.0))

produces a result such as "record complex_5(2)".

Some built-in values have string images consisting of the keyword that produces the value. For example,

    image()

produces "&null".

The image of a co-expression includes its serial number and the number of times it has been activated in parentheses. The serial number for &main is 1. For example,

    image(&main)

produces "co-expression_1(1)", assuming &main has not been activated since its initial activation to start program execution.

EXERCISES

10.1   Assuming that each line of the input file is supposed to be a single number, write a program that checks the input file to be sure it contains only numeric values.

10.2* Write a procedure hexcvt(s) that converts strings representing hexadecimal numbers to their numerical equivalents. For example, hexcvt("a7") should produce 167.

10.3   Write a program that writes the lines of the input file that contain duplicate characters.

10.4   Write a procedure that does what the function find(s1, s2, i1, i2) does.

10.5   Write a procedure that produces a completely duplicated copy of its argument, including structures nested to arbitrary levels.

11

Input and Output

FILES

All reading and writing in earlier examples are from *standard input* to *standard output*. In an interactive system, standard input often comes from the user's terminal and standard output often is written to this terminal. These standard files are implicit in reading and writing operations; they are the default files that are used in case no specific files are given.

Values of type file are used to reference actual files of data that are external to the program. There are three predefined values of type file:

&input	standard input
&output	standard output
&errout	standard error output

The values of these keywords cannot be changed. Standard input and output normally are used for input and output. On most systems standard input and standard output can be connected to specific files when the Icon program is run. This allows a program to use any input and output files without having to incorporate the names of the files in the text of the program. By convention, standard error output is used for error messages so that such messages are not mixed up with normal output.

While many programs can be written using just standard input and output, sometimes it is necessary to use other files. For example, some programs must read from several files or write to several files.

How files are named is a property of the operating system under which Icon runs, not a property of Icon itself. For example, when Icon runs under UNIX, UNIX file naming conventions apply.

The name of a file is specified when it is opened for reading or writing; at this point a value of type file is created in the program and connected with the actual file that is to be read or written. The function

open(s1, s2)

opens the file named s1 according to options given in s2 and produces a value of type file that can be used to reference the named file.

The options given in s2 specify how the file is to be used. Some options can be used in combination. These options are inherently somewhat dependent on the operating system, although some options are common to all operating systems. The two basic options for opening files are:

"r"	open for reading
"w"	open for writing

Other options are:

"b"	open for reading and writing (bidirectional)
"a"	open for writing in append mode
"c"	create and open for writing
"t"	open in translated mode
"u"	open in untranslated mode
"p"	open pipe

The "b" option usually applies to interactive input and output at a terminal that behaves like a file that is both written and read. With the "p" option, the first argument is passed to an operating-system shell for execution. Not all operating systems support pipes. If a file is opened for writing but not for reading, "c" is implied. The "c" and "a" options have no effect on pipes. Upper- and lowercase letters are equivalent in option specifications. The translated and untranslated modes and pipes are described later in this chapter.

If the option is omitted, "r" is assumed. For example,

intext := open("shaw.txt")

opens the file shaw.txt for reading and assigns the resulting file to intext. The omission of the second argument with the subsequent default to "r" is common practice in Icon programming.

A file that is opened for reading must already exist; if it does not, open() fails. A file that is opened for writing may or may not already exist. If it does not exist, a new file with the name s1 is created. If this is not possible (there may be various reasons, depending on the environment), open() fails. If the file does exist, the previous contents of the file are destroyed unless the "a" option is used, in which case new output is written at the end of old data. Some files may be protected to prevent them from being modified; open() fails if an attempt is made to open such a file for writing.

Since open() may fail for a variety of reasons, it is good practice to check for possible failure, even if it is not expected. An example is

if not(intext := open("shaw.txt")) then stop("cannot open shaw.txt")

This also can be formulated as

(intext := open("shaw.txt")) | stop("cannot open shaw.txt")

The function close(f) closes the file f. This has the effect of physically completing output for f, such as flushing output buffers, and making the file inaccessible for further input or output. A file that has been closed can be opened again for input or output.

If several files are used, it is good practice to close files when they are no longer needed, since most operating systems allow only a limited number of files to be open at the same time. All open files are closed automatically when program execution terminates.

INPUT

The function read(f) reads the next line from the file referenced by f. If f is omitted, standard input is assumed, as is illustrated in earlier examples. For example, the following program copies shaw.txt to standard output.

```
procedure main()
    (intext := open("shaw.txt")) | stop("cannot open shaw.txt")
    while write(read(intext))
end
```

In text files, line terminators separate the lines. These line terminators are discarded by read(f) and are not included in the strings it produces.

When there is no more data in a file, read() fails. This end-of-file condition can be used to terminate a loop in which the read occurs, as illustrated in earlier examples.

The operation !f generates the lines from the file f, terminating when an end of file is reached. As with read(), line terminators are discarded. For example,

every line := !&input do ...

is equivalent to

while line := read() do ...

Sometimes it is useful to be able to read a fixed number of characters instead of lines. This is done by

> reads(f, i)

where f is the file that is read and i specifies how many characters are to be read. If f is omitted, standard input is assumed. If i is omitted, 1 is assumed. The function reads(f, i) reads a string of i characters; line terminators are not discarded and they appear in the string that is read. If there are not i characters remaining, only the remaining characters are read. In this case the value produced is shorter than i. The function reads() fails if there are no characters remaining in the file.

There is no limit to the length of a string that can be produced by read() or reads() except for the amount of memory needed to store it.

OUTPUT

The function

> write(x1, x2, ..., xn)

writes strings. What write() does depends on the types of its arguments. The simplest case is

> write(s)

which simply writes a line consisting of the string s to standard output. The function write() automatically appends a line terminator, so s becomes a new line at the end of the file.

If there are several string arguments, as in

> write(s1, s2, ..., sn)

then s1, s2, ..., sn are written in sequence and a line terminator is appended to the end. Therefore, the line consists of the concatenation of s1, s2, ..., sn, although the concatenation is done on the file, not in the Icon program. When several strings are written in succession to form a single line, it is much more efficient to use write() with several arguments than to actually concatenate the strings in the program.

The most general case is

> write(x1, x2, ..., xn)

where x1, x2, ..., xn may have various types. If the *i*th argument, xi, is not a string, it is converted to a string if possible and then written. If xi is a file, subsequent output is directed to that file. The following program, for example, copies shaw.txt to standard output and also copies it to shaw.cpy:

```
procedure main()
  (intext := open("shaw.txt")) | stop("cannot openshaw.txt")
  (outtext := open("shaw.cpy", "w")) | stop("cannot open shaw.cpy")
  while line := read(intext) do {
    write(line)
    write(outtext,line)
    }
end
```

The output file can be changed in midstream. Therefore,

```
write(&errout, s1, &output, s2)
```

writes s1 to standard error output and s2 to standard output. A separate line is written to each file; a line terminator is appended whenever the file is changed.

If the ith argument, xi, is not a file and is not convertible to a string, program execution terminates with a diagnostic message. There is one exception; the null value is treated like an empty string. Therefore,

```
write()
```

writes an empty line (a line terminator) to standard output.

The function

```
writes(x1, x2, ..., xn)
```

is like write(), except that a line terminator is not appended to the end. One line on a file can be built up using writes() several times. Similarly, prompting messages to users of interactive programs can be produced with writes() to allow the user at a computer terminal to enter input on the same visual line as the prompt. For example, the following program prompts the user for the names of the input and output files for a file copy:

```
procedure main()
  writes("specify input file: ")
  while not(intext := open(read())) do
    writes("cannot open input file, respecify: ")

  writes("specify output file: ")
  while not(outtext := open(read(), "w")) do
    writes("cannot open output file, respecify: ")

  while write(outtext, read(intext))
end
```

In addition to writing, write() and writes() produce the last value written. For example,

last := write("The final value is ", count)

assigns the value of count to last.

There is no limit to the length of a string that can be written by write() or writes() except for the amount of file space needed for it.

TEXT FILES AND BINARY FILES

Text files are usually thought of as files composed of lines that contain printable characters, while binary files (such as executable programs) have no line structure and may contain nonprintable characters. While this view of text and binary files fits most situations well, in reality the distinction is not that clear.

Some computer systems, notably UNIX, do not differentiate at all between text and binary files. On these systems, a file is simply a sequence of characters. Other computer systems distinguish between text and binary files, and a file can be opened in either text or binary mode. How a file is opened determines how it is treated during input and output.

For historical reasons, it also is common on ASCII-based systems to think of text characters as being only those in the first half of the character set (that is, those with the high-order bit not set). However, 128 different characters have proved too few for modern applications, and many systems use almost all of the 256 characters for text. Consequently, the important matter is not the characters that a file contains, but whether or not it is viewed as consisting of lines. When a file is viewed as text, it is thought of as consisting of lines, while there is no such structure in binary files. Conceptually, a line is a sequence of characters followed by a line terminator. When a line is read, the sequence of characters up to the line terminator is returned and the line terminator is discarded. When the line is written, a line terminator is appended to become part of the file.

Unfortunately, not all computer systems use the same line terminator. On UNIX and the Amiga, lines are terminated by linefeed characters (hex 0A). On MS-DOS and the Atari ST, lines are terminated by two characters: return/linefeed pairs (hex 0D/hex 0A). On the Macintosh, lines are terminated by return characters (hex 0D). On some computer systems, the line terminator is not even composed of characters.

Notice that except for the characters actually in the file, the effect is the same when reading and writing lines, regardless of the nature of the line terminator: It is discarded on input and appended on output. As long as line-oriented input/output is done on text files, there is no need to worry about line terminators. Note that writes() does not append a line terminator, so it can be used to build up lines incrementally.

As mentioned previously, on UNIX systems line terminators are linefeed characters, which are represented literally by "\n". Thus,

write(line1, "\n", line2, "\n", line3)

writes three lines, since separating line terminators are provided. Suppose a program containing this expression is run on an MS-DOS system, where line terminators are pairs (represented literally as "\r\n"). It may be surprising to learn that a single "\n" works as a line terminator on MS-DOS also. This is because the input/output system that stands between Icon and the actual file translates line terminators automatically, converting (in MS-DOS) the linefeed to a return/line feed pair.

This translation is a property of the mode in which a file is opened — the *translated* mode, which is the default. This translation can be prevented by opening a file in the untranslated mode, using the "u" option, as in open("run.log", "uw"). The default translated mode can be given explicitly with the "t" option, and the same situation applies to opening a file for reading. Note that "u" and "t" options are irrelevant on systems for which the line terminator is the linefeed character. Standard input, standard output, and standard error output are translated.

Normally a text file is not opened in untranslated mode. However, in order to read or write a binary file on a system for which the line terminator is not the linefeed character, the file must be opened in untranslated mode. Otherwise, the data will be corrupted by translation. It is worth noting that some input/output systems treat characters other than line terminators in special ways. This is another reason for being careful to use the untranslated mode for binary data.

Binary input and output usually are done using reads() and writes(). Using reads() prevents line terminators from being discarded. It also usually is needed for reading binary data, because any line terminator characters that exist in binary data usually are unrelated to the amount of data you want to read — in fact, if there are no line terminator characters in a binary file, read() reads the entire file in one piece. (No line terminator is required after the last "line" of a file.) On the other hand, reads() permits the reading of a binary file in fixed-sized pieces.

Using read() and write() with files opened in the translated mode, while using reads() and writes() with files opened in the untranslated mode, follows from the usual properties of files. It is not a physical or logical necessity. However, adhering to these conventions produces the correct results and avoids problems in most cases.

PIPES

Some operating systems (notably UNIX) support *pipes*, which allow the output of one process to be the input of another process ("piped into it"). In UNIX commands, pipes are indicated by the character | between processes. For example,

ls | grep dat

is a command that pipes the output of ls into grep. The program ls writes the names of the files in the current directory, and grep writes only the ones containing the string in its argument (dat here).

On systems that support pipes, a command string can be opened as a pipe by using the open option "p". For example,

iconfiles := open("ls *.icn", "p")

assigns a pipe to iconfiles corresponding to the command line above. Consequently,

while write(read(iconfiles))

writes out the names of all files that end in .icn.

A pipe can be opened for reading ("pr") or writing ("pw"), but not both. Opening for reading is the default, and the "r" can be omitted.

An example of writing to a pipe is

listprocs := open("grep procedure", "pw")

so that

while write(listprocs, read())

pipes the lines from standard input into grep procedure, which writes only those containing the substring "procedure". Notice that a command string opened as a pipe need not contain any pipes itself.

On systems that support pipes, opening command strings as pipes provides a very powerful technique for using other programs during the execution of an Icon program. The use of pipes in Icon programs, however, requires not only an understanding of the programs that are used, but also the system's command-line interpreter ("shell"), how programs work when connected by pipes, and how Icon's input and output work with pipes.

KEYBOARD FUNCTIONS

On systems that support console input and output, there are three keyboard functions.

The function getch() waits until a character is entered from the keyboard and then produces the corresponding one-character string. The character is not displayed. The function getche() is the same as getch() except that the character is displayed.

The function kbhit() succeeds if a character is available for getch() or getche() but fails otherwise.

RANDOM-ACCESS INPUT AND OUTPUT

There are two functions related to random-access input and output, in which information does not have to be accessed sequentially.

The function **seek**(f, i) seeks to position i in file f. As with other positions in Icon, a nonpositive value of i can be used to reference a position relative to the end of f. i defaults to 1. The Icon form of position identification is used; the position of the first character of a file is 1, not 0 as it is in some other random-access facilities. **seek**(f, i) produces f but fails if an error occurs. The function **where**(f) produces the current byte position in the file f.

Random-access input and output may produce peculiar results in the translated mode on systems that have multi-character line terminators. Seeking only the positions previously produced by **where**(f) minimizes this risk.

OPERATIONS ON FILES

Files can be removed or renamed during program execution. The function **remove**(s) removes the file named s. Subsequent attempts to open the file fail, unless it is created anew. If the file is open, the behavior of **remove**(s) is system dependent. **remove**(s) fails if it is unsuccessful.

The function **rename**(s1, s2) causes the file named s1 to be known subsequently by the name s2. The file named s1 is effectively removed. If a file named s2 exists prior to the renaming, the behavior is system-dependent. **rename**(s1, s2) fails if unsuccessful, in which case if the file existed previously it is still known by its original name. Among the other possible causes of failure that are system-dependent are a file currently open or a necessity to copy the file's contents to rename it.

EXERCISES

11.1   Write a procedure laminate(f1, f2, f3) that performs a line-by-line concatenation of corresponding lines from f1 and f2 and writes the result to f3. If the files are of different lengths, provide empty lines for the shorter file.

11.2   Write a program that copies a binary file from standard input to standard output. Do it in a manner that will work on any computer system.

11.3   Write procedures to read and write integers as binary data.

11.4   Write a program for interactively examining a binary file and printing selected portions of its contents in a reasonable format.

12

Running an Icon Program

In most cases, running an Icon program is a simple matter. On systems that use a command-line interface, it is usually just a matter of typing a command or two. There are, however, several options that provide flexibility and handle special situations.

Icon has been implemented on many systems, and there are necessarily some differences between systems in how Icon is run. File naming conventions vary from system to system, as does command syntax. Some systems support environment variables, while others do not, and so on. This chapter describes the essential aspects of running Icon under most command-line interfaces. User manuals for Icon on specific systems provide more information.

BASICS

The name of a file that contains an Icon source program must end with the suffix .icn, as in hello.icn. The .icn suffix is used by the Icon compiler to distinguish Icon source programs from other kinds of files.

The Icon compiler is named icont. To compile hello.icn, all that is needed is

        icont hello.icn

The suffix .icn is assumed if none is given, so that this can be written more simply as

        icont hello

The result is an *icode* file that can be executed. The name of the icode file depends on the system on which Icon is run. On some systems, notably UNIX, the name is the same as the name of the source file, but without the suffix. On these systems, the compilation of hello.icn produces an icode file named hello. On other systems, the icode file has the suffix .icn replaced by .icx, as in hello.icx.

On some systems, again notably UNIX, icode files are executable, so that after compilation, entering

        hello

causes the program to be executed. Invoking an icode file this way is called *direct execution*. On other systems, it is necessary to run an "executor", iconx, with the icode file as an argument.

        iconx hello

Use of the executor also works on systems on which icode files are executable, and this form is used in the remainder of this chapter. The icode suffix, if any, is optional on the iconx command line. For example, on systems with the icode suffix .icx, the following two lines are equivalent:

        iconx hello.icx
        iconx hello

An Icon program can be compiled and run in a single step using the −x option following the program name. For example,

        icont hello −x

compiles and executes hello.icn. An icode file also is created, and it can be executed subsequently without recompiling the source program.

INPUT AND OUTPUT REDIRECTION

As described in Chapter 11, most input and output is done using standard input, standard output, and standard error output. When a program is run from a terminal, standard input is read from the keyboard and standard output and standard error output are written to the screen.

Most systems allow redirection of standard input and standard output so that files can be used in place of the terminal. For example,

        iconx hello < hello.dat > hello.out

executes hello with hello.dat as standard input and hello.out as standard output. (The directions that the angular brackets point relative to the program are suggestive of the information flow.)

Standard error output can be redirected to a file by the –e option, followed by the desired file name. For example,

    iconx –e prog.err prog

runs prog and redirects error output to prog.err. This option cannot be used with direct execution.

It is important to understand that matters like input/output redirection and how they are specified are properties of the system on which Icon runs and have nothing to do with Icon itself. Icon is just another program, and it behaves like other programs in these respects.

COMMAND-LINE ARGUMENTS

Arguments on the iconx command line following the icode file name are available to the executing Icon program in the form of a list of strings. This list is the argument to the main procedure. For example, suppose args.icn consists of

```
procedure main(L)
   every write(!L)
end
```

This program simply prints the arguments on the command line on which it executed. Thus,

```
icont args
iconx args Hello world
```

writes

```
Hello
world
```

Arguments are separated by blanks. The treatment of special characters, methods of embedding blanks in arguments, and so forth, vary from system to system.

It is common practice to use arguments that begin with a dash to communicate options to Icon programs. For example,

```
procedure main(opt)
   if opt[1] = = "–L" then
      limit := integer(opt[2]) | stop("option error")
         ·
         ·
         ·
```

uses an argument of the form −L to specify the following argument as an integer limit for processing, as in

      iconx prog −L 20

This method of specifying options follows a convention that arose in the UNIX environment. However, its common use by Icon programs enhances the portability of Icon programs among different systems.

LIBRARIES

The term "compilation" as it applies to Icon programs refers to two processes: the translation of a source program to an intermediate form (called *ucode*) and the linking of one of more ucode files to produce an icode file.

Ucode files consist of instructions for an Icon "virtual machine"; they resemble assembly language. Normally icont deletes ucode files after they have been linked to produce icode files. However, the process can be stopped after translation, leaving the ucode files intact. The ucode files then can be linked with other programs. This provides a library facility, since ucode files can be linked with other programs.

The compilation process is stopped before linking by using the −c option before the source program file name. For example

      icont −c graphics

translates the source program graphics.icn, but does not link it.

The translation of a source program produces two ucode files with suffixes .u1 and .u2 in place of .icn. The .u1 file contains the virtual machine instructions and data for the program, while the .u2 file contains global information about the program.

These ucode files can be linked with a program in two ways: by including them on the command line along with the source file with which they are to be linked, or by listing them in a link declaration in the program itself. Using the first method, the suffix .u is included to allow icont to distinguish ucode files from source files. For example,

      icont hello graphics.u

causes the program hello.icn to be compiled and linked with graphics.u1 and graphics.u2 to form a single program that includes the code from graphics.icn.

A better method of including ucode files, at least from an organizational viewpoint, is to specify them in the program that uses them. This is done with the link declaration, which lists the ucode files (without suffixes). For example, the declaration link graphics

causes the ucode files graphics.u1 and graphics.u2 to be linked. If such a declaration appears in hello.icn,

icont hello

causes the ucode files from graphics.icn to be linked automatically.

Ucode files from several programs can be specified in link declarations, either by using a comma-separated list of names or by using several link declarations. For example,

link time, signon, signoff

causes ucode files from time.icn, signon.icn, and signoff.icn to be linked.

Since a program can only have one procedure by a given name, care must be taken to use distinct procedure names in libraries.

The names specified in link declarations must satisfy the syntax for Icon identifiers. Not all file names satisfy this requirement, however. For example, sign–on.icn is a legal file name on most systems, but sign–on is not a legal Icon identifier. In this case, the name can be enclosed in quotes in the link declaration, as in

link "sign–on"

To assist in building libraries, the names in link declarations can include paths (which must be enclosed in quotes). An example is

link "/usr/icon/lib/time"

Path syntax varies from system to system; Icon merely passes the string on to the system on which it runs.

The location of one or more libraries can be established in the environment in which icont is run. If the operating system environment variable IPATH is set, it is used in searching for ucode files. IPATH is a blank-separated list of paths. For example, using the UNIX *csh*,

setenv IPATH "/usr/icon/lib /usr/icon/newlib"

IPATH is set so that /usr/icon/lib and /usr/icon/newlib are searched for ucode files listed in link declarations. The search is in order of paths given in IPATH, but the current working directory (in which icont is executed) is always searched first.

OTHER ASPECTS OF COMPILATION

Command-Line Options

There are several command-line options that are useful in some situations. Options must appear before file names on the icont command line.

The command-line option −s suppresses the informative messages. Normally, both informative messages and error messages are sent to standard error output

The command-line option −u causes warning messages to be issued for undeclared identifiers. The warnings are issued during the linking phase.

The command-line option −o *name* causes the icode file to be named *name*. For example,

```
icont −o prog.icx comp
```

causes comp.icn to be compiled and the resulting icode file to be named prog.icx.

The command-line option −m causes source files to be preprocessed by the *m4* macro processor before translation. This option is available only on UNIX systems. If this option is used, error messages refer to line numbers in the output of *m4*, not in the source file.

COMPILATION ERRORS

Errors During Translation

Syntactic errors in an Icon source program are detected during translation. Each such error produces an explanatory message and the location at which the error was detected. Since some errors cannot be detected until after the point at which the actual error occurred, previous portions of the program should be examined if the problem at the specified location is not obvious.

Translation continues following the detection of a syntax error, but an icode file is not produced. Since some kinds of errors cause a cascade of apparent errors in subsequent program text, it often is advisable to correct only the first error and attempt to compile the program again.

There is one warning message, which occurs if the dereferencing operation is applied to a numeric literal, as in .25.

Errors During Linking

Some errors are not evident until ucode files from more than one source file are combined to form a single icode file. These errors are detected by the linker:

inconsistent redeclaration
invalid field name

These errors prevent the production of an icode file.

As mentioned earlier, if the −u option is used, the linker produces the message

undeclared identifier

for identifiers that are not declared. This message is only a warning; it does not prevent the use of the resulting icode file.

Table Overflow

Icon has several tables related to the translation and linking of programs. These tables are large enough for most programs, but their sizes can be changed, if necessary, by the −S option. This option has the form −Scn, where c is a letter that specifies the table and n is the number of storage units to allocate for the table. The tables and their usual default sizes are:

c	constant table	100
f	field table	100
g	global symbol table	200
i	identifier table	500
l	local symbol table	100
n	line number space	1000
r	field table for records	100
s	string space	20000
t	tree space	15000
C	code buffer	15000
F	file name table	10
L	label table	500

The units depend on the table involved, but the default values can be used as a general guide for appropriate settings of −S without knowing the units. For example,

icont −Sg400 prog

compiles prog.icn with twice the default space for the global symbol table.

The error message **parse stack overflow** indicates there is not enough space to parse an Icon procedure. The size of the stack cannot be changed. Instead, the procedure being translated when this message occurs must be simplified or made into several simpler procedures.

VERSION INCOMPATIBILITY

Different versions of Icon may be incompatible for several reasons, such as differences in function repertoire or differences in the internal representation of structures. Since ucode and icode files may not be used until long after they are produced, they contain version identifications so that Icon can check for incompatibilities.

If a ucode file (from a library, for example) is not compatible with the current linker, the error is noted and no icode file is produced. In such a case, the offending ucode file should be replaced by recompiling the corresponding source file with the current version of Icon.

An icode file also may be incompatible with the current executor. If this happens, the error is noted and the icode file is not executed. The offending icode file should be replaced by recompiling the corresponding source file with the current version of Icon.

STORAGE MANAGEMENT

Storage is allocated automatically during program execution as strings and other objects are created. Garbage collection occurs automatically when more space is needed; it reclaims space used by objects that are no longer in use [7].

This automatic management of storage normally is transparent to persons writing and running Icon programs. However, Icon programs vary widely in their utilization of storage, and the amount of computer memory available to Icon programs varies from system to system. For these reasons, some understanding of how Icon manages storage may be useful.

Storage Regions

The storage Icon allocates is divided into four parts:

1. Co-expressions and operating-system uses

2. Strings

3. Blocks for all other data objects (csets, lists, and so forth)

4. Workspace for the garbage collector

There are two forms of allocation, depending on the system on which Icon is allocated: fixed regions and expandable regions.

With fixed-region allocation, the storage used by Icon is fixed when a program begins allocation. There are separate fixed-sized regions for strings, blocks, and garbage-collector workspace. Space for co-expressions and operating-system use is obtained from the operating system as needed and is beyond Icon's control. With fixed-region allocation, the string and block regions must be large enough to hold all the data needed at any one time by an Icon program. Program execution terminates with an error if there is not enough space in a region (after garbage collection) to create an object.

With expandable-region allocation, there are separate static, string, and block regions. Strings and blocks are handled in the same manner as for fixed-region allocation, but space for co-expressions and operating-system use is provided by Icon from the static region. Garbage-collector workspace is obtained from the system as needed. However, if more space is needed in a region that is available, the region is expanded. Program execution only terminates for lack of storage if memory is not available to expand a region.

Expandable-region allocation offers more flexibility than fixed-region allocation. Not only do regions expand to accommodate programs that need a large amount of memory, but the initial sizes of regions can be small for all programs.

Fixed- or expandable-region allocation is a property of a particular implementation of Icon; it is not under user control. Persons using an implementation of Icon with fixed-region allocation may need to pay more attention to memory management because of its comparative inflexibility. The type of allocation used by an implementation can be determined from the user's manual or by the keyword &features, described later in this chapter.

The default initial sizes of Icon's storage regions vary somewhat from implementation to implementation. For most implementations, the default sizes for the string and block regions are 65,000 bytes. In fixed-region implementations, the size of the garbage-collector workspace usually is 5,000 bytes. In expandable-region implementations, the initial size of the static region usually is 20,480 bytes.

Setting Initial Region Sizes

The default initial sizes for the storage regions can be changed by using operating system environment variables. The maximum permissible size to which a storage region can be set depends on the implementation. This information is contained in user guides.

If the environment variable STRSIZE is set, it determines the initial size, in bytes, of the string region. For example, with UNIX *csh*,

```
setenv STRSIZE 1000000
```

sets the initial size of the string region to one million bytes.

The environment variable BLKSIZE determines the initial size, in bytes, of the block region.

On expandable-region implementations, STATSIZE determines the initial size, in bytes, of the static region. STATINCR is the increment for expanding the static region. Its default is one-fourth the initial size of the static retion. On fixed-region implementations, QLSIZE determines the size of the workspace used by the garbage collector.

Stacks

Icon uses two stacks: an evaluation stack and a system stack. The evaluation stack contains intermediate results of computations and procedure call information. The system stack contains calls of C functions (Icon is implemented in C).

The evaluation stack grows as a result of procedure calls and suspended expressions. The system stack grows as a result of suspended expressions and during garbage collection.

There is an evaluation stack and a system stack for execution that starts with the initial call of the main procedure (in the co-expression &main). Each newly created co-expression also has its own evaluation stack and system stack. The stacks for user-created co-expressions normally are smaller than those for &main.

The evaluation stack may overflow in programs with deeply nested (or runaway) procedure calls. Its default size usually is 10,000 words, which is ample for most programs. This size can be changed by setting the environment variable MSTKSIZE. For example, with UNIX *csh*,

    setenv MSTKSIZE 20000

sets the size of the main evaluation stack to 20,000 words.

The system stack may overflow if there are too many simultaneously suspended expressions. This may happen, for example, if there are many expressions in conjunction in string scanning. The system stack also may overflow if long chains of pointers are encountered during garbage collection.

The size of the system stack depends on the implementation. On a computer with a large amount of memory, the system stack usually is very large and overflow is unlikely. On personal computers with a limited amount of memory, the system stack may be small and overflow may be a problem.

Unfortunately, system stack overflow may not be detected. If this happens, adjacent memory may be overwritten, resulting in program or system malfunction. On some systems, it is possible to set the size of the system stack when execution begins. The method of setting the system stack size varies and is described in user guides.

The problems with stack overflow often is more severe in co-expressions. The default size for co-expressions usually is 2,000 words, with the space divided evenly between an evaluation stack and a system stack. Thus, both are much smaller than for &main. Furthermore, overflow detection is less effective in program-created co-expressions. The size of co-expressions can be set using the environment variable COEXPSIZE. For example, with UNIX *csh*,

    setenv COEXPSIZE 4000

doubles the default size of co-expressions.

Although the size of co-expressions can be increased, the amount of space they require makes a size comparable to &main impractical on most systems. It therefore is advisable to avoid deeply nested procedure calls and many simultaneously suspended expressions within a co-expression that is created during program execution (as opposed to &main).

Storage Trade-Offs

On systems where the amount of available memory is small, it may be necessary to make trade-offs among the various uses of memory.

The factors involved are the size of the icode file (which resides in memory during program execution), the sizes of the string and block regions, the amount of space needed for co-expressions, the amount of space needed by the operating system itself (mainly for i/o buffers), and the size of evaluation and system stacks for &main. As mentioned earlier, expandable-region implementations offer more flexibility, since the sizes of the static, string, and block regions increase automatically if more space is required. Their sizes therefore can safely be set to small values.

Another important consideration is transient program data as opposed to persistent data. For example, a program that processes a file on a line-by-line basis, but does not store all the lines, may allocate a large amount of space for strings. However, such a program may not need a large string region, since space for previously processed strings can be reclaimed by the garbage collector. On the other hand, a program that builds a large dictionary using a table may require large block and string regions, since all the data for the dictionary is in use and cannot be garbage-collected.

There is a trade-off between the size of storage regions and time required for garbage collection. With larger regions, garbage collection is less frequent (it occurs only when there is not enough space for a newly created object). As a general rule, less time is required to handle the same amount of data for fewer garbage collections with larger regions.

It is worth noting, however, that garbage collection is fastest when most data objects are transient. Garbage collection actually does not collect unneeded data objects; instead it accumulates and rearranges them. Garbage collection is slowest when there is a large amount of persistent data.

While the implementation of storage management in Icon attempts to avoid "thrashing", it may occur in situations where there is barely enough collectible space to satisfy the needs of newly created objects. In this situation, garbage collection may occur frequently (and successfully) at a considerable penalty in execution time.

Three keywords can be used to measure the utilization of storage during program execution. The keyword &collections generates four values: the total number of garbage collections to date, followed by the number caused by allocations in the static, string, and block regions respectively. For example, write(&collections)

writes the total number of garbage collections that have occurred.

    Since **&collections** is a generator, using a list to collect its results may be helpful. For
example, the following procedure writes all the values with identifying labels:

```
procedure notecol()
  local coll
  coll := [ ]
  every put(coll, &collections)
  write("static: ", coll[2])
  write("string: ", coll[3])
  write("block: ", coll[4])
  write("total: ", coll[1])
  return
end
```

    The keyword **&regions** generates the sizes of the static, string, and block regions. For
fixed-region implementations, which do not have a static region, the first value generated by
&regions is not meaningful.

    The keyword **&storage** generates the amount of space currently occupied in the static,
string, and block regions. The first value is not meaningful and is included only for
consistency with **&regions**. The values produced by **&storage** give the space occupied;
some of that space may be collectible.

    Sometimes it is useful to force a garbage collection — for example to find out how
much space is available for future allocation. The function collect(i1, i2) causes a garbage
collection, requesting i2 bytes of storage in region i1. The regions are identified by integers:
1 for the static region, 2 for the string region, and 3 for the block region. The function fails
if i bytes are not available in the region after collection. If i1 is 0, a garbage collection is done,
and contributes to the count of garbage collections, but no region is identified and i2 has no
effect. Both i1 and i2 default to zero, so that collect() performs an "anonymous" collection
and always succeeds.

OTHER EXECUTION SETTINGS

There are three operating-system environment variables that affect the execution of Icon
programs.

    Normally, standard error output is buffered. Consequently, error messages may not be
written as soon as they are produced. If the environment variable NOERRBUF is set,
standard error output is not buffered.

    For implementations that support direct execution (notably UNIX), iconx is run auto-
matically and its location is built into the icode file. This may cause a problem if iconx is

moved after the icode file is created, or if a different version of iconx is needed. If the environment variable ICONX is set, its value is used for iconx. For example, with UNIX *csh*

> setenv ICONX /usr/icon/altbin/iconx

the version of iconx at /usr/icon/altbin/iconx is used, regardless of the location specified in an icode file. The order of searching for iconx is the value of ICONX, if set, then the built-in path, if present, and finally locations specified in the PATH environment variable.

If the environment variable ICONCORE is set, a core dump is produced if an Icon program terminates with an error. This environment variable is intended for debugging Icon itself and normally is not needed by Icon programmers. It is effective only with some implementations of Icon.

THE EXECUTION ENVIRONMENT

Tracing

Tracing is the main debugging tool in Icon. Tracing is controlled by &trace. If &trace is zero (its initial value), there is no tracing. If the value of &trace is nonzero, a diagnostic message is written to standard error output each time a procedure is called, returns, suspends, or is resumed. The value of &trace is decremented by 1 each time a message is written, so the value assigned to &trace can be used to limit the amount of trace output. On the other hand,

> &trace := −1

allows tracing to continue indefinitely or until another value is assigned to &trace.

The command-line option −t causes &trace to have the value of −1 when program execution begins.

If the environment variable TRACE is set, &trace has its value at the beginning of program execution. TRACE overrides the −t option to icont. For example, with UNIX *csh*

> setenv TRACE   −1

causes &trace to have the initial value of −1.

The diagnostic messages produced by tracing show the name of the file containing the program, the line in that file, procedures called, values returned, and so on. The vertical bars indicate, by way of indentation, the level of procedure call.

An example of tracing for the first method of computing the Fibonacci numbers given in Chapter 8 is:

```
fib.icn:      9  |  fib(5)
fib.icn:      3  |  |  fib(4)
fib.icn:      3  |  |  |  fib(3)
fib.icn:      3  |  |  |  |  fib(2)
fib.icn:      2  |  |  |  |  fib returned 1
fib.icn:      3  |  |  |  |  fib(1)
fib.icn:      2  |  |  |  |  fib returned 1
fib.icn:      3  |  |  |  fib returned 2
fib.icn:      3  |  |  |  fib(2)
fib.icn:      2  |  |  |  fib returned 1
fib.icn:      3  |  |  fib returned 3
fib.icn:      3  |  |  fib(3)
fib.icn:      3  |  |  |  fib(2)
fib.icn:      2  |  |  |  fib returned 1
fib.icn:      3  |  |  |  fib(1)
fib.icn:      2  |  |  |  fib returned 1
fib.icn:      3  |  |  fib returned 2
fib.icn:      3  |  fib returned 5
fib.icn:     10  main failed
```

The name of the file containing the program is fib.icn. The initial call, fib(5), is on line 9, which is in the main procedure used for testing. Note the redundant computations.

Tracing Co-Expressions

Co-expression activation and return also is traced if the value of &trace is non-zero. As for procedure calls and returns, the value of &trace is decremented for each trace message. The form of co-expression tracing is illustrated by the following program:

```
procedure main()
   local lower, upper
   &trace := −1
   lower := create !&lcase
   upper := create !&ucase
   while write(@lower, " ", @upper)
end
```

If this program is in the file trace.icn, the trace output is:

```
trace.icn:    6 | main; co-expression_1 : &null @ co-expression_2
trace.icn:    4 | main; co-expression_2 returned "a" to co-expression_1
trace.icn:    6 | main; co-expression_1 : &null @ co-expression_3
trace.icn:    6 | main; co-expression_1 : &null @ co-expression_2
trace.icn:    4 | main; co-expression_2 returned "b" to co-expression_1
trace.icn:    6 | main; co-expression_1 : &null @ co-expression_3
trace.icn:    5 | main; co-expression_3 returned "B" to co-expression_1
trace.icn:    6 | main; co-expression_1 : &null @ co-expression_2
                       .
                       .
                       .
trace.icn:    6 | main; co-expression_1 : &null @ co-expression_3
trace.icn:    5 | main; co-expression_3 returned "Z" to co-expression_1
trace.icn:    6 | main; co-expression_1 : &null @ co-expression_2
trace.icn:    4 | main; co-expression_2 failed to co-expression_1
trace.icn:    7 main failed
```

Serial numbers that identify different co-expressions follow the underscores. See Chapter 10 for more information about serial numbers. Note that activation really is transmission of the null value.

Procedure Calls

&level is the current level of procedure call. It starts at 1 for the initial call of the main procedure and increases and decreases as procedures are called and return.

The function display(i, f) writes the image of the current co-expression, followed by a list of local identifiers and their values in i levels of procedure calls, starting at the current level, followed by the program's global identifiers and their values. The output is written to the file f. An omitted value of i defaults to &level, whose value is the current level of procedure. An omitted value of f defaults to &errout. The function call display(1) includes only local identifiers in the currently active procedure. The function call display(&level) includes local identifiers for all procedure calls leading to the current procedure call, while display(0) includes only global identifiers.

An example of the output of display() is given by the following program:

```
procedure main()
  local intext
  (intext := open("build.icn")) | stop("cannot open input file")
  write(linecount(intext))
end
```

```
procedure linecount(file)
  local count, line
  count := 0
  while line := read(file) do
    if find("stop", line) then break
    else count +:= 1
  display()
  return count
end
```

which produces the display output

```
co-expression_1(1)

linecount local identifiers:
  file = file(build.icn)
  count = 585
  line = "   then stop(\"ca..."

main local identifiers:
  intext = file(build.icn)

global identifiers:
  main = procedure main
  linecount = procedure linecount
  open = function open
  stop = function stop
  write = function write
  read = function read
  find = function find
  display = function display
```

Note that values are displayed in the manner of image(x).

Time and Date

The value of &date is the current date in the form *yyyy*/*mm*/*dd*. For example, the value of &date for October 15, 1989 is "1989/10/15".

The value of &dateline is the date and time of day in a format that is easy to read. An example is

```
Sunday, October 15, 1989  7:21 am
```

The value of &clock is the current time in the form *hh:mm:ss*. For example, the value of &clock for 7:21 p.m. is 19:21:00.

The value of &time is the elapsed CPU time in milliseconds, measured from the beginning of program execution.

Icon Identification

The value of &host is the location, operating system, and computer on which Icon is running. The format of the information varies from implementation to implementation. An example is

> University of Arizona, UNIX 4.3BSD, VAX 8650

The value of &version is the version number and creation date of the Icon implementation. An example is

> Icon Version 8.0. December 20, 1989

Environment Variables

Some operating systems support environment variables that can be set to different values in order to communicate information about the environment in which a program executes. The function getenv(s) produces the value of the environment variable s, but fails if the environment variable s is not set. For example,

> write(getenv("TRACE"))

prints the value of the environment variable TRACE, provided it is set.

The function getenv() also fails on systems that do not support environment variables.

PROGRAM TERMINATION

The execution of an Icon program may be terminated for several reasons: completion, programmer-specified termination, or error.

The normal way to terminate program execution is by return from the main procedure. This produces a normal exit code for the process whether the main procedure returns or fails.

Execution of the function exit(i) causes an Icon program to terminate with exit code of i. If i is omitted, the normal exit code is produced. This function is useful for terminating program execution in situations where it is not convenient to return to the main procedure.

The function stop(x1, x2, ..., xn) writes output in the manner of write() and then terminates program execution with an error exit code. Output is written to standard error output unless another file is specified.

Run-Time Errors

When a run-time error occurs, a diagnostic message is produced indicating the nature of the error, where in the program the error occurred, and, when possible, the offending value. Next, a trace back of procedure calls is given, followed by the offending expression.

For example, suppose the following program is contained in the file max.icn:

```
procedure main()
  i := max("a", 1)
end

procedure max(i, j)
  if i > j then i else j
end
```

The execution of this program produces the following output:

```
Run-time error 102
File max.icn; Line 6
numeric expected
offending value: "a"
Trace back:
  main()
  max("a", 1) from line 2 in max.icn
  {"a" > 1} from line 6 in max.icn
```

Error Conversion

Most run-time errors can be converted to expression failure, rather than causing termination of program execution.

If the value of &error is zero (its initial value), errors cause program termination as shown above. If the value of &error is nonzero, errors are treated as failure of expression evaluation and &error is decremented. For example, if the value of &error had been nonzero when the expression i > j was executed in the previous example, the expression simply would have failed.

There are a few errors that cannot be converted to failure: arithmetic overflow and underflow, stack overflow, and errors during program initialization.

When an error is converted to failure, the value of &error is decremented and the values of three other keywords are set:

- &errornumber is the number of the error (for example, 101).
- &errortext is the error message (for example, "integer expected").
- &errorvalue is the offending value. References to &errorvalue fail if there is no offending value associated with the error.

A reference to any of these keywords fails if there has not been an error.

The function errorclear() removes the indication of the last error. Subsequent references to the keywords above fail until another error occurs.

Error conversion is illustrated by the following procedure, which could be used to process potential run-time errors:

```
procedure ErrorCheck()
   write("\nRun-time error ", &errornumber)
   write(&errortext)
   write("offending value: ", image(&errorvalue))
   writes("\nDo you want to continue? (n)")
   if map(read()) == ("y" | "yes") then return
   else exit(&errornumber)
end
```

For example,

```
&error := −1
   ⋮
   ⋮
write(s) | ErrorCheck()
```

could be used to check for an error during writing, while

```
(L := sort(T, 3)) | ErrorCheck()
```

could be used to detect failure to sort a table into a list (for lack of adequate storage).

A run-time error can be forced by the function runerr(i, x), which causes program execution to terminate with error number i as if a corresponding run-time error had occurred. If i is the number of a standard run-time error, the corresponding error text is printed; otherwise no error text is printed. The value of x is given as the offending value. If x is omitted, no offending value is printed.

This function makes it possible for library procedures to terminate in the same fashion as built-in operations. It is advisable to use error numbers for programmer-defined errors that are well outside the range of numbers used by Icon itself. Error number 500 has the predefined text "program malfunction" for use with runerr(). This number is not used by Icon itself.

A call of runerr() is subject to conversion to failure like any other run-time error.

Program Location Information

The keywords &file and &line contain, respectively, the name of the file and line number in that file for the currently executing expression.

For example,

write("File ", &file, "; Line ", &line)

writes out the current file name and the line number in it.

The file name and line number normally are taken from the file when it is compiled. Note that a program may consist of several parts that are compiled from different files.

A comment that starts at the beginning of a line and has the form

#line *n* "*f*"

changes the line number to *n* and the file name to *f*. For example,

#line 100 "prog.icn"

changes the line number to 100 and the file name to **prog.icn**. The line number subsequently is incremented until another **#line** comment is encountered. The file name may be omitted on a **#line** comment. If it is omitted, the file name is not changed.

The **#line** comment is useful for Icon programs that produce Icon programs which need to report location information different from that in the output file.

EXECUTING COMMANDS

The function **system(s)** executes the command given by the string **s** as if it were entered on the command line. This facility allows an Icon program to execute other programs and in particular to perform system-dependent operations that are not part of Icon itself. The value returned by **system(s)** is the exit status returned by the command-line interpreter. For example with UNIX

system("ls −l ∗.icn")

lists, in long form, the files whose names end in .icn. The value returned is 0, whether or not there are any such files, since **ls** returns this exit code in either case. Exit codes vary considerably, depending on the system and the specific program.

EXECUTABLE IMAGES

Some implementations of Icon, notably many of those for Berkeley UNIX, support a facility for saving an executable image of an Icon program. This facility is especially useful for programs that do a large amount of initialization.

The function **save(s)** creates an executable image and stores it in the file **s**. The function fails if the file cannot be written. If the function succeeds, it returns the number of bytes in the executable image. Execution of the program continues after the executable image is saved.

The saved file can be run like any other program. Execution begins in the main procedure of the saved program. An example is

```
global hello

procedure main()
  initial {
    hello := "Hello world!"
    save("greeting") | stop("cannot save\"greeting\"")
    hello := "Bad news."
    exit()
    }
  write(hello)
end
```

When this program is run, the initial clause in the main procedure is executed, assigning a value to the global variable hello and then saving an executable image in the file greeting. Assuming the file is written, the value of hello is changed and the program then exits. When the program greeting is run, execution begins in the main procedure again, but since its initial clause has already been executed, control goes immediately to the following expression, which writes Hello world!. Note that this is the value of hello when the executable image was saved. The subsequent change to the value of hello in the initial clause does not affect the executable image. Similarly, if hello had not been a global or static identifier, its value would have been lost, since the second invocation of the main procedure, when greeting is executed, produces a new copy of its dynamic local identifiers.

When an executable image is executed, the arguments on its command line are passed to the main procedure in the same manner as for executing an Icon program. Consequently, arguments can be passed to an executable image in the same manner as for an Icon program. The values of environment variables, such as those to set the values of storage regions, are not used when an executable image is run; the values are those in effect when the executable image is saved.

Since executable images contain the Icon executor iconx, the icode file, and all of Icon's storage regions, they may be quite large.

EXTERNAL FUNCTIONS AND CALLING ICON

Icon provides an interface for calling functions written in other languages. Since Icon is written in C, such external functions usually are written in C, although it is possible to provide interfaces to functions written in other programming languages. The mechanism for accessing functions external to Icon and passing data to and from them depends on the system and applications involved. See Reference 8 and user guides for more information.

The Icon function callout(x, x1, …, xn) calls the external function designated by x and passes it the arguments x1, …, xn. Different methods are used for designating external functions. On some systems, they may be designated by their string names, while on others they may be indicated by integer indexes into a function vector.

An external function may produce a value, which is returned by callout() as for any other Icon function, or it may fail. An external function cannot suspend, however.

It is also possible to call Icon as a subprogram of another program. The way to do this is described in Reference 8.

The mechanism for calling Icon from another program and calling external functions from Icon is general. Such calls can be freely interleaved and can be recursive.

MEMORY MONITORING

Storage allocation and garbage collection in Icon are instrumented. Normally, this instrumentation is not activated and it has no effect on the execution of Icon programs. If the instrumentation is activated, a detailed history of storage allocation is written to a file. The instrumentation is active if the environment variable MEMMON (for "memory monitoring") is set. The allocation history is written to the file that is the value of MEMMON. For example, with UNIX *csh*,

> setenv MEMMON prog.history

causes the allocation history to be written to the file prog.history.

There are several tools for processing Icon allocation history files, including ones for producing interactive visualizations of the storage management process with allocated values shown in color by type. Three functions add user-specified information to allocation history files. The function mmpause(s) causes a pause in interactive visualizations, displaying the identification s. If s is omitted, the identification is "programmed pause".

The function mmshow(x, s) redraws the object x in a color specified by s. The color specifications are:

"b"	black
"g"	gray
"w"	white
"h"	highlight: blinking black and white
"r"	redraw in normal color

The default is "r".

The function mmout(s) writes s as a line in the allocation history file without any interpretation. This function may be used to add comments or additional information for special purposes.

EXERCISES

12.1   Write a procedure that causes a garbage collection and generates the amount of space available for allocation in the string and block regions respectively.

12.2   Trace acker(3, 3) for the solutions to Exercises 8.4 and 8.7 in Chapter 8.

12.3*   Write a procedure that produces a trace of the depth of recursion in the computation of Ackermann's function. Do not use tabulation.

12.4   Write a program that prints the values of the environment variables whose names are given as command-line arguments.

12.5*   Write a procedure pause(i) that loops for i milliseconds before returning.

13

Programming with Generators

Generators, used in combination with iteration and goal-directed evaluation, allow complex computations to be expressed in a concise and natural manner. In many cases they internalize computations that otherwise would require complicated loops, auxiliary identifiers, and tedious comparisons.

Most programming languages do not have generators. Consequently, using the full capacity of generators requires new programming techniques and nontraditional ways of approaching problems. This chapter describes ways to use generators and provides several idioms for computations that are natural in Icon.

NESTED ITERATION

Many problems that require the production of all possible solutions can be formulated using nested iteration. For example, many word puzzles depend on the intersection of two words in a common character. In constructing or solving such puzzles, all the places that two words intersect may be of interest.

Given two words **word1** and **word2**,

    i := upto(word2, word1)

produces the position in **word1** of one intersection. In this expression, the string value of **word2** is automatically converted to a cset consisting of the possible characters at which an intersection in **word1** can occur. While i gives the position of such an intersection in **word1**, the position in word2 is needed also. The pair of positions can be determined by

```
if i := upto(word2, word1)
then j := upto(word1[i], word2)
```

This computation can be cast in terms of a procedure that locates the positions and displays the intersection:

```
procedure cross(word1, word2)
  local i, j
  if i := upto(word2, word1)
  then {
    j := upto(word1[i], word2)
    every write(right(word2[1 to j − 1], i))
    write(word1)
    every write(right(word2[j + 1 to *word2], i))
    write()
    }
  return
end
```

For example, cross("lottery", "boat") produces

```
    b
l o t t e r y
    a
    t
```

This approach produces at most one intersection. All intersections can be produced by using nested iteration:

```
every i := upto(word2, word1) do
  every j := upto(word1[i], word2) do {
    every write(right(word2[1 to j − 1], i))
    write(word1)
    every write(right(word2[j + 1 to *word2], i))
    write()
    }
```

In this procedure, i iterates over the positions in word1 at which there is a character in word2, while j iterates over the positions in word2 at which this character occurs. The results written for cross("lottery", "boat") are:

```
   b
l o t t e r y
   a
   t

      b
      o
      a
l o t t e r y

         b
         o
         a
l o t t e r y
```

This nested iteration can be reformulated using a single iteration and conjunction:

```
every (i := upto(word2, word1)) & (j := upto(word1[i], word2)) do {
  every write(right(word2[1 to j – 1], i))
  write(word1)
  every write(right(word2[j + 1 to *word2], i))
  write()
}
```

The effect is the same as for nested iteration, because suspended generators are resumed in a last-in, first-out manner, which is the same in a single iteration with conjunction as it is in nested iterations.

GOAL-DIRECTED EVALUATION AND SEARCHING

Goal-directed evaluation is one of the more powerful programming techniques for solving problems that involve searching through many possible combinations of values. Goal-directed evaluation is commonly used in Icon for "small-scale" computation, such as finding common positions in two strings. The real power of goal-directed evaluation is evident in larger problems in which solutions are best formulated in terms of searches over "solution spaces".

The classical problem of this kind consists of placing eight queens on a chessboard so that no two queens are on the same column, row, or diagonal. The solution to this problem involves generation of possible solutions: Goal-directed evaluation to find mutually consistent solutions and data backtracking to reuse previous partial solutions. One solution of this problem is:

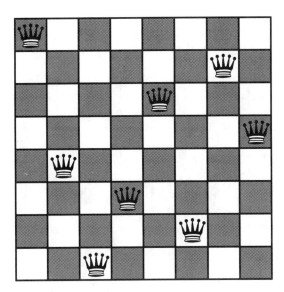

Since there can be only one queen on the same column, a natural approach to solving this problem is to assign one queen to each column. The queens then can be placed consecutively, starting with the first queen in the first column.

The first queen can be placed in any row, since there are no other queens on the board yet. The natural place to put the first queen is in row one. The second queen cannot be placed in row one, since the first queen is in this row, nor in row two, since the first queen is on a diagonal through this position. Row three is an acceptable place for the second queen, however. Continuing this process, each successive queen is placed on the first free row. When an attempt is made to place the sixth queen, however, there are no free rows:

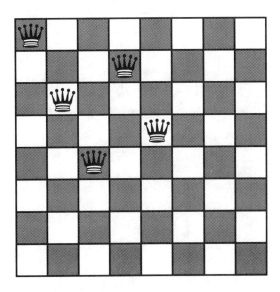

Some previously placed queen must be moved to another position. This is accomplished by backtracking to the previous queen, which can be placed in row eight instead of row four:

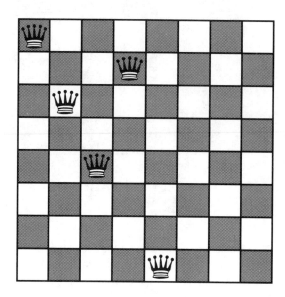

Another attempt is now made to place the sixth queen. No row is free, however, and backtracking takes place to the fifth queen again. There are no more free rows for the fifth queen, so backtracking takes place to the fourth queen, which is now placed in row seven:

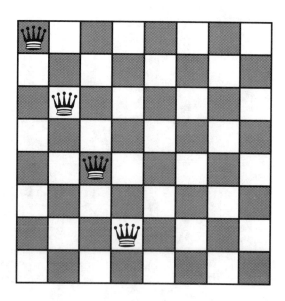

Now placement of the fifth queen is attempted anew. Eventually, through backtracking, the positions are finally adjusted so that all eight queens are placed, as shown on the board at the beginning of this section. Notice that it is not necessary to try all queens in all positions; a queen is moved only when its position cannot lead to a final solution.

This informal description of the placement process corresponds to the way that arguments are evaluated in Icon: left-to-right evaluation with last-in, first-out resumption to obtain alternative results. The solution of the eight-queens problem therefore can be formulated in terms of functions that place the queens according to the method described. A way of representing the chessboard and of determining free positions is needed, however.

The geometrical representation of the chessboard as an eight-by-eight array is not particularly useful. Instead, the important matter is the occupancy of columns, rows, and diagonals. The columns are taken care of by the assignment of one queen to each column. A list provides a natural way of representing the rows:

row := list(8, 0)

where row [i] is zero if there is no queen on it and nonzero otherwise.

The diagonals are slightly more difficult, since there are 30 of them in all. One approach is to divide the diagonals into two groups [9]. Fifteen of the diagonals are downward facing, with their left ends lower than their right ends:

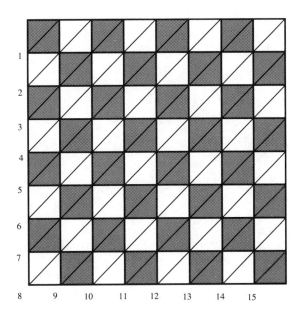

The other 15 diagonals are upward facing:

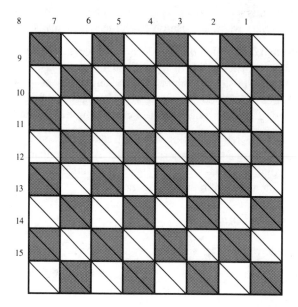

In each case, the diagonals can be represented by lists:

down := list(15, 0)
up := list(15, 0)

with zero or nonzero values assigned as for the rows.

In placing a queen c on row r, it is necessary to assure that row, down, and up for that position are zero. The expression

r + c − 1

selects the correct downward facing diagonal, while

8 + r − c

selects the correct upward facing diagonal. A queen c can be placed on row r if the following comparison succeeds:

row[r] = down[r + c −1] = up[8 + r − c] = 0

To place a queen, a nonzero value is assigned to the corresponding positions in row, down, and up. The row number is a convenient value to use, since it records the row on which the queen is placed and can be used in displaying the resulting solution:

row[r] <- down[r + c − 1] <- up[8 + r − c] <- r

Reversible assignment is used so that the queen can be removed automatically during backtracking. The complete program is

```
procedure main()
   write(q(1), q(2), q(3), q(4), q(5), q(6), q(7), q(8))
end

procedure q(c)
   suspend place(1 to 8, c)   # look for a row
end

procedure place(r, c)
   static up, down, row
   initial {
      up := list(15, 0)
      down := list(15, 0)
      row := list(8, 0)
      }
   if row[r] = down[r + c −1] = up[8 + r − c] = 0     # place if free
   then suspend row[r] <- down[r + c − 1] <- up[8 + r − c] <- r
end
```

The procedure q(c) corresponds to the queen on column c. The procedure place(r, c) places queen c on row r if that position is free. If place(r, c) is successful, it suspends so that if it is resumed because the next queen cannot be placed, the queen is removed by reversing the assignment.

The expression

write(q(1), q(2), q(3), q(4), q(5), q(6), q(7), q(8))

serves to place the queens. When all the queens are successfully placed, the row positions are written:

15863724

All possible solutions can be obtained by iteration:

every write(q(1), q(2), q(3), q(4), q(5), q(6), q(7), q(8))

There are 92 solutions in all, although only 12 are unique because of symmetries.

See Appendix F for a more general solution to the n-queens problem using co–expressions.

RECURSIVE GENERATORS

Recursion is a powerful programming tool. While recursive procedure calls are widely used, the use of recursion in generation is not as obvious.

Consider the problem of generating all the strings from a set of characters with the strings produced in the order of their length. For example, the results for "abc" would be "", "a", "b", "c", "aa", "ab", "ac", "ba", ... A procedure that produces these results is

```
procedure star(chars)
  suspend "" | (star(chars) || !chars)
end
```

In order to understand the sequence of results for this procedure, consider

```
star("abc")
```

The first result is the empty string, produced by suspending with "". The subsequent results consist of each result in the results for star("abc") followed by each character in "abc". Since !chars is repeatedly resumed for each value produced by star(chars), each character in chars is appended to the first value in the results for star(chars). Therefore, the results are "", "a", "b", "c", ... When star(chars) is resumed for its second result, it produces "a", onto which are appended "a", "b", and "c", and so on.

Recursive generators also can be used to produce the sequences for many recursively defined functions. For example, the Fibonacci numbers are generated by fibseq(1, 1) using the following procedure:

```
procedure fibseq(i, j)
  suspend i | fibseq(j, i + j)
end
```

Other examples of recursive generators are given in subsequent chapters.

EXERCISES

13.1   Extend the procedure cross() so that it finds all the intersections of three words in a common character. Devise a way to display the results.

13.2   Trace the solution of the 8-queens problem and observe the backtracking process.

13.3   Modify the solution of the 8-queens problem to display the placement of the queens in a visually attractive way.

13.4   Modify the solution of the 8-queens problem to keep track of how many times a queen is placed at each position. Display the results in a way that is easily understood.

13.5   Write a program that determines all the ways that eight rooks can be placed on a chessboard so that no two rooks are on the same column or row.

13.6   Trace the call of star("abc") and observe the interaction between generation and recursion.

13.7*   Write a procedure gensubstr(s) that generates all the nonempty substrings of s. Do not generate the same substring in the same position more than once, but generate all substrings even if there are duplicates. For example, gensubstr("aaa") should generate "a", "aa", "aaa", "a", "aa", "a" (or the same results in a different order).

13.8   Describe the transformation from the recursive definition for the Fibonacci numbers to the procedure for generating them. To what kinds of recursively defined functions does this transformation apply?

13.9   Write a program that transforms recursively defined functions as given in the preceding exercise into corresponding recursive generators.

13.10   Write an iterative version of fibseq(). Show that recursive generation serves only to transfer values between the two arguments.

13.11   Write a generator that produces the prime numbers in sequence.

13.12   Write a recursive generator for the following recurrence:

$$xseq(1) = c_1$$
$$xseq(2) = c_2$$
$$xseq(3) = c_3$$
$$xseq(i) = i + xseq(i-1) - xseq(i-2) + 2xseq(i-3) \quad \text{for } i > 3$$

where c_1, c_2, and c_3 are integer constants. The initial call of the generator should have the form xseq(i1, i2, i3). For example, xseq(1, 2, 4) should generate 1, 2, 4, 8, 13, 19, 29, 44, 62, 86, ...

14

String Scanning and Pattern Matching

Although string scanning involves only a few functions and operations, its apparent simplicity is deceptive. Except for generators, string scanning adds more to the power of Icon and influences programming techniques more than any other feature of the language. Furthermore, some of the ways that string scanning can be used are not obvious. This chapter explores string scanning, concentrating on examples and techniques that exploit its potential and lead to good programming style.

ARITHMETIC EXPRESSIONS

Arithmetic expressions are usually written in infix form with operators between the arguments and with parentheses used for grouping. Rules of precedence and associativity for operators are used to avoid excessive numbers of parentheses. Icon's syntax itself is typical in this respect. Such a syntax is designed for human use. In computer processing, it is more convenient to dispense with precedence and associativity rules and to use parentheses to group all arguments with their operators or to use some other equivalent representation. Furthermore, it often is convenient to have operators appear before or after their arguments, that is, to have operations in prefix form or suffix form rather than the infix form that is easier for human beings to read. The conversion of strings from one form to another provides a good example of string scanning.

Some typical infix operators with their relative precedences and associativities are

operator	precedence	associativity
^	3	right to left
*	2	left to right
/	2	left to right
+	1	left to right
−	1	left to right

For example, the fully parenthesized form of

"x−y−z*delta"

is

"((x−y)−(z*delta))"

and

"u+v/n^e^2"

is equivalent to

"(u+(v/(n^(e^2))))"

The prefix forms of these two expressions are:

"−(−(x, y),*(z,delta))"
"+(u /(v,^(n,^(e,2))))"

Note that the variables and constants have the same form in both infix and prefix notation.

A typical problem is to convert infix expressions with the preceding operators into prefix form. There may be superfluous parentheses, but the infix expressions otherwise are assumed to be well formed (that is, syntactically correct). The general approach to the problem is recursive, with a procedure fix(exp) that converts an infix expression exp into prefix form. Therefore, the transformation has the form

expr1 operator expr2 → *operator* (fix(*expr1*), fix(*expr2*))

The first problem is to remove any outer parentheses that may occur around the argument of fix(). Since there may be superfluous parentheses, this process must be repeated. One approach is:

```
while exp ?:= {
  2(="(", tab(bal(')'))), pos(−1))
  }
```

As long as exp begins with a left parenthesis, the balanced string up to a right parenthesis is matched, and pos(−1) checks that this parenthesis is the last character of the string being scanned. If the right parenthesis is the last character of the string being scanned, the scanning expression succeeds. The value produced by tab(bal(')')) is assigned to exp, and the while loop continues with exp being scanned again.

The next step is to analyze exp to get the proper operator for the pattern

expr1 operator expr2

This pattern may occur in an infix expression in many ways. For example, in

"x−y∗2"
 ↑ ↑

the pattern occurs in two ways, as indicated by the arrows beneath the operators. Precedence is used to select the correct operator. The first occurrence of the pattern is the correct one in this example, since multiplication has higher precedence than subtraction, and hence y is an argument of the multiplication, not the subtraction. The correct pattern therefore is obtained by looking for the operators of lowest precedence first.

A similar problem occurs in selecting among several operators of equal precedence. Therefore, in "x−y−z" there are two ways the pattern could be applied. Since subtraction is left-associative, this expression is equivalent to "(x−y)−z" and the rightmost left-associative operator is the correct one. On the other hand, the opposite is true of right-associative operators. For example, "x^e^2" is equivalent to "x^(e^2)".

In summary, there are two rules:

1. Look for the operator of lowest precedence first and then for operators with increasingly higher precedence.

2. Locate the rightmost left-associative operator but the leftmost right-associative operator.

Since string scanning operates from left to right, it is easiest to handle right-associative operators. A procedure is:

```
procedure rassoc(exp, op)
  return exp ? {
    form(tab(bal(op)), move(1), tab(0))
    }
end
```

where form(arg1, op, arg2) constructs the desired prefix expression:

```
procedure form(arg1, op, arg2)
  return op || "(" || fix(arg1) || "," || fix(arg2) || ")"
end
```

Note that form(arg1, op, arg2) performs the necessary rearrangement of the strings produced by scanning.

The rightmost left-associative operator can be located by iterating over the result sequence for the positions of all such operators to find the last one:

```
procedure lassoc(exp, op)
  local j

  return exp ? {
    every j := bal(op)
    form(tab(\j), move(1), tab(0))
    }
end
```

The expression \j determines whether any value was assigned to j in the every loop. If bal(op) does not produce any result, the initial null value of j is not changed, tab(\j) fails, and lassoc() fails, indicating that op does not occur in exp.

The procedures rassoc() and lassoc() must be applied in the correct order. The obvious approach is:

```
if exp := lassoc(exp, '+ −') then return exp
else if exp := lassoc(exp, '*/') then return exp
else if exp := rassoc(exp, '^') then return exp
else return exp
```

Note that the second arguments of lassoc() and rassoc() are character sets, allowing all operators in a class to be processed at the same time. The final component of this expression returns exp unchanged if it contains no operators, that is, if it is an identifier or a constant. This presumes, of course, that exp is well formed.

The preceding program segment can be made considerably more concise by using goal-directed evaluation in the return expression:

```
return lassoc('+ −' | '*/') | rassoc(exp, '^') | exp
```

The argument of the return expression consists of the possible alternatives, which are evaluated from left to right. Notice that the argument of lassoc() also contains two alternatives, an application of the fact that

$$p(expr1) \mid p(expr2)$$

and

$$p(expr1 \mid expr2)$$

are equivalent.

The procedure to convert infix expressions into prefix form first removes outer parentheses and then applies lassoc() and rassoc(), as shown previously:

```
procedure fix(exp)
  while exp ?:= {
    2(="(", tab(bal(')')), pos(-1))
    }
  return lassoc(exp, '+ -' | '*/') | rassoc(exp, '^') | exp
end
```

The rest of the program for infix-to-prefix conversion is:

```
procedure main()
  while write(fix(read()))
end

procedure lassoc(exp, op)
  local j

  return exp ? {
    every j := bal(op)
    form(tab(\j), move(1), tab(0))
    }
end

procedure rassoc(exp, op)
  return exp ? {
    form(tab(bal(op)), move(1), tab(0))
    }
end

procedure form(arg1, op, arg2)
  return op || "(" || fix(arg1) || "," || fix(arg2) || ")"
end
```

Note that the prefix form is determined in form(); suffix or fully parenthesized infix forms can be produced by rearranging the concatenation.

PATTERN MATCHING

The operations for transforming infix to prefix forms in the preceding sections use patterns such as

expr1 operator expr2

to describe the structure of the string and to identify its components.

A pattern is a powerful conceptual tool for describing the structure of a string. This section develops a methodology for describing and implementing patterns using string scanning.

Matching Expressions

The functions tab(i) and move(i) are called matching functions because they change the position in the subject and produce the substring of the subject between the old and new positions. While the value of i in tab(i) can be computed in many ways using string analysis functions, actual matching is done only by tab(i) and move(i).

Matching expressions that extend the repertoire of matching functions provide a way of expressing more complicated matching operations. Matching expressions must obey a protocol that allows them to be used like matching functions. The protocol for a matching expression *expr* is as follows:

1. Evaluation of *expr* does not change the subject.

2. If *expr* succeeds, it produces the substring of the subject between the positions before and after its evaluation.

3. If *expr* does not produce a result, it leaves the position where it was prior to the time *expr* was evaluated.

The first rule assumes that matching expressions all apply to the same subject. The second rule is concerned with the values produced by matching expressions, while the third rule assures that alternative matches start at the same place in the subject. The third rule includes the possibility that a matching expression may change the position but later restore it if a subsequent match is unsuccessful. The three rules are largely independent.

For example,

   tab(upto(',')) || move(1)

is a matching expression, but

   tab(upto(',')) || move(−1)

is not, since the value it produces is not the substring between the old and new positions. Similarly,

   tab(upto(',')) & move(1)

is not a matching expression, since it does not produce the substring of the subject between the positions before tab(upto(',')) is evaluated and after move(1) is evaluated. The expression

   &subject[.&pos:&pos := upto(',')]

is not a matching expression either, since, if it is resumed, it does not restore the previous position. On the other hand,

&subject[.&pos:&pos <– upto(',')]

is a matching expression, since, if it is resumed, the reversible assignment operation restores the previous position. Note that in both cases the first occurrence of &pos in the range specification must be dereferenced before a new value is assigned to &pos.

In general, bounded expressions prevent restoration of the position, so that

{s := move(1); s || tab(0)}

is not a matching expression even though it produces the matched substring.

When using string scanning to do pattern matching, it is generally good practice to use matching expressions. Most pattern matching is done from left to right. In such cases,

expr1 || *expr2*

should be used instead of

expr1 & *expr2*

since the former expression produces the matched substring, while the latter does not. Both operations perform data backtracking, however. If production of matched substrings is not important, conjunction may be used in place of concatenation.

Matching Procedures

A *matching procedure* is a procedure whose call is a matching expression. As an example, consider a procedure that does what the function tab(i) does.

```
procedure tab(i)
    suspend .&subject[.&pos:&pos <– i]
end
```

Such a procedure is merely an encapsulation of a matching expression and satisfies all the rules of protocol for matching expressions. The value returned is dereferenced; otherwise the result would be a variable to which a value could be assigned to change the subject.

The matching function move(i) can be written as a procedure in an analogous manner.

Using this technique, a variety of matching procedures can be written. For example,

```
procedure arb()
    suspend .&subject[.&pos:&pos <– &pos to *&subject + 1]
end
```

matches any string from the current position through the end of the subject. Note that arb() may generate more than one value. Therefore,

> arb() || ="load" || arb() || ="r6"

matches any string that contains the substring "load" followed by the substring "r6"; "load" need not appear at the beginning of the subject, and "load" and "r6" need not be consecutive substrings.

A similar procedure that matches the longest possible string first is

```
procedure rarb()
    suspend .&subject[.&pos: &pos <- ((*&subject + 1) to &pos by −1)]
end
```

For example,

> rarb() || ="."

matches the string up to the last period in the subject.

Another example is a matching procedure that matches any one of several strings in a list:

```
procedure lmatch(slist)
    suspend =!slist
end
```

For example,

> lmatch(["black", "white", "gray"])

matches "black", "white", or "gray".

One advantage of using a matching procedure for high-level string processing is that a procedure is a value. As such, it can be used as an argument to other matching procedures. An example of such a use is given by:

```
procedure arbno(p)
    suspend "" | (p() || arbno(p))
end
```

The procedure arbno(p) matches zero or more instances of whatever p() matches. The first alternative, the empty string, corresponds to zero matches of p(). The second alternative matches whatever p() matches, concatenated with whatever arbno(p) matches: zero or more instances of whatever p() matches. For example, given

```
procedure shades()
  suspend arb() || lmatch(["black", "white", "gray"])
end
```

then arbno(shades) matches strings that contain zero or more occurrences of "black", "white", or "gray".

The argument of arbno() must be a matching procedure. It cannot be an arbitrary matching expression, since the argument is called in the body of the procedure for arbno(). For example, in

arbno(lmatch(["black", "white", "gray"]))

the call of lmatch() is evaluated before arbno() is called. Not only is this order of evaluation incorrect, but also the value assigned to the parameter p is a string, not a procedure.

Note that arbno() is a recursive generator. Compare it to star() given in Chapter 13.

GRAMMARS AND LANGUAGES

A pattern characterizes a set of strings—the strings that it matches. A set of strings is called a language. The strings in a language (its "sentences") are derived or described according to grammatical rules.

Natural languages, such as English, are very complex. The grammatical rules of such languages (their syntax) describe these languages only superficially. In fact, there are many aspects of natural languages that defy precise description. There are, however, many interesting languages, including programming languages, in which the structure can be defined by precise and comparatively simple grammatical rules.

Patterns and the grammars for languages have a close relationship. For some kinds of grammars, there is a direct mapping from the rules of the grammar to patterns that match strings in the corresponding language.

A language for a simple class of arithmetic expressions can be described informally in terms of mutually recursive definitions:

1. An *expression* is a *term* or a *term* followed by a + followed by an *expression*.

2. A *term* is an *element* or an *element* followed by a * followed by a *term*.

3. An *element* is one of the characters x, y, z or an *expression* enclosed in parentheses.

Words in italics, like *element*, describe sets of strings and are called nonterminal symbols. Specific strings, like x, are called terminal symbols.

These definitions can be expressed more formally in terms of a grammar as follows: Let X, T, and E stand for *expression*, *term*, and *element*, respectively. Then a grammar corresponding to the preceding definitions is:

X ::= T | T+X
T ::= E | E*T
E ::= x | y | z | (X)

Uppercase letters are used here to denote nonterminal symbols, while other characters, including parentheses, stand for themselves. The symbol ::= stands for "is defined to be". The concatenation of symbols replaces "followed by" in the informal definition, and the vertical bar replaces "or". Note the similarity of this use of the vertical bar to the alternation control structure in Icon. In a grammar, the vertical bar has lower precedence than concatenation.

Each nonterminal symbol defines its own language: A language for expressions defined by X, a language for terms defined by T, and a language for elements defined by E. One nonterminal symbol is designated as a "goal" for the language of interest. X is the goal in the examples that follow.

In deriving the strings for the language defined by a nonterminal symbol, the symbol ::= in the grammar means that an instance of the nonterminal symbol on its left can be replaced by any one of the alternatives on the right. For example, T can be replaced by E or E*T. Starting with the goal symbol X, a possible derivation of a sentence is:

X	goal
T+X	second alternative for X
T+T	first alternative for X
E+T	first alternative for first instance of T
x+T	first alternative for E
x+E	first alternative for T
x+(X)	fourth alternative for E
x+(T)	first alternative for X
x+(E*T)	second alternative for T
x+(y*T)	second alternative for E
x+(y*E)	first alternative for T
x+(y*z)	third alternative for E

Since there are no more nonterminal symbols in this string, x+(y*z) is a sentence in the language defined by X.

The alternatives in the preceding derivation were chosen at random. Application of all the rules in all possible ways produces all strings in the language. As in most interesting languages, the language for X contains an infinite number of strings.

Recognizers

Recognition is the process of determining whether or not a string belongs to a language and is the converse of derivation. In the context here, this amounts to matching the strings that are in a language and only those strings.

In the case of grammars like the preceding one, there is a straightforward and mechanical way of producing patterns that match the strings in the language:

1. Terminal symbols are matched by corresponding matching expressions for the specific strings. For example, x is matched by ="x".

2. Nonterminal symbols are matched by matching procedures. For example, X is matched by X(). The form of such matching procedures is given later.

3. A concatenation of symbols is matched by the concatenation of the matching expressions for the individual symbols. For example, T+X is matched by

$$T() \mid\mid ="+" \mid\mid X()$$

4. Alternatives are matched by the alternation of matching expressions. For example,

$$E\mid E*T$$

is matched by

$$E() \mid (E() \mid\mid ="*" \mid\mid T())$$

5. A matching procedure encapsulates the matching expression for the corresponding nonterminal symbol. For example, the matching procedure for

$$X ::= T\mid T+X$$

is:

```
procedure X()
   suspend T() | (T() || ="+" || X())
end
```

These rules can be used to convert any context-free grammar of the kind given previously directly into matching procedures.

The procedure for the nonterminal goal symbol is called within a scanning expression. Since recognition requires that the entire string be matched, not just an initial substring of it, the scanning operation has the form

```
line ? {
   X() & pos(0)
   }
```

A program to recognize strings in the language defined by X is:

```
procedure main()
  while writes(line := read()) do
    if line ? {
      X() & pos(0)
      }
    then write(" accepted") else write(" rejected")
end
```

The kind of recognizer given here is called a top-down, recursive-descent recognizer with backtracking. This kind of recognizer has two problems: It is inefficient, and it cannot handle left recursion in the grammar. Left recursion occurs when the definition of a nonterminal symbol has an alternative that begins with a nonterminal symbol leading back to itself. For example, in a rule such as

$$X ::= X+T|T$$

the matching procedure

```
procedure X()
  suspend (X() || ="+" || T()) | T()
end
```

calls itself indefinitely, which causes internal stack overflow and program termination with an error message.

Despite these problems, this approach to recognizing strings is sometimes useful. It also provides insights into the relationship between grammars and pattern matching.

There are other possibilities. The previous matching procedures have no arguments. By adding arguments, recognizers can be constructed for classes of languages that are more general than context-free ones. Consider, for example, the program

```
procedure main()
  while writes(line := read()) do
    if line ? {
      ABC("") & pos(0)
      }
    then write(" accepted") else write(" rejected")
end

procedure ABC(s)
  suspend =s | (="a" || ABC("b" || s) || ="c")
end
```

This program matches sentences in the language $a^n b^n c^n$ for $n = 0, 1, \ldots$: the empty string, abc, aabbcc, aaabbbccc, ... This is a well-known context-sensitive language, which cannot be derived from any context-free grammar. While there are much more obvious ways of recognizing such strings than the procedure given above, it is representative of a general class of recognizers for context-sensitive languages.

Tracing provides insight into the matching process. For the input line **aaabbbccc**, the trace output is:

```
abc.icn:    4  |  ABC("")
abc.icn:   10  |  ABC suspended ""
abc.icn:    4  |  ABC resumed
abc.icn:   10  |  |  ABC("b")
abc.icn:   10  |  |  |  ABC("bb")
abc.icn:   10  |  |  |  |  ABC("bbb")
abc.icn:   10  |  |  |  |  ABC suspended "bbb"
abc.icn:   10  |  |  |  ABC suspended "abbbc"
abc.icn:   10  |  |  ABC suspended "aabbbcc"
abc.icn:   10  |  ABC suspended "aaabbbccc"
```

Parsers

The process of recognizing strings in a language has limited usefulness. Recognition produces only a "yes" or a "no", but no information is produced about how the string is matched or how its structure is related to the grammar.

It is relatively easy to convert matching procedures like those given previously into parsing procedures that produce a "parse tree" that retains the structure of the match. The technique produces lists of matched strings rather than concatenations of matched strings. A matching procedure such as

```
procedure X()
   suspend T() | (T() || ="+" || X())
end
```

can be rewritten as a parsing procedure:

```
procedure X()
   suspend [T()] | [T(), ="+", X()]
end
```

Since parsing procedures produce lists, the result is a list of lists, or a tree, that shows the details of the parse. For example, the value produced for the string "x+(y*z)" is

$$[[["x"]], "+", [[["(", [[["y"], "*", [["z"]]]], ")"]]]]$$

Such a list is more easily understood if it is drawn as a tree:

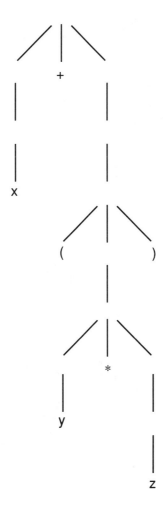

It may be useful to provide a tag as the first value in each list in order to identify the nonterminal symbol. With this addition, the parsing procedures for the grammar in the preceding section are:

```
procedure T()
   suspend ["T", E()] | ["T", E(), ="*", T()]
end

procedure E()
   suspend ["E", =!"xyz"] | ["E", ="(", X(), =")"]
end
```

```
procedure X()
  suspend ["X", T()] | ["X", T(), ="+", X()]
end
```

Note that the more compact formulation

=!"xyz"

is used in place of the direct translation

="x" | ="y" | ="z"

The tree produced for the preceding example is:

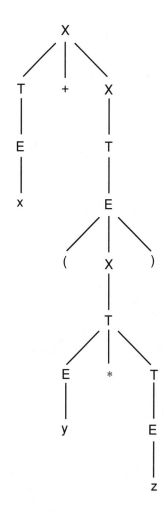

EXERCISES

14.1   Modify the procedures for processing expressions in infix form to produce postfix form instead of prefix form.

14.2   Write a procedure fields(s, c) that generates the substrings of s that are separated by characters in c.

14.3   Suppose *expr1* and *expr2* are matching expressions. Which of the following are matching expressions?

> *expr1* | *expr2*
> |*expr1*
> *expr1* \ 1
> if *expr1* then *expr2*
> if pos(1) then *expr1* else *expr2*

14.4   Write a matching procedure that does what the function move(i) does.

14.5*   Write a matching procedure limit(p, i) that matches at most the first i strings matched by the matching procedure p.

14.6   Write a matching procedure select(p, i) that matches only the ith string matched by the matching procedure p.

14.7*   Generalize the procedure arbno(p) so that arguments for p can be provided.

14.8   Suppose that the protocol for matching expressions is relaxed so that they can produce any string, not just a matched string. How does this affect matching procedures? What would be the consequences of relaxing the protocol even further so that the result produced by a matching expression can be any type of value?

14.9   Consider the following procedure:

```
procedure ABC(A, B, C)
  suspend (=A || =B || =C) | ABC("a" || A, "b" || B, "c" || C)
end
```

The expression

```
line ? {
  ABC("", "", "") & pos(0)
  }
```

matches strings of the form $a^n b^n c^n$ for $n = 0, 1, 2, \ldots$. It is not a recognizer, however. Explain the problem.

14.10*   Write a recognizer for strings of the form $a^n b^n c^n d^n$ for $n = 0, 1, 2, \ldots$.

14.11   Write a program that lists an Icon source program, annotating each line with the level of nesting of braces in effect. Account for braces in quoted literals and comments.

14.12   Write a program that reads a context-free grammar and produces an Icon program that recognizes strings in the language described by this grammar. Provide a means of specifying the goal symbol.

14.13   Write a program as specified in the preceding exercise but produce a parser instead of a recognizer.

15

Using Structures

Icon provides the facilities that are needed for processing structures, such as the parse trees that were developed in Chapter 14. This chapter describes how records, lists, sets, and tables can be used for representing and manipulating trees, graphs, and other structures.

TREES

A tree is a collection of nodes connected by directed arcs. At most one arc can be directed into any node, although there may be many arcs directed out of a node. One node, the *root*, has no arcs directed into it. Nodes that have no arcs directed out of them are *leaves*. A value usually is associated with each node.

A common way to represent trees with strings corresponds to the way that arithmetic expressions are given in prefix form (see Chapter 14). For example, the arithmetic expression

"(a/b)+(c–d)"

has the prefix form

"+(/(a,b),–(c,d))"

and corresponds to the tree

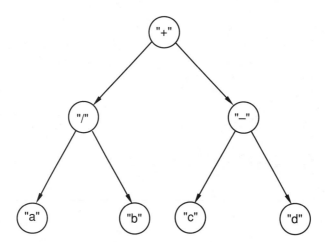

As shown here, trees usually are drawn with the root at the top. This is a binary tree. That is, there are two arcs out of all nodes except the leaves.

When a tree is represented by a string, the parentheses and commas indicate the structural relationships. The string representation of a tree is compact, but it is awkward to process for many purposes. There are several ways that a tree can be represented with structures. A natural method uses lists, as in

["+", ["/", ["a"], ["b"]], ["–", ["c"], ["d"]]]

In this representation each node of the tree is represented by a list. The first value in each list is the value that is associated with the node, and subsequent values in a list correspond to arcs to other nodes. Note that this representation is somewhat different from the one used for parse trees in Chapter 14. In that representation, leaves are represented by strings, not lists. The representation here is more general.

A more structured way of representing a binary tree is to use records for the nodes:

record node(value, lptr, rptr)

where the lptr and rptr fields contain pointers to the left and right subtrees, respectively.

Using this representation, the tree shown above can be constructed as follows:

```
leaf1 := node("a")
leaf2 := node("b")
leaf3 := node("c")
leaf4 := node("d")
inode1 := node("*", leaf1, leaf2)
inode2 := node("–", leaf3, leaf4)
root := node("+", inode1, inode2)
```

Of course, this tree could be constructed in a single large expression.

While such a representation of a tree is useful for processing data within a program, information read into a program and written out of a program consists of strings. Consequently, procedures are needed to convert between the string and record representations of trees. A procedure to do this is naturally recursive, since the structure of a tree is recursive.

A procedure to convert the string representation of a tree to its corresponding record representation is:

```
procedure rtree(stree)
  local R

  stree ? {
    if R := node(tab(upto('('))) then {      # new node
      move(1)                                # skip paren
      R.lptr := rtree(tab(bal(',')))         # left subtree
      move(1)                                # skip comma
      R.rptr := rtree(tab(bal(')')))         # right subtree
      }
    else R := node(tab(0))                   # leaf
    }
  return R
end
```

This formulation assumes that the string representation of the tree is well-formed. The two branches of the selection expression differentiate between interior and leaf nodes. For interior nodes, rtree() is called recursively to construct the subtrees. Note that the fields lptr and rptr have null values for leaf nodes.

Conversion from the record representation of a tree to the corresponding string representation is similar in structure, with concatenation replacing assignments to fields:

```
procedure stree(rtree)
  if /rtree.lptr then return rtree.value        # leaf
  else return rtree.value || "(" || stree(rtree.lptr) || "," || stree(rtree.rptr) || ")"
end
```

This formulation assumes that if one pointer from a node is null the other one is also.

For some purposes it is useful to be able to visit all the nodes (subtrees) of a tree. This can be done easily with a generator:

```
procedure visit(rtree)
  suspend rtree
  suspend visit(\(rtree.lptr | rtree.rptr))     # not leaf, continue
end
```

Note that this procedure is a recursive generator, reflecting the recursive definition of a tree. The root node itself is produced first, followed by the nodes for its subtrees. Here it is more convenient to check that each pointer is non-null.

The procedure visit(rtree) can be used in a variety of ways. For example,

```
every write(stree(visit(rtree)))
```

writes all the subtrees in rtree, while

```
every write(visit(rtree).value)
```

writes the values of all nodes in the tree. Similarly,

```
every R := visit(rtree) do
   if /R.lptr then write(R.value)
```

writes the values of all leaves in rtree.

Sometimes it is necessary to know whether or not two trees have the same structure and the same node values, that is, if they are equivalent. The operation

```
R1 === R2
```

does not determine whether or not two trees are equivalent, but only if they are identical; that is, if R1 and R2 are the same record (see Chapter 10). A procedure to compare two trees for equivalence is

```
procedure rtreeq(R1,R2)
   if R1 === R2 then return R2              # identical subtrees
   else if /(R1 | R2) then fail             # only one is null
   else if {
     R1.value === R2.value &                # check values and subtrees
     rtreeq(R1.lptr, R2.lptr) &
     rtreeq(R1.rtpr, R2.rptr)
     }
     then return R2
   else fail
end
```

The first test checks whether R1 and R2 are identical. If they are, it is not necessary to check anything else. If this fails, the values and subtrees are checked for equivalence, calling rtreeq() recursively. The recursion terminates for equivalent trees when null-valued pointers (for leaf nodes) are compared. If all subtrees are the same, R2 is returned, conforming to the convention for built-in comparison operations.

DAGS

A directed acyclic graph, or *dag*, is a graph in which there are no loops leading from a node back to itself. A *rooted* dag is like a tree except that there may be several arcs directed into any node other than the root. Rooted dags occur, for example, as the result of common subexpression elimination, where a subtree that is the same as another is eliminated and the two arcs are directed to one of the subtrees. For example, the infix expression

$$(a/b)+((a/b)-b)$$

has the tree

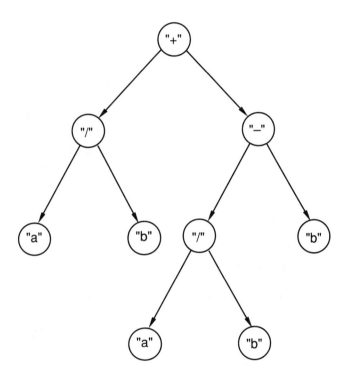

Duplicate subtrees can be eliminated by converting this tree to a dag:

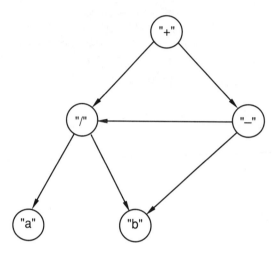

Instead of converting a tree to a dag, it is easier to construct the dag in the first place. The technique used here is to tabulate the parts of the structure that have been built already and to direct arcs to them rather than constructing equivalent parts:

```
procedure rdag(stree,done)
   local R

   /done := table()                           # new table
   if R := \done[stree] then return R         # return part already done
   stree ? {
      if R := node(tab(upto('('))) then {      # new node
         move(1)                               # skip paren
         R.lptr := rdag(tab(bal(','')), done)  # left subdag
         move(1)                               # skip comma
         R.rptr := rdag(tab(bal(')')), done)   # right subdag
         }
      else R := node(tab(0))                   # leaf
      }
   return done[stree] := R
end
```

The table **done** keeps track of portions of the dag that already have been constructed. Its keys are strings and its values point to the corresponding nodes. When rdag() is called to construct a dag for **stree**, the second argument is omitted, since no parts of the dag have been constructed yet. Thus, the table is created on the initial call of rdag(). The recursive call of rdag() includes the table **done** as its second argument, passing the table of the parts that have been constructed. Finally, the newly constructed dag is added as the value corresponding to the key **stree**.

The method of handling the table of constructed parts deserves note. Since the table done is created at the "top-level" call of rdag() and subsequently passed as an argument to recursive calls of rdag(), done is local to the processing of a particular tree. If it were global instead, independent uses of rdag() might interfere with each other. The table cannot be constructed in an initial clause for the same reason.

Note that the tree-processing functions in the preceding section all work properly on rooted dags. The procedure stree() processes dags as well as trees, effectively "unfolding" them. Similarly, rtreeq() works properly on dags. The procedure visit() works on dags, although nodes with more than one arc into them are visited once for each arc. This causes a dag to appear to be a tree.

GRAPHS

In general, directed graphs have cycles and unconnected subgraphs, as in:

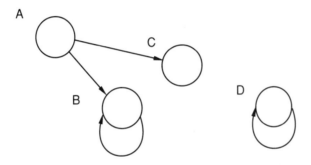

One way to build the corresponding structure is to represent each node in the graph by a set. Then the values in the set are pointers — arcs to the nodes to which the node points. For ex- ample, the program structures for the graph shown above are:

```
A := set()
B := set()
C := set()
D := set()
insert(A, B)
insert(A, C)
insert(B, B)
insert(D, D)
```

The important conceptual point is that a set is a collection of pointers to other sets. A slightly different visualization of the structures in the programming domain illustrates this:

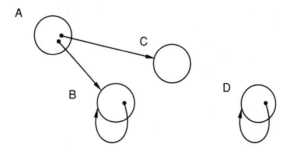

Thus, an arc is represented by (a pointer to) a set and a node is represented by the values in the set.

The ease of manipulating this representation of graphs is illustrated by a procedure to compute the transitive closure of a node (the node and all nodes reachable from it by a succession of arcs):

```
procedure closure(n, S)
   local n1

   /S := set()
   insert(S, n)
   every n1 := !n do
      member(S, n1) | closure(n1, S)
   return S
end
```

Note that a set also is used to keep track of nodes as they accumulate.

Several problems arise in computations on graphs that may require a somewhat more sophisticated representation of structures. For example, values may be associated with arcs:

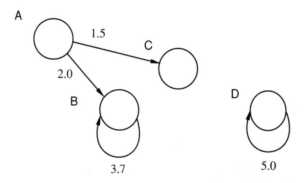

In this case, the set-of-sets approach is inadequate. However, a record type can be used for arcs, as in

    record arc(value, node)

where the **value** field contains the value associated with the arc and the **node** field contains the set to which the arc points. Then the graph can be represented in a program as follows:

    insert(A, arc(2.0, B))
    insert(A, arc(1.5, C))
    insert(B, arc(3.7, B))
    insert(D, arc(5.0, D))

TWO-WAY TABLES

Programs that manipulate graphs generally need to be able to read a representation of a graph in string form and write the results in string form. For example, the (unweighted) form of the graph in the preceding section might be represented by strings such as:

    "A–>B"
    "A–>C"
    "B–>B"
    "D–>D"

One problem is associating labels for the nodes with corresponding program structures. The natural solution in Icon is to use a table in which the keys are the labels and the corresponding values are the corresponding sets. Written out explicitly for the graph above, this might be:

    Node := table()
    Node["A"] := A
    Node["B"] := B
    Node["C"] := C
    Node["D"] := D

Consequently, Node["A"] produces the node (set) labeled A. Such a table might be used, for example, in constructing a graph from its string representation.

On the other hand, the converse association may be needed. For example, in writing out the results of a computation on a graph (such as the transitive closure of a node), the labels associated with nodes may be needed.

Since any kind of value can be used as a key, a table with the keys and corresponding values reversed can be used:

```
Label := table()
Label[A] := "A"
Label[B] := "B"
Label[C] := "C"
Label[D] := "D"
```

It is not necessary to have two tables, however. Since the keys in a table need not all be of the same type, the same table can be keyed with both the labels and the nodes (sets):

```
Graph := table()
Graph["A"] := A
Graph["B"] := B
Graph["C"] := C
Graph["D"] := D
Graph[A] := "A"
Graph[B] := "B"
Graph[C] := "C"
Graph[D] := "D"
```

Such a "two-way" table keeps all the information needed to associate labels with nodes and vice versa in one structure. Subscripting it with a label produces the corresponding node, and subscripting it with a node produces the corresponding label.

EXERCISES

15.1   Modify rtree() to verify that the string representation of the tree is well-formed.

15.2   Generalize the record representation of trees to allow *n*-ary trees in which there may be one or many arcs from an interior node. Write procedures for converting between the string and record representations of such trees, and for comparing record representations for equality.

15.3* Write a procedure that determines the maximum depth of a binary tree; that is, the longest series of arcs from the root to a leaf.

15.4   Write a procedure that prints a binary tree, indenting according to the depth in the tree.

15.5* Write a procedure that copies a binary tree.

15.6   Describe in detail the possible effects of keeping a global table of the constructed parts of a dag.

15.7* Write a procedure that produces the number of nodes in a dag.

15.8   Write a procedure that generalizes the function image(x) by producing a detailed and understandable representation of any structure, including lists, sets, tables, and records.

15.9   Write a procedure to convert the string representation of an unweighted graph to the corresponding program structures. Do the same for a weighted graph.

15.10   Write a procedure to convert the set representation of an unweighted graph to the corresponding string representation. Do the same for a weighted graph.

15.11   Devise a representation for graphs in which there may be more than one arc from a node to another node.

16

Mappings and Labelings

MAPPING TECHNIQUES

The function map(s1, s2, s3) usually is used to perform a character substitution on s1 by replacing characters in s1 that occur in s2 by the characters of s3 that are in corresponding positions to those in s2. In this kind of use, s2 and s3 are parameters that characterize the substitution, and s1 varies, as in

map(line, "aeiou", "*****")

which replaces all lowercase vowels in line by asterisks.

If s1 and s2 are considered to be parameters and s3 is allowed to vary, some surprising results are possible.

Transpositions

If the value of labels is a string of distinct characters (that is, containing no duplicates), and the value of trans is a rearrangement, or *transposition*, of the value of labels, then

map(trans, labels, s3)

produces the corresponding transposition of s3. For example,

map("654321", "123456", s3)

produces the reversal of the value of s3. Suppose the value of s3 is "quotas" as in

map("654321", "123456", "quotas")

Then the "6" in the first argument is replaced by the character corresponding to the "6" in the second argument, that is, "s". Similarly, the character "5" in the first argument is replaced by the character corresponding to the "5" in the second argument, that is, "a", and so on:

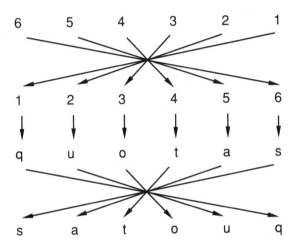

The value produced is "satouq", the reversal of "quotas", since the specified transposition, "654321", is the reversal of the labeling string, "123456". If the transposition is different, as in

map("561234", "123456", s3)

the result produced is correspondingly different. In this case it is the rotation of s3 two characters to the right (or four to the left).

Any characters can be used for the labeling as long as there are no duplicates. The maximum size of a transposition is limited to 256. The more important restriction is that the sizes of the second and third arguments must be the same. Therefore,

map("654321", "123456", s3)

only can be used to reverse six-character strings. In many cases, however, the transposition of longer strings can be performed piece by piece. That is,

reverse(s1 || s2) == (reverse(s2) || reverse(s1))

Although there is a built-in function reverse(s), a corresponding procedure using mapping techniques provides a model for a variety of transpositions. A procedure is:

```
procedure reverse(s)
  static labels, trans, max

  initial {
    labels := "abcdefghijklmnopqrstuvwxyz"
    trans := "zyxwvutsrqponmlkjihgfedcba"
    max := *labels
    }

  if *s <= max then return map(right(trans, *s), left(labels, *s), s)
    else return reverse(right(s, *s – max)) || map(trans, labels, left(s, max))
end
```

The values chosen for labels and trans are two strings of reasonable size that are easy to write. If s is not too long, it can be reversed by one application of map(). The expression

```
left(labels, *s)
```

truncates s at the right and produces a labeling of the correct length. The expression

```
right(trans, *s)
```

produces the corresponding transposition from the other end of trans. Subscripting expressions also could also be used for these purposes.

If s is too long to be reversed by one application of map(), recursion is used. Piece-by-piece reversals of long strings can be done iteratively, of course; recursion simply provides a more compact solution for the purposes of illustration.

The reversal process is more efficient for longer values of labels and trans. The longest possible labeling is 256, as mentioned earlier. Strings of all 256 characters are impractical to write out literally, but they can be computed by

```
labels := string(&cset)
trans := ""
every trans := !labels || trans
```

A more sophisticated approach is to obtain the longest labeling and transposition strings by bootstrapping, starting with short labeling and transposition strings. For example,

```
labels := "12"
trans := "21"
```

characterizes reversal. The procedure reverse() can be modified to perform the bootstrapping in its initial clause:

```
procedure reverse(s)
    static labels, trans, max

    initial {
        labels := "12"                        # short label
        trans := "21"                         # short transposition
        max := *labels
        trans := reverse(string(&cset))       # long transposition
        labels := string(&cset)               # long label
        max := *labels                        # new length
    }
        .
        .
        .
```

When reverse() is called the first time, it calls itself to change short values of labels and trans to the longest possible values. Note that labels, trans, and max must be defined consistently when reverse() calls itself in its initial clause.

The two strings

```
labels := "12"
trans := "21"
```

characterize the reversal of two-character strings. The extension of this transposition to the reversal of strings of arbitrary length depends on the way substrings of labels and trans are selected and on the handling of the case in which s is too long to be transposed by a single call of map(). Consider a transposition in which every odd-numbered character is swapped with its even-numbered neighbor. For six-character strings, this has the form

```
map("214365", "123456", s3)
```

This transposition also can be characterized by

```
labels := "12"
trans := "21"
```

which is the same labeling as used for reversal. The procedure to swap characters is very similar to reverse(). The two procedures differ in the way that substrings of labels and trans are selected and in the handling of strings that are too long to be transposed by a single call of map(), which is based on

```
swap(s1 || s2) == (swap(s1) || swap(s2))
```

The complete procedure for swapping adjacent characters is:

```
procedure swap(s)
  static labels, trans, max
  initial {

    labels := "12"
    trans := "21"
    max := *labels
    trans := swap(string(&cset))
    labels := string(&cset)
    max := *labels
    }

  if *s <= max then return map(left(trans, *s), left(labels, *s), s)
    else return swap(left(s, *s – max)) || map(trans, labels, right(s, max))
end
```

This procedure only works properly if the size of **s** is even; see Exercise 16.2.

It is reasonable to question the use of mapping techniques for transpositions of this kind, since the procedures are relatively complicated and many transpositions can be written concisely using more conventional techniques. Mapping techniques have two advantages. First they are fast, especially when the same transposition is performed many times, overcoming the initialization overhead for procedures. Second, mapping techniques also provide a clear characterization of the transposition process.

Positional Transformations

For transpositions like

    map(trans, labels, s3)

labels cannot contain duplicate characters and **trans** must be a transposition of **labels**. If these two constraints are relaxed, other kinds of *positional transformations* are possible [10].

The strings **trans** and **labels** do not have to be the same size. If some characters in **labels** are omitted from **trans**, the corresponding characters in **s3** are omitted from the result. For example,

    map("124578", "12345678", s3)

deletes the third and sixth characters of an eight-character string, **s3**. Therefore,

    map("124578", "12345678", "03:56:42")

produces "035642". In cases like this, labels that are more mnemonic make the intent clearer. Furthermore, the labels that correspond to deleted characters can be anything; they need not be distinct. An equivalent positional transformation is:

map("HhMmSs", "Hh:Mm:Ss", s3)

If there are characters in trans that do not occur in labels, these characters are added to the result. Consequently,

map("Hh:Mm:Ss", "HhMmSs", "035642")

produces "03:56:42".

If labels contains duplicate characters, the rightmost correspondences with characters in s3 apply. For example,

map("be", "beeeeee", s3)

produces the first and last characters of strings s3 of length seven.

Characters in labels also can be duplicated in trans. For instance,

map("123321", "123", s3)

produces the three-character string s3 followed by its reversal. An example is:

map("123321", "123", "−∗|")

which produces " − ∗||∗ −" .

LABELINGS

In the preceding sections, characters are used as labels to identify positions of characters in strings. Characters can also be used to stand for objects. Since there are only 256 different characters, their use to label objects is limited, but when they can be used they often allow a compact representation and efficient manipulation. Two examples follow.

Manipulating Decks of Cards

Since a standard deck of playing cards consists of 52 different cards, it is a natural candidate for representation by characters, such as

deck := string(&letters)

In this string, the correspondence between characters and individual playing cards is arbitrary. For example, "a" might correspond to the ace of clubs, "b" to the two of clubs, "n" to the ace of diamonds, and so on.

To illustrate the ease of performing computations on such a representation, consider shuffling a deck of cards. One approach is:

```
procedure shuffle(deck)
  local i

  every i := *deck to 2 by −1 do
    deck[?i] :=: deck[i]
  return deck
end
```

In order to display a shuffled deck or any hand of cards, the implied correspondence between characters and cards must be converted to a readable format. Suppose that in a "fresh" deck the first 13 characters are clubs, the second 13 are diamonds, and so on. Then if

```
fresh := string(&letters)
```

and

```
suits := repl("C", 13) || repl("D", 13) || repl("H", 13) || repl("S", 13)
```

the mapping

```
map(deck, fresh, suits)
```

produces a string showing the suit of each card in deck. Similarly, if the denominations in each suit of a fresh deck are arranged with the ace first, followed by the two, and so on through the jack, queen, and king, then

```
denoms := repl("A23456789TJQK", 4)
```

used in the mapping

```
map(deck, fresh, denoms)
```

produces a string showing the denomination of each card in deck. A complete procedure for displaying the cards with suits on one line and denominations below is:

```
procedure disp(deck)
  static fresh, suits, denoms

  initial {
    fresh := string(&letters)
    suits := repl("C", 13) || repl("D", 13) || repl("H", 13) || repl("S", 13)
    denoms := repl("A23456789TJQK", 4)
    }

  write(map(deck, fresh, suits))          # suits
  write(map(deck, fresh, denoms))         # denominations
end
```

A typical display might be:

```
CDCHSS...
53KTQ8...
```

While such a display is understandable, it is not attractive. Consider the problem of displaying a bridge hand in the conventional way, with each suit given separately. One way to extract all the cards of a given suit from a hand is to map all characters that are not in that suit into a single character. A blank provides a convenient representation for all cards in the suits that are not of interest. If the first 13 cards in a fresh deck are clubs, then in ASCII

```
clubs := "ABCDEFGHIJKLM" || repl(" ", 39)
```

characterizes the clubs. If hand contains characters from fresh, then

```
map(hand, fresh, clubs)
```

maps all clubs in hand into distinct characters and all other characters in hand into spaces. Characters that do not correspond to clubs are "filtered out". Diamonds can be obtained by using

```
diamonds := repl(" ", 13) || "ABCDEFGHIJKLM" || repl(" ", 26)
```

in a similar manner. Since the same string is used to label the characters in both suits, corresponding clubs and diamonds are mapped into the same characters. These characters correspond to the ranks of the card in the suit: Cards of the same rank in different suits are mapped into the same character. Furthermore

```
string(cset(map(hand, fresh, clubs)))
```

places the clubs in order. Any blanks are condensed into a single blank which, because of the order of the ASCII characters, is at the beginning of the resulting string. This blank is essentially "invisible".

See Appendix F for a program that deals and displays randomly selected bridge hands.

Manipulating Graphs

Chapter 15 presented a general way of representing directed graphs. In many cases, a considerably more concise representation is possible. If the number of nodes in a graph is small and only the structural properties of graphs are of interest, a graph can be represented by labeling each node with a different character. An arc from one node to another can be represented by the two characters for the nodes, in order according to the direction of the arc.

For example, the graph

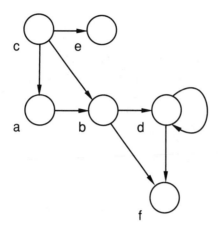

can be represented by the string

　　　g := "abbdbfcacbcedddf"

where "ab" represents the arc from a to b, "bd" represents the arc from b to d, and so on.

Many computations are particularly simple if such a representation is used. For example, the number of arcs in a graph g is given by

　　　*g/2

and the number of nodes is given by

　　　*cset(g)

This representation assumes there is no isolated node that has no arc into it or out of it. If such a node exists, a separate list of nodes is necessary.

Computing transitive closure illustrates the methods of manipulating this representation of directed graphs. The first step in determining transitive closure is to obtain the immediate successors of a set of nodes (those to which there is an arc from any of the nodes in the set):

```
procedure successors(graph, nodes)
  local snodes

  snodes := ''                    # start with none
  graph ? repeat {
    if tab(any(nodes)) then snodes ++:= move(1)
    else move(2) | break     # exit at end of string
    }
  return snodes
end
```

The successor of every odd-numbered character in graph that is contained in nodes is added to snodes by the augmented assignment operation.

Transitive closure starts with the single node of interest and successively expands the set of nodes that can be reached from it until no new nodes are added:

```
procedure closure(graph, nodes)
  local snodes

  snodes := nodes                     # start with given nodes
  while snodes ~=== (nodes ++:= successors(graph, nodes)) do
    snodes := nodes                   # update if changed
  return nodes
end
```

Note that at each step all the successors that can be reached from any node currently in the closure are added to the closure.

This procedure can be simplified considerably by using augmented assignment:

```
procedure closure(graph, nodes)
  while nodes ~===:= (nodes ++:= successors(graph, nodes))
  return nodes
end
```

EXERCISES

16.1 One simple form of enciphering messages transposes characters in fixed-length blocks of a message. Design a transposition cipher and write procedures that encipher and decipher messages using this cipher.

16.2 Determine the result that is produced by swap(s) if the size of s is odd. Modify the procedure so that the last character of s is not transposed if the size of s is odd.

16.3 Write a procedure that interleaves the characters of two strings. For example, the result of interleaving "abc" and "xyz" should be "axbycz". Decide what to do if the two strings are not the same size.

16.4* One way to underscore printed text on typewriter-like devices is to precede each character of the text by an underscore and a backspace. For example,

> write("_\bt_\be_\bx_\bt")

writes <u>text</u>. Write a procedure that produces underscored text.

16.5* One way to print boldface text is to overstrike each character of the text several times (four overstrikes usually are sufficient to produce the appearance of boldface text on typewriter-like devices). Write a procedure that produces boldface text.

16.6 Write a program that underscores words in its input that are preceded by "_" and boldfaces words preceded by "!".

16.7 Write a procedure that reverses strings using character-by-character concatenation. Compare timings of this procedure with those for the procedure reverse() given at the beginning of this chapter. Plot the times versus the length of the string that is reversed.

16.8 Write a procedure that displays hands of cards with each suit sorted in the manner that is conventional for the game of bridge. Such a display might be

```
S  7
H  A J 2
D  A J 9 7 4 3
C  K Q 2
```

16.9 Modify the method for extracting cards according to suit and ordering the result to work on EBCDIC systems.

16.10 Write a procedure that compares the rank of two poker hands.

16.11 Write a procedure that produces the nodes of a graph in topological order so that if there is an arc from node a to node b, a appears before b. Note that not all graphs can be topologically sorted.

16.12 The representation of the arcs of a graph by character pairs is hard to prepare and difficult to read. A more natural representation uses arrows and punctuation. For example, the graph shown previously could be represented by

> "a–>b;b–>d;b->f;c–>a;c–>b;c–>e;d–>d;d–>f;"

Write procedures that convert this representation to the pair representation and conversely.

17

Programming with Strings and Structures

As shown in previous chapters, strings and structures provide many ways of representing and manipulating data. Choosing a good data representation is important but often difficult. Using strings and structures in combination is often the key to writing good programs to solve complicated problems. This chapter contains examples of different ways of representing data and the influences such choices have on programming techniques. It also contains an example in which strings and structures are used in combination to deal with complex relationships in data.

LARGE INTEGERS

Some implementations of Icon support large integers, which are not limited in size by computer architecture. This section illustrates ways of representing and manipulating large integers. The procedures given here illustrate aspects of programming in Icon and are not intended for computation with large integers.

Representing Large Integers

Consider the integer 3,793,234,045. This base-10 notation represents the coefficients of a polynomial:

$$3*10^9 + 7*10^8 + 9*10^7 + 3*10^6 + 2*10^5 + 3*10^4 + 4*10^3 + 0*10^2 + 4*10^1 + 5*10^0$$

This number also can be represented using a larger base, for example 10,000:

$$37*10{,}000^2 + 9{,}323*10{,}000^1 + 4{,}045*10{,}000^0$$

Therefore, the coefficients in base-10,000 notation are 37, 9323, and 4045. Numerical computations can be performed on integers using the base 10,000 in the same manner as used with the base 10. This allows numerical computations on large integers to be performed on segments of manageable size.

Segmented large integers can be represented in several ways. Strings and lists are the obvious ways. The representation of a large integer as a string of digits is straightforward and makes input and output of large integers trivial. For example, the integer 3,793,234,045 is represented by the string "3793234045".

A list of coefficients, such as

[37, 9323, 4045]

is nearly as straightforward as the string representation, but it requires conversion on input and output.

Addition of Large Integers

There are two kinds of numerical computations: base-10, which for addition corresponds to

i1 + i2

and base-n, for which a procedure call such as

add(x1, x2)

is needed. To avoid ambiguity, the term *sum* is used for base-10 addition, while the term *addition* is used for base-n addition. The value 10,000 is used for n for purposes of illustration.

String Representation.   Consider the problem of adding 213,504,961,785 and 581,465,035,213. In the string representation, this amounts to

("2135" + "5814") || ("0496" + "6503") || ("1785" + "5213")

Note that in such an expression, strings are automatically converted to integers, and vice versa. This case is simple, since both integers are of the same length, there are no carries, and all sums produce four digits. If any of these conditions do not hold, there are complications that must be handled.

As with longhand addition, the general approach is to start with the rightmost coefficients (segments), performing a sum with a possible carry to the left. Since the base is a power of 10, the size of a segment is just the number of digits in the base less 1. Two global identifiers are used for these values:

```
global base, segsize
```

which can be initialized in the main procedure as

```
base := 10000
segsize := *base − 1
```

The addition procedure begins as follows:

```
procedure add(s1, s2, carry)
   local size, sum

   if *s1 > *s2 then s1 :=: s2
   size := *s2
   if size <= segsize then return s1 + s2 + carry
     .
     .
     .
```

Since s1 and s2 may be of different sizes, their values are exchanged, if necessary, so that s2 always is at least as long as s1. If the size of the longest is less than or equal to the size of a segment, an ordinary sum is returned. This value is one digit longer than the length of a segment if a new carry is produced; it merely is the beginning of a new segment on the left.

In the general case, the two strings must be segmented. To make processing easier, leading zeros are added to s1, if necessary, to make it the same length as s2:

```
s1 := right(s1, size, "0")
```

the sum of the rightmost segments is:

```
sum := right(right(s1, segsize) + right(s2, segsize) + carry,
   segsize + 1, "0")
```

This computation makes use of the fact that right() truncates its argument on the left if the string is longer than the specified size. The resulting sum may be larger than the base. The values for the remaining digits and the carry are, respectively:

```
right(sum, segsize)
left(sum, 1)
```

The process then is applied to the next segment to the left, and so on. This process is simplest to formulate recursively:

```
add(left(s1, size − segsize), left(s2, size − segsize), carry) || seg
```

Here left() is used to truncate s1 and s2 at the right, while right() is used to provide leading zeros for **seg** that may be deleted in its computation.

One problem remains. A carry ordinarily is specified only when **add()** calls itself recursively. If the third argument is omitted in the call, carry has the null value. This possibility is taken care of by

```
/carry := 0
```

The complete procedure is

```
procedure add(s1, s2, carry)
   local size, sum

   /carry := 0                              # default carry
   if *s1 > *s2 then s1 :=: s2
   size := *s2
   if size <= segsize then return s1 + s2 + carry
   s1 := right(s1, size, "0")
   sum := right(right(s1, segsize) + right(s2, segsize) + carry,
      segsize + 1, "0")
   return add(left(s1, size – segsize), left(s2, size – segsize),
      left(sum, 1) || right(sum, segsize)
end
```

List Representation.   There are several problems with the string representation. Strings representing large integers are constantly broken down and reconstructed during addition. Furthermore, string-to-integer conversion is required when sums are formed, and integer-to-string conversion is required when the sums are concatenated. All of these computations are expensive. Finally, addition begins with the least significant digits, which are at the right ends of the strings. Although right(s, segsize) extracts these digits, the process is conceptually awkward, since string processing normally proceeds from left to right.

Some of these problems can be overcome (or exchanged for other problems) by using a list representation. Here it is more convenient to place the least significant digits first, so that 3,793,234,045 is represented by

```
[4045, 9323, 37]
```

rather than with the coefficients in the opposite order suggested earlier.

Now the sum of two coefficients can be computed directly by an expression such as

```
L1[i] + L2[i]
```

No string-to-integer or integer-to-string conversion is required, but procedures are needed to convert strings to lists on input and to perform the converse conversion on output.

To produce a list of coefficients, the least significant coefficient is needed first, since the lengths of the strings generally are not even multiples of the segment length. This provides a good example of the usefulness of the ability to move from the right toward the left in string scanning:

```
procedure large(s)
  local L

  L := [ ]
  s ? {
    tab(0)                      # start at right end
    while not pos(1) do         # add remaining digits
      put(L, integer(move(–segsize)) | tab(1))
    }
  return L
end
```

Note that the segments are converted to integers as they are put on the list.

The procedure to add two large integers in the list representation is similar to that for the string representation, except for a number of details and special cases that must be handled differently. In the procedure that follows, the carry is represented as a list with one value, either 0 or 1. The process is recursive, with the first values in the two lists being summed and pushed onto the list that results from adding the remaining sections of the lists. Special cases occur when the remaining sections are empty; an empty list is equivalent to zero in this representation.

```
procedure add(L1, L2, carry)
  local sum

  /carry := [0]                    # default carry
  if *L1 = *L2 = 0 then return if carry[1] ~= 0 then carry else [ ]
  if *L1 > *L2 then L1 :=: L2
  if *L1 = 0 then return add(carry, L2)
  sum := L1[1] + L2[1] + carry[1]
  carry := [sum / base]
  return push(add(L1[2:0], L2[2:0], carry), sum % base)
end
```

The function push() produces the list produced by add(). Note that add() eventually is called with an argument that is an empty list, which terminates the recursion.

In order to write a large integer represented by a list, it must be converted to a string. One approach is:

```
procedure lstring(L)
   local s
   static nonzero

   initial nonzero := ~'0'

   s := " "
   every s := right(!L, segsize, "0") || s
   s ?:= {
      tab(upto(nonzero) | -1) & tab(0)
      }
   return s
end
```

This procedure iterates through the list, padding the segments to the required length. If this were not done, a small coefficient such as 0 would produce an erroneous string representation. However, appending the leading zeros to the segments may produce leading zeros in the final result. Removing leading zeros is somewhat tricky, since a single zero should be produced if the result is composed entirely of zeros. The scanning expression in the procedure does this by tabbing to the first nonzero character if possible, but otherwise tabbing to the next-to-last character. The desired result is the remainder of the string.

Linked-List Representation. The list representation used in the preceding section relies on Icon's capability to increase the size of a list by pushing values onto it. Another representation that allows an automatic increase in size is a linked list. Such a linked list is composed of records with two fields, one field for the coefficient and the other field for the next record (a pointer to it). While lists of size two can be used instead of records, records allow processing in a more mnemonic manner. The declaration

```
record largint(coeff, ptr)
```

provides a largint type with the two fields coeff and ptr.

The linked-list representation of a large integer such as 3,793,234,045 can be pictured as:

As for the list representation, there are special cases to be handled in dealing with the linked-list representation. For example, the null value for ptr indicates the end of a linked list. In this representation, the null value is equivalent to zero. The addition procedure otherwise is similar to the one for the list representation:

```
procedure add(g1, g2, carry)
  local sum

  /carry := largint(0)                          # default carry
  if /g1 & /g2 then return if carry.coeff ~= 0 then carry else &null
  if /g1 then return add(carry, g2)
  if /g2 then return add(g1, carry)
  sum := g1.coeff + g2.coeff + carry.coeff
  carry := largint(sum / base)
  return largint(sum % base, add(g1.ptr, g2.ptr, carry))
end
```

As for the list representation, conversion on input and output are required. In both cases, recursion provides compact solutions:

```
procedure large(s)
  if *s <= segsize then return largint(integer(s))
  else return largint(right(s, segsize), large(left(s, *s – segsize)))
end
```

```
procedure lstring(g)
  local s
  static nonzero

  initial nonzero := ~'0'

  if /g.ptr then s := g.coeff
  else s := lstring(g.ptr) || right(g.coeff, segsize, "0")
  s ?:= {
    tab(upto(nonzero) | –1) & tab(0)
    }
  return s
end
```

Multiplying Large Integers

The multiplication of large integers is formulated easily by following the longhand method. The least significant coefficient of the first large integer is multiplied by the second large integer, and this result is added to the result of multiplying the remaining portion of the first large integer by the second large integer.

A procedure for multiplying large integers in the linked-list representation is:

```
procedure mpy(g1, g2)
   local prod

   if /(g1 | g2) then return &null                # zero product
   prod := g1.coeff * g2.coeff
   return largint(prod % base, add(mpy(largint(g1.coeff), g2.ptr),
      mpy(g1.ptr, g2), largint(prod / base)))
end
```

Note that if either **g1** or **g2** has the null value, which is equivalent to zero, the procedure produces the null value.

Procedures for multiplying large integers in the string and list representations are similar.

RANDOM STRINGS

The grammar in Chapter 14 shows how infinitely many strings can be characterized by a finite grammar. Pattern matching, derived directly from the grammatical rules, can determine whether a particular string is among those that can be derived from the grammar.

It is also possible to generate the strings for a grammar, but the recursive nature of the grammatical rules prevents a straightforward approach to producing strings that are representative of all portions of the grammar. One way to circumvent this problem is to generate strings "at random".

The following program generates strings at random, using a grammar as a basis. The program reads grammatical rules (productions) and generates strings on request.

Representing Grammars

There are two problems to be considered: the form in which the definitions are provided to the program and the form in which they are represented internally.

Grammar Input. A notation for grammars was introduced in Chapter 14. The advantage of such a formal notation is that it is unambiguous and can be analyzed easily. The notation used in Chapter 14, in which uppercase letters stand for nonterminal symbols, is not general enough to represent many languages of interest. One problem is that many languages contain uppercase letters as terminal symbols. Another problem is that a single letter is inadequate for representing nonterminal symbols; longer, more mnemonic names are needed.

An alternative notation for grammars encloses nonterminal names in angular brackets. The grammar in Chapter 14 can be rephrased in this notation as:

```
<expr>::=<term>|<term>+<expr>
<term>::=<element>|<element>*<term>
<element>::=x|y|z|(<expr>)
```

Any character to the right of a ::= that is not a vertical bar or enclosed in angular brackets is a terminal symbol. In particular, spaces are valid terminal symbols.

Internal Representation of Grammars.   The random generation process involves selecting alternatives for nonterminal symbols from their definitions. A grammar could be represented in a program by strings such as

```
expr := "<term>|<term>+<expr>"
```

Such a representation, however, is not easy to use for the random generation of strings. For example, the determination of nonterminal symbols requires analysis of the string. Selection of a random alternative requires counting the number of alternatives (the number of vertical bars plus one) and then analyzing the string to select an alternative at random. Since such operations are performed repeatedly during generation, it is better to analyze the definitions once and put them in a form in which the desired operations can be performed easily and quickly.

One way to distinguish terminal symbols from nonterminal symbols is to use strings for terminal symbols and records for nonterminal symbols. With the declaration

```
record nonterm(name)
```

an instance of the nonterminal symbol <expr> is represented by

```
nonterm("expr")
```

A natural way to represent the definition for a nonterminal symbol is to use a list — a list of the alternatives in which each value is a list of the terminal and nonterminal symbols for that alternative. For the preceding grammar, this amounts to:

```
expr1 := [nonterm("term")]
expr2 := [nonterm("term"), "+", nonterm("expr")]
expr := [expr1, expr2]
term1 := [nonterm("element")]
term2 := [nonterm("element"), "*", nonterm("term")]
term := [term1, term2]
element1 := ["x"]
element2 := ["y"]
element3 := [ "z"]
element4 := ["(", nonterm("expr"), ")"]
element := [element1, element2, element3, element4]
```

These definitions are in a form that can be accessed readily. For example, **?expr** produces a randomly selected alternative for **<expr>**.

Given a nonterminal symbol, there must be a way to obtain its definition. This can be accomplished if the definitions are put in a table rather than assigned to identifiers:

```
defs := table()
defs["expr"] := [expr1, expr2]
defs["term"] := [term1, term2]
defs["element"] := [element1, element2, element3, element4]
```

Processing Grammars

In the previous example, the table and lists for the grammar are written explicitly. A program for generating random strings must read in the grammar and construct the table and lists. This is primarily a string scanning problem.

The general form of a line is

<name> ::= definition

where the definition has the form

alternative | alternative | ... | alternative

and each alternative is, in turn, a sequence of symbols. A line of input first must be analyzed to identify the name and the corresponding definition. The desired transformation is

<name>::= definition → defs[*name*] := alts(*definition*)

where **alts** produces a list of alternatives from the definition. If **defs** is a global variable, this transformation can be performed directly by:

```
procedure define(line)
  return line ? {
    defs[="<" & tab(find(">::="))] := (move(4) & alts(tab(0)))
    }
end
```

That is, the key for **defs** is the value of the second expression in the conjunction

```
="<" & tab(find(">::="))
```

namely,

```
tab(find(">::="))
```

The assigned value is the remainder of the line after the ::= , once it has been processed:

    alts(tab(0))

Note that **define**() fails if **line** is not a syntactically valid definition.

The procedure **alts**() constructs the list of alternatives for the definition. To construct this list, it is easiest to start with an empty list and add values using the queue access method:

```
procedure alts(defn)
   local alist

   alist := [ ]
   defn ? repeat {
      put(alist, syms(tab(upto('|') | 0)))
      move(1) | break
      }
   return alist
end
```

The procedure **syms**() produces a list of symbols. It is similar to **alts**(), except that it is necessary to distinguish terminal symbols from nonterminal symbols:

```
procedure syms(alt)
   local slist
   static nonbrack

   initial nonbrack := ~'<'

   slist := [ ]
   alt ? {
      while put(slist, tab(many(nonbrack)) |
         nonterm(2(="<", tab(upto('>')), move(1))))
      }
   return slist
end
```

Note that **nonterm** records are added to the list for nonterminal symbols and that a string of terminal symbols is treated as a single symbol.

The Generation Process

Generating random strings from a grammar involves starting with a goal, such as <expr>. As illustrated in Chapter 14, a nonterminal symbol can be replaced by any one of the alternatives in its definition. If this process is repeated, a string of terminal symbols may result. If the alternatives are selected at random, the string is a "randomly selected" string in the language.

It is easiest always to make the replacement for the leftmost nonterminal symbol. A possible sequence of steps leading from **<expr>** to a terminal string is:

```
<expr>
↑
<term>
↑
<element>
↑
(<expr>)
↑
(<term>+<expr>)
↑
(<element>+<expr>)
↑
(x+<expr>)
   ↑
(x+<term>)
   ↑
(x+<element>)
   ↑
(x+y)
      ↑
```

The arrows indicate the division between terminal symbols on the left and the next nonterminal symbol to be processed on the right. When there are no more nonterminal symbols to be processed, the generation is complete.

In summary, the process is:

1.   Start with the nonterminal goal symbol.

2.   Working from left to right, replace the leftmost nonterminal symbol by a randomly chosen alternative for it.

A recursive definition may get out of hand. In fact, there is no guarantee that the process will terminate: The sequence of symbols may become longer and longer with more and more nonterminal symbols. The probability of the random selection process "converging" to a string, as opposed to continuing indefinitely, can be computed from the structure of the grammar. It depends on the amount and nature of recursion in the definitions. This problem is not considered here, but see Exercise 17.10.

The actual generation process operates on the internal structures given earlier:

```
procedure gener(goal)
  local pending, symbol

  pending := [nonterm(goal)]
  while symbol := get(pending) do {
    if type(symbol) == "string" then writes(symbol)
    else (pending := ?\defs[symbol.name] ||| pending) |
      stop("*** undefined nonterminal <", symbol.name, ">")
    }
  write()
end
```

The list **pending** initially consists of the nonterminal goal symbol. Symbols are removed from the left of **pending**. A terminal symbol is written (without a newline), while a nonterminal symbol is replaced by a randomly selected alternative from its definition. The process terminates when **pending** is empty.

Generation Specifications

Some way is needed to specify the generation of strings from a nonterminal goal symbol. One is to choose a syntax for specifying generation that is different from the syntax for grammatical definition and let the program determine whether to generate or define. Here a nonterminal symbol followed by an integer specifies how many strings are to be generated from the language defined by the nonterminal symbol. Therefore, the input line

```
<expr>10
```

specifies the generation of 10 <expr>s. A procedure to process generation specifications is:

```
procedure generate(line)
  local goal, count

  if line ? {
    ="<" &
    (goal := tab(upto('>')) \ 1) &
    move(1) &
    count := integer(tab(0))
    }
  then {
    every 1 to count do
      gener(goal)
    return
    }
  else fail
end
```

The main processing loop can be written as

```
while line := read() do
   (define | generate)(line)
```

Note that define() is applied to a line of input first; if define(line) fails, indicating an invalid definition, generate() is applied to the line.

This program allows nonterminal symbols to be redefined. Definitions also can be interspersed with generation specifications. Therefore, a grammar can be built, tested, and modified incrementally.

A complete listing of a similar program for generating random sentences, including some additional features, is contained in Appendix F.

EXERCISES

17.1   What determines the maximum value that can be used for the base in large integer computations?

17.2*   Write a procedure that verifies that a string is a valid large integer.

17.3*   Write a procedure that inserts commas to separate three-digit groups in the string representation of large integers.

17.4   Write procedures that compare the magnitudes of large integers in each of the three representations given in this chapter.

17.5   Write a procedure that copies large integers in the linked-list representation.

17.6   Write procedures that perform large integer addition iteratively for each of the representations.

17.7   Write procedures that subtract and divide large integers in each of the representations.

17.8   Modify the procedure fibseq() in Chapter 13 that generates the Fibonacci sequence so that it handles large integers. Generate the first 100 Fibonacci numbers.

17.9*   Take any positive integer, reverse the order of its digits, and add it to itself. Repeat the process until the result is palindromic, that is, until the sum reads the same backward and forward. For example, starting with 37, the sums are $37 + 73 = 110$, and $110 + 011 = 121$, which is a palindrome. There is a conjecture that all such sequences eventually terminate in palindromes. Write a procedure palseq(i) that generates the sequence of sums as described. For example, the results generated by palseq(37) should be 110 and 121. Test your solution on the integers from 1 to 100. *Caution:* The conjecture may be false. Some integers, such as 196, are not known to produce sequences that terminate.

17.10   As mentioned earlier, the random generation process may not terminate. See Reference 11 for a discussion of this problem. One way to circumvent the termination problem is to provide a means of weighting the selection process toward alternatives that are more likely to lead to terminal symbols. Provide a mechanism that allows the specification of weights in grammars.

17.11   Write a "pretty printer" for Icon programs that arranges them in a standard format with proper indentation of nested expressions.

17.12   Design and implement a preprocessor for Icon that supports conditional compilation and the definition of constants and macros.

17.13   Write a "keyword in context" program to show all words in the input file in the contexts in which they appear. Write out lines in the alphabetical order of the words they contain, with each occurrence of the word in column 40 and the line rotated correspondingly. If a word appears in more than one line, give the contexts for the lines in order of input.

A

Syntax

The description of the syntax of Icon that follows uses an italic typeface to denote syntactic classes, such as *program*, and a sans-serif typeface to denote literal program text, such as global. An optional symbol is denoted by the subscript *opt*, so that

$$(expression_{opt})$$

denotes an optional expression that is enclosed in parentheses.

Alternatives are denoted by vertical stacking. For example,

program:
    declaration
    declaration program

defines a *program* to be a *declaration* or a *declaration* followed by a *program*. In effect, a program is a sequence of one or more declarations.

PROGRAMS

declaration:
    link-declaration
    global-declaration
    record-declaration
    procedure-declaration

link-declaration:
    link *link-list*

link-list:
    file-name
    file-name , link-list

file-name:
    identifier
    string-literal

global-declaration:
    global *identifier-list*

identifier-list:
    identifier
    identifier , identifier-list

record-declaration:
    record *identifier* (*field-list$_{opt}$*)

field-list:
    field-name
    field-name , field-list

procedure-declaration:
    header locals$_{opt}$ initial-clause$_{opt}$ expression-sequence end

header:
    procedure *identifier* (*parameter-list$_{opt}$*) ;

parameter-list:
    identifier-list
    identifier-list$_{opt}$ identifier [ ]

locals:
    local-specification identifier-list
    local-specification identifier-list ; locals

local-specification:
    local
    static

initial-clause:
    initial *expression*

expression-sequence:
    expression$_{opt}$
    expression$_{opt}$ *; expression-sequence*

expression:
    parenthesized-expression
    compound-expression
    list-expression
    field-reference-expression
    subscripting-expression
    invocation-expression
    mutual-evaluation-expression
    prefix-expression
    infix-expression
    to-by-expression
    create-expression
    return-expression
    break-expression
    next-expression
    case-expression
    if-then-else-expression
    loop-expression
    identifier
    keyword
    literal

parenthesized-expression:
    (*expression*$_{opt}$)

compound-expression:
    { *expression-sequence* }

list-expression:
    [*expression-list*]

expression-list:
    expression$_{opt}$
    expression$_{opt}$, *expression-list*

field-reference-expression:
    expression . *field-name*

subscripting-expression:
    expression [*expression*]
    expression [*range-specification*]

range-specification:
    expression : *expression*
    expression +: *expression*
    expression −: *expression*

invocation-expression:
    expression$_{opt}$ (*expression-list*)
    expression$_{opt}$ { *expression-list* }

mutual-evaluation-expression:
    (*expression-list*)

prefix-expression
    prefix-operator expression

infix-expression
    expression infix-operator expression

to-by expression:
    expression to *expression by-clause*$_{opt}$

by-clause:
    by *expression*

create-expression:
    create *expression*

return-expression
    return *expression*$_{opt}$
    suspend *expression*$_{opt}$ *do-clause*$_{opt}$
    fail

do-clause:
    do *expression*

break-expression:
    break *expression*~*opt*~

next-expression:
    next

case-expression:
    case *expression* **of** { *case-list* }

case-list:
    case-clause
    case-clause ; *case-list*

case-clause:
    expression : *expression*
    default : *expression*

if-then-else expression:
    if *expression* **then** *expression else-clause*~*opt*~

else-clause:
    else *expression*

loop-expression:
    repeat *expression*
    while *expression do-clause*~*opt*~
    until *expression do-clause*~*opt*~
    every *expression do-clause*~*opt*~

LANGUAGE ELEMENTS

The most elementary components of Icon expressions are identifiers, reserved words, key-words, and literals.

Identifiers

An identifier must begin with a letter or an underscore, which may be followed by any number of letters, underscores, and digits. Upper- and lowercase letters are distinct. The syntax for field names is the same as the syntax for identifiers.

Reserved Words

Reserved words may not be used as identifiers or field names. Reserved words are all lowercase. The reserved words are:

break	global	record
by	if	repeat
case	initial	return
create	link	static
default	local	suspend
do	next	then
else	not	to
end	of	until
every	procedure	while
fail		

Keywords

Keywords consist of an ampersand followed by one of a selected set of identifiers. Keyword meanings are summarized in Appendix C. The keywords, which are lowercase, are:

&ascii	&errout	&output
&clock	&fail	&pos
&collections	&features	&random
&cset	&file	&regions
&current	&host	&source
&date	&input	&storage
&dateline	&lcase	&subject
&digits	&letters	&time
&error	&level	&trace
&errornumber	&line	&ucase
&errortext	&main	&version
&errorvalue	&null	

Literals

There are two categories of literals:

literal:
    numeric-literal
    quoted-literal

Numeric literals, in turn, are divided into two categories:

numeric-literal:
    integer-literal
    real-literal

Integer literals have two forms:

> *integer-literal:*
>   *digit-literal*
>   *radix-literal*

Digit literals consist of one or more digits. Radix literals allow the radix for digits to be specified:

> *radix-literal:*
>   *digit-literal radix-specification digit-specification*

> *radix-specification:*
>   r
>   R

The value of the digit literal specifies the radix and must be between 2 and 36, inclusive. The digit specification consists of a sequence of digits and letters, where a stands for 10, b stands for 11, and so forth through z. Upper- and lowercase letters in digit specifications are equivalent. The characters in digit specifications must stand for values that are less than the radix.

Real literals have two forms:

> *real-literal:*
>   *decimal-literal*
>   *exponent-literal*

> *decimal-literal:*
>   *digit-literal . digit-literal*$_{opt}$

> *exponent-literal:*
>   *digit-literal exponent-specification sign*$_{opt}$ *digit-literal*
>   *decimal-literal exponent-specification sign*$_{opt}$ *digit-literal*

> *exponent-specification:*
>   e
>   E

> *sign:*
>   +
>   −

An expression such as .25 is not a real literal; it is an integer literal preceded by the dereferencing operator.

Quoted literals are divided into two categories:

quoted-literal:
    cset-literal
    string-literal

A cset literal consists of a string of characters enclosed in single quotes. A single quote may not appear within the enclosing quotes unless it is escaped. Escape sequences are described below.

A string literal consists of a string of characters enclosed in double quotes. A double quote may not appear within the enclosing quotes unless it is escaped.

Escape sequences allow characters to be included in string literals that otherwise would be awkward or impossible to include. An escape sequence consists of a backslash followed by one or more characters that are given special meanings. The escape sequences and the characters that they stand for are as follows:

\b	backspace
\d	delete
\e	escape
\f	formfeed
\l	linefeed
\n	newline
\r	return
\t	horizontal tab
\v	vertical tab
\'	single quote
\"	double quote
\\	backslash
\ddd	*octal code*
\xdd	*hexadecimal code*
\^c	*control code*

The linefeed and newline characters are the same in ASCII; both are included to accommodate the terminologies of different computer systems.

The sequence \ddd stands for the character with octal code *ddd*, where *d* is an octal digit 0, 1, ..., 7. The sequence \xdd stands for the character with hexadecimal code *dd*, where *d* is a hexadecimal digit 0, 1, ..., A, ... F. Upper- and lowercase hexadecimal digits, such as a and A, are equivalent. Only enough digits need to be given to specify the desired octal or hexadecimal number, provided the characters that follow cannot be considered as part of the escape sequence. For example, \43 specifies the ASCII character #, and \xA is equivalent to \x0A.

The control code sequence \^c stands for the ASCII character control-*c*. For example, \^A stands for control-A. Specifically, \^c stands for the character corresponding to the five low-order bits of *c*.

If the character following a backslash is not one of those in the preceding list, the backslash is ignored. Therefore, \a stands for a.

LAYOUT

White Space

Program text that has no meaning in itself is collectively called "white space". Except in quoted literals, blanks and tabs serve as white space to separate tokens that otherwise could be construed as a single token. For example,

ifnot *expr1* then *expr2*

is syntactically erroneous, since ifnot is interpreted as an identifier rather than two reserved words.

Blanks otherwise have no significance. For example, blanks can appear between a prefix operator and its argument. Blanks can also be used as optional separators to improve the visual appearance of a program. Blanks are necessary to separate infix operators from prefix operators in situations that are ambiguous. For example,

expr1||*expr2*

might be interpreted in two ways, as concatenation or as alternation followed by repeated alternation of the second expression. The Icon translator resolves such potential ambiguities by taking the longest legal sequence of operator symbols to be a single token, so this example is interpreted as concatenation. A blank between the two bars would cause the expression to be interpreted as alternation followed by repeated alternation.

A #, except in a quoted literal, introduces a comment, which terminates at the end of the line. A comment is considered to be white space by the Icon compiler.

Semicolons and Line Breaks

The Icon compiler generally is indifferent to program layout, but it automatically inserts a semicolon at the end of a line if an expression ends on that line and the next line begins with another expression. Therefore,

```
x := 1
y := 2
z := 0
```

is equivalent to

```
x := 1; y := 2; z := 0
```

Because the compiler inserts semicolons at the ends of lines where possible, it usually is not necessary to use semicolons explicitly. However, care must be taken in splitting an expression between two lines. In the case of an infix operation, the operator should be placed at the end of the first line, not the beginning of the second. Therefore,

expr1 || expr2

should be split as

expr1 ||
   expr2

The compiler does not insert a semicolon at the end of the first line, since the expression at the end of that line is not complete. However, in

expr1
   || expr2

a semicolon is inserted at the end of the first line, since

expr1; || expr2

is syntactically correct. Here || is two prefix repeated alternation operators.

Identifiers can be arbitrarily long, but they must be contained on one line. A quoted literal can be continued from one line to the next by placing an underscore after the last character of the literal on a line and omitting the closing quote. If a quoted literal is continued in this way, the underscore as well as any white space at the beginning of the next line are ignored. For example,

```
cons := "bcdfghjklmn_
        pqrstvwxyz"
```

is equivalent to

```
cons := "bcdfghjklmnpqrstvwxyz"
```

PRECEDENCE AND ASSOCIATIVITY

Icon has many operators. Precedence determines how different operators, in combination, group with their arguments. Associativity determines whether operations group to the left or to the right.

The list that follows gives operators by precedence from highest to lowest. Operators with the same precedence are grouped together; lines separate groups. Most infix operators are left-associative. Those that associate to the right are marked as such.

It is difficult to remember all the precedences and associativities; if in doubt, use parentheses to insure that expressions group in the intended way.

(*expr*)
{ *expr1*; *expr2*; ... }
[*expr1*, *expr2*, ...]
expr. *f*
expr1 [*expr2*]
expr1 [*expr2* : *expr3*]
expr1 [*expr2* +: *expr3*]
expr1 [*expr2* −: *expr3*]
expr (*expr1*, *expr2*, ...)
expr { *expr1*, *expr2*, ... }

---

not *expr*
| *expr*
! *expr*
* *expr*
+ *expr*
− *expr*
. *expr*
/ *expr*
\ *expr*
= *expr*
? *expr*
~ *expr*
@ *expr*
^ *expr*

---

expr1 \ *expr2*
expr1 @ *expr2*
expr1 ! *expr2*

---

expr1 ∧ *expr2*   (right associative)

---

expr1 * *expr2*
expr1 / *expr2*
expr1 % *expr2*
expr1 ** *expr2*

---

expr1 + *expr2*
expr1 − *expr2*
expr1 ++ *expr2*
expr1 −− *expr2*

---

expr1 || *expr2*
expr1 ||| *expr2*

---

expr1 < *expr*2
expr1 <= *expr2*
expr1 = *expr2*
expr1 >= *expr2*
expr1 > *expr2*
expr1 ~= *expr2*
expr1 << *expr2*
expr1 <<= *expr2*
expr1 == *expr2*
expr1 >>= *expr2*
expr1 >> *expr2*
expr1 ~== *expr2*
expr1 === *expr2*
expr1 ~=== *expr2*

---

expr1 | *expr2*

---

expr1 to *expr2* by *expr3*

---

expr1 := *expr2*	(right associative)
expr1 <− *expr2*	(right associative)
expr1 :=: *expr2*	(right associative)
expr1 <−> *expr2*	(right associative)
expr1 op:= *expr2*	(right associative)

---

expr1 ? *expr2*

---

expr1 & *expr2*

---

break *expr*
case *expr* of { *expr1* : *expr2*; *expr3* : *expr4*; ... }
create *expr*
every *expr1* do *expr2*
fail
if *expr1* then *expr2* else *expr3*
next
repeat *expr*
return *expr*
suspend *expr1* do *expr2*
until *expr1* do *expr2*
while *expr1* do *expr2*

B

Characters

The following chart shows the decimal, octal, and hexadecimal codes for the 256 characters, followed by the ASCII and EBCDIC graphics associated with these codes. ASCII control characters, which are associated with the first 32 codes, are shown also.

Several different sets of EBCDIC graphics are in use. The most commonly used correspondences are shown in the following chart.

Some computers, such as the Macintosh, support different "fonts" with many more graphics than are shown here.

decimal	octal	hex	ASCII	EBCDIC	ASCII controls
000	000	00			control-@ (null)
001	001	01			control-A
002	002	02			control-B
003	003	03			control-C
004	004	04			control-D
005	005	05			control-E
006	006	06			control-F
007	007	07			control-G (bell)
008	010	08			control-H (backspace)
009	011	09			control-I (tab)
010	012	0a			control-J (linefeed)
011	013	0b			control-K (vertical tab)
012	014	0c			control-L (formfeed)
013	015	0d			control-M (return)
014	016	0e			control-N
015	017	0f			control-O
016	020	10			control-P
017	021	11			control-Q
018	022	12			control-R
019	023	13			control-S
020	024	14			control-T
021	025	15			control-U
022	026	16			control-V
023	027	17			control-W
024	030	18			control-X
025	031	19			control-Y
026	032	1a			control-Z
027	033	1b			control-[(escape)
028	034	1c			control-\
029	035	1d			control-]
030	036	1e			control-^
031	037	1f			control-_
032	040	20	(blank)		
033	041	21	!		
034	042	22	"		
035	043	23	#		
036	044	24	$		
037	045	25	%		
038	046	26	&		
039	047	27	'		
040	050	28	(		

decimal	octal	hex	ASCII	EBCDIC
041	051	29	)	
042	052	2a	*	
043	053	2b	+	
044	054	2c	,	
045	055	2d	−	
046	056	2e	.	
047	057	2f	/	
048	060	30	0	
049	061	31	1	
050	062	32	2	
051	063	33	3	
052	064	34	4	
053	065	35	5	
054	066	36	6	
055	067	37	7	
056	070	38	8	
057	071	39	9	
058	072	3a	:	
059	073	3b	;	
060	074	3c	<	
061	075	3d	=	
062	076	3e	>	
063	077	3f	?	
064	100	40	@	(blank)
065	101	41	A	
066	102	42	B	
067	103	43	C	
068	104	44	D	
069	105	45	E	
070	106	46	F	
071	107	47	G	
072	110	48	H	
073	111	49	I	
074	112	4a	J	¢
075	113	4b	K	.
076	114	4c	L	<
077	115	4d	M	(
078	116	4e	N	+
079	117	4f	O		
080	120	50	P	&

decimal	octal	hex	ASCII	EBCDIC
081	121	51	Q	
082	122	52	R	
083	123	53	S	
084	124	54	T	
085	125	55	U	
086	126	56	V	
087	127	57	W	
088	130	58	X	
089	131	59	Y	
090	132	5a	Z	!
091	133	5b	[	$
092	134	5c	\	*
093	135	5d	]	)
094	136	5e	^	;
095	137	5f	_	¬
096	140	60	`	−
097	141	61	a	/
098	142	62	b	
099	143	63	c	
100	144	64	d	
101	145	65	e	
102	146	66	f	
103	147	67	g	
104	150	68	h	
105	151	69	i	
106	152	6a	j	
107	153	6b	k	,
108	154	6c	l	%
109	155	6d	m	_
110	156	6e	n	>
111	157	6f	o	?
112	160	70	p	
113	161	71	q	
114	162	72	r	
115	163	73	s	
116	164	74	t	
117	165	75	u	
118	166	76	v	
119	167	77	w	
120	170	78	x	

decimal	octal	hex	ASCII	EBCDIC
121	171	79	y	
122	172	7a	z	:
123	173	7b	{	#
124	174	7c	|	@
125	175	7d	}	`
126	176	7e	~	=
127	177	7f		"
128	200	80		
129	201	81		a
130	202	82		b
131	203	83		c
132	204	84		d
133	205	85		e
134	206	86		f
135	207	87		g
136	210	88		h
137	211	89		i
138	212	8a		
139	213	8b		
140	214	8c		
141	215	8d		
142	216	8e		
143	217	8f		
144	220	90		
145	221	91		j
146	222	92		k
147	223	93		l
148	224	94		m
149	225	95		n
150	226	96		o
151	227	97		p
152	230	98		q
153	231	99		r
154	232	9a		
155	233	9b		
156	234	9c		
157	235	9d		
158	236	9e		
159	237	9f		
160	240	a0		

decimal	octal	hex	ASCII	EBCDIC
161	241	a1		~
162	242	a2		s
163	243	a3		t
164	244	a4		u
165	245	a5		v
166	246	a6		w
167	247	a7		x
168	250	a8		y
169	251	a9		z
170	252	aa		
171	253	ab		
172	254	ac		
173	255	ad		[
174	256	ae		
175	257	af		
176	260	b0		
177	261	b1		
178	262	b2		
179	263	b3		
180	264	b4		
181	265	b5		
182	266	b6		
183	267	b7		
184	270	b8		
185	271	b9		
186	272	ba		
187	273	bb		
188	274	bc		
189	275	bd		]
190	276	be		
191	277	bf		
192	300	c0		{
193	301	c1		A
194	302	c2		B
195	303	c3		C
196	304	c4		D
197	305	c5		E
198	306	c6		F
199	307	c7		G
200	310	c8		H

decimal	octal	hex	ASCII	EBCDIC
201	311	c9		I
202	312	ca		
203	313	cb		
204	314	cc		
205	315	cd		
206	316	ce		
207	317	cf		
208	320	d0		{
209	321	d1		J
210	322	d2		K
211	323	d3		L
212	324	d4		M
213	325	d5		N
214	326	d6		O
215	327	d7		P
216	330	d8		Q
217	331	d9		R
218	332	da		
219	333	db		
220	334	dc		
221	335	dd		
222	336	de		
223	337	df		
224	340	e0		\
225	341	e1		
226	342	e2		S
227	343	e3		T
228	344	e4		U
229	345	e5		V
230	346	e6		W
231	347	e7		X
232	350	e8		Y
233	351	e9		Z
234	352	ea		
235	353	eb		
236	354	ec		
237	355	ed		
238	356	ee		
239	357	ef		
240	360	f0		0

decimal	octal	hex	ASCII	EBCDIC
241	361	f1		1
242	362	f2		2
243	363	f3		3
244	364	f4		4
245	365	f5		5
246	366	f6		6
247	367	f7		7
248	370	f8		8
249	371	f9		9
250	372	fa		
251	373	fb		
252	374	fc		
253	375	fd		
254	376	fe		
255	377	ff		

C

Reference Manual

This reference manual summarizes the built-in operations of Icon. The descriptions are brief; they are intended for quick reference only.

The operations fall into four main categories: functions, operators, keywords, and control structures. Functions, operators, and keywords perform computations, while control structures determine the order of computation. Function names provide a vocabulary used with a common syntax in which computations are performed on argument lists. Different operators, on the other hand, have different syntactic forms. They are divided into prefix operators, infix operators, and operators with distinctive syntax. Keywords, like functions, all have a common syntax, but they have no argument lists.

Data types are important in Icon, especially the types of data a function or operation expects and the type it returns. Types are indicated by letters as follows:

c	cset	C	co-expression
f	file	L	list
i	integer	N	numeric (i or r)
n	null	R	record (any record type)
p	procedure	S	set
r	real	T	table
s	string	X	any structure type (L, R, S, or T)
x	any type		

Numeric suffixes are used to distinguish different arguments of the same type. For example,

center(s1, i, s2)

indicates that center has three arguments. The first and third are strings; the second is an integer.

The type of the result produced by a function follows the function, with a separating colon. For example,

center(s1, i, s2) : s3

indicates that center produces a string. The format of entries for operators and keywords is similar.

The results for generators are indicated by a sequence, as in

!s : s1, s2, ..., sn

Some operations, such as variable(s) and s[i], produce variables to which values can be assigned.

Icon performs type conversion automatically when an argument does not have the expected type, so the types of arguments may be different from the expected type and still be acceptable. For example, center(s1, 10, s2) and center(s1, "10", s2) produce the same result, since the string "10" is converted to the integer 10.

Default values are provided automatically in some cases when an argument is omitted (or has the null value). For example, the default for the second argument of center() is 1, while the third argument defaults to a single blank. Consequently, center(s1) is equivalent to center(s1, 1, " "). Refer to the entry for center() to see how this information is shown.

Errors may occur for a variety of reasons. The possible errors and their causes are listed for each function and operation. Again, see the entry for center() for examples. In particular, note that a phrase such as "s not string" means s is neither a string nor a type that can be converted to a string.

In addition to the errors listed in the entries that follow, an error also can occur if there is not enough space to convert an argument to the expected type. For example, converting a very long string to a real number for use in a numerical computation conceivably could run out of memory space. Such errors are unlikely.

Cross references among entries have two forms. Most cross references refer to functions and operations that perform related computations, such as center(), left(), and right(). There also are cross references among operators and control structures with similar syntax, such as *x and N1 * N2, even though the computations performed are not related.

A list of generators appears at the end of this appendix.

FUNCTIONS

The arguments of functions are evaluated from left to right. If the evaluation of an argument fails, the function is not called. Some functions may generate a sequence of results for a given set of arguments. If an argument generates more than one value, the function may be called repeatedly with different argument values.

A few functions are not available in some implementations of Icon. These are identified by the symbol † to the left of the function name. See Appendix E for more information about implementation differences.

---

abs(N) : N   compute absolute value

abs(N) produces the absolute value of N.

Error: 102   N not numeric

---

acos(r1) : r2   compute arc cosine

acos(r1) produces the arc cosine of r1 in the range of 0 to π for r1 in the range of -1 to 1.

Errors: 102   r1 not real
              205 |r1| greater than 1

See also: cos()

---

any(c, s, i1, i2) : i3   locate initial character

any(c, s, i1, i2) succeeds and produces i1 + 1, provided s[i1] is in c and i2 is greater than i1. It fails otherwise.

Defaults: s   &subject
              i1   &pos if s is defaulted, otherwise 1
              i2   0

Errors: 101   i1 or i2 not integer
              103   s not string
              104   c not cset

See also: many() and match()

args(p) : i   get number of procedure arguments

args(p) produces the number of arguments for procedure p. For built-in procedures with a
variable number of arguments, the value produced is −1. For declared procedures with a
variable number of arguments, the value returned is the negative of the number of formal
parameters.

Error: 106   p not procedure

See also: proc()

---

asin(r1) : r2   compute arc sine

asin(r1) produces the arc sine of r1 in the range of $-\pi/2$ to $\pi/2$ for r1 in the range −1 to 1.

Errors: 102   r1 not real
              205 |r1| greater than 1

See also: sin()

---

atan(r1, r2) : r3   compute arc tangent

atan(r1, r2) produces the arc tangent of r1 / r2 in the range of $-\pi/2$ to $\pi/2$ with the sign of
r1.

Default: r2   1.0

Error: 102   r1 or r2 not real

See also: tan()

---

bal(c1, c2, c3, s, i1, i2) : i3, i4, ..., in   locate balanced characters

bal(c1, c2, c3, s, i1, i2) generates the sequence of integer positions in s preceding a character of c1 in s[i1:i2] that is balanced with respect to characters in c2 and c3, but fails if there
is no such position.

Defaults: c1   &cset
              c2   '('
              c3   ')'
              s   &subject
              i1   &pos if s is defaulted, otherwise 1
              i2   0

Errors: 101   i1 or i2 not integer
              103   s not string
              104   c1, c2, or c3 not cset

See also: find() and upto()

callout(x, x1, x2, ..., xn): xm   call external function

callout(x, x1, x2, ..., xn) calls the external function specified by x with arguments x1, x2, ..., xn. The mechanism for locating the function specified by x is system dependent.

Error: 216   specified function not found

---

center(s1, i, s2) : s3   position string at center

center(s1, i, s2) produces a string of size i in which s1 is centered, with s2 used for padding at left and right as necessary.

Defaults: i   1
              s2   " " (blank)

Errors: 101   i not integer
              103   s1 or s2 not string
              205   i < 0
              306   inadequate space in string region

See also: left() and right()

---

char(i) : s   produce character

char(i) produces a one-character string whose internal representation is i.

Errors: 101   i not integer
              205   i not between 0 and 255, inclusive
              306   inadequate space in string region

See also: ord()

---

close(f) : f   close file

close(f) closes f.

Error: 105   f not file

See also: open()

collect(i1, i2) : n   perform garbage collection

collect(i1, i2) causes a garbage collection in region i1, requesting i2 bytes of space in that region. It fails if the requested space is not available. The regions are identified as follows:

i1	region
1	static
2	string
3	block

If i1 is 0, a collection is done, but no region is identified and i2 has no effect. The value of i2 is ignored for the static region.

Defaults:	i1	0
	i2	0

Errors:	101	i1 or i2 not integer
	205	i1 not between 0 and 3 inclusive or i2 < 0.

---

copy(x1) : x2   copy value

copy(x1) produces a copy of x1 if x1 is a structure; otherwise it produces x1.

Error: 307   inadequate space in block region

---

cos(r1) : r2   compute cosine

cos(r1) produces the cosine of r1 in radians.

Error: 102   r1 not real

See also: cos()

---

cset(x) : c   convert to cset

cset(x) produces a cset resulting from converting x, but fails if the conversion is not possible.

Error: 307   inadequate space in block region

---

delete(X, x) : X   delete element

If X is a set, delete(X, x) deletes x from X. If X is a table, delete(X, x) deletes the element for key x from X. delete(X, x) produces X.

Error: 122   X not set or table.

See also: insert() and member()

detab(s1, i1, i2, ..., in) : s2   remove tabs

detab(s1, i1, i2, ..., in) produces a string based on s1 in which each tab character is replaced by one or more blanks. Tab stops are at i1, i2, ..., in, with additional stops obtained by repeating the last interval.

Default: i1   9

Errors: 101   i1, i2, ..., in not integer
              103   s1 not string
              210   i1, i2, ..., in not positive or in increasing sequence
              306   inadequate space in string region

See also: entab()

---

display(i, f) : n   display variables

display(i, f) writes the image of the current co-expression and the values of the local variables in the current procedure call. If i is greater than 0, the local variables in the i preceding procedure calls are displayed as well. After all local variables are displayed, the values of global variables are displayed. Output is written to f.

Defaults: i   &level
              f   &errout

Errors: 101   i not integer
              105   f not file
              205   i < 0
              213   f not open for writing

---

dtor(r1) : r2   convert degrees to radians

dtor(r1) produces the radian equivalent of r1 given in degrees.

Error: 102   r1 not real

See also: rtod()

entab(s1, i1, i2, ..., in) : s2   insert tabs

entab(s1 ,i1, i2, ..., in) produces a string based on s1 in which runs of blanks are replaced
by tabs. Tab stops are at i1, i2, ..., in, with additional stops obtained by repeating the last
interval.

Default: i1   9

Errors: 101   i1, i2, ..., in not integer
              103   s1 not string
              210   i1, i2, ..., in not positive or in increasing sequence
              306   inadequate space in string region

See also: detab()

---

errorclear() : n   clear error indication

errorclear() clears the indications of the last error.

See also: &error

---

exit(i)   exit program

exit(i) terminates program execution with exit status i.

Default: i   normal exit (machine dependent)

Error: 101   i not integer

See also: stop()

---

exp(r1) : r2   compute exponential

exp(r1) produces *e* raised to the power r1.

Errors: 102   r1 not real
              204   overflow

See also: log() and N1 ^ N2

find(s1, s2, i1, i2) : i3, i4, ..., in   find string

find(s1, s2, i1, i2) generates the sequence of integer positions in s2 at which s1 occurs as a substring in s2[i1 :i2], but fails if there is no such position.

Defaults:	s2	&subject
	i1	&pos if s2 is defaulted, otherwise 1
	i2	0

Errors:	101	i1 or i2 not integer
	103	s1 or s2 not string

See also: bal(), match(), and upto()

---

get(L) : x   get value from list

get(L) produces the leftmost element of L and removes it from L, but fails if L is empty. get is a synonym for pop.

Error: 108   L not list

See also: pop(), pull(), push(), and put()

---

† **getch() : s**   get character

getch() waits until a character has been entered from the keyboard and then produces the corresponding one-character string. The character is not displayed. The function fails on an end of file.

See also: getche() and kbhit()

---

† **getche() : s**   get and echo character

getche() waits until a character has been entered from the keyboard and then produces the corresponding one-character string. The character is displayed. The function fails on an end of file.

See also: getch() and kbhit()

---

getenv(s1) : s2   get value of environment variable

getenv(s1) produces the value of the environment variable s1, but fails if s1 is not set.

Error: 103   s1 not string

iand(i1, i2) : i3   compute bit-wise *and*

iand(i1, i2) produces an integer consisting of the bit-wise *and* of i1 and i2.

Error: 101   i1 or i2 not integer

See also: icom(), ior(), ishift(), and ixor()

---

icom(i1) : i2   compute bit-wise complement

icom(i1) produces the bit-wise complement of i1.

Error: 101   i1 not integer

See also: iand(), ior(), ishift(), and ixor()

---

image(x) : s   produce string image

image(x) produces a string image of x.

Error: 306   inadequate space in string region

---

insert(X, x1, x2) : X   insert element

If X is a table, insert(X, x1, x2) inserts key x1 with value x2 into X. If X is a set, insert(X, x1) inserts x1 into X. insert(X, x1, x2) produces X.

Default: x2   &null

Errors: 122   X not set or table
              307   inadequate space in block region

See also: delete() and member()

---

integer(x) : i   convert to integer

integer(x) produces the integer resulting from converting x, but fails if the conversion is not possible.

See also: numeric() and real()

---

ior(i1, i2) : i3   compute bit-wise inclusive *or*

ior(i1, i2) produces the bit-wise inclusive *or* of i1 and i2.

Error: 101   i1 or i2 not integer

See also: iand(), icom(), ishift(), and ixor()

ishift(i1, i2) : i3   shift bits

ishift(i1, i2) produces the result of shifting the bits in i1 by i2 positions. Positive values of i2 shift to the left, negative to the right. Vacated bit positions are zero-filled.

Error: 101   i1 or i2 not integer

See also: iand(), icom(), ior(), and ixor()

---

ixor(i1, i2) : i3   compute bit-wise exclusive *or*

ixor(i1, i2) produces the bit-wise exclusive *or* of i1 and i2.

Error: 101   i1 or i2 not integer

See also: iand(), icom(), ior(), and ishift()

---

† **kbhit() : n**   check for keyboard character

kbhit() succeeds if a character is available for getch() or getche() but fails otherwise.

See also: getch() and getche()

---

key(T) : x1, x2, ..., xn   generate keys from table

key(T) generates the keys in table T.

Error: 124   T not table

---

left(s1, i, s2) : s3   position string at left

left(s1, i, s2) produces a string of size i in which s1 is positioned at the left, with s2 used for padding at the right as necessary.

Defaults: i   1
                s2   " " (blank)

Errors: 101   i not integer
                103   s1 or s2 not string
                205   i < 0
                307   inadequate space in block region

See also: center() and right()

list(i, x) : L   create list

list(i, x) produces a list of size i in which each value is x.

Defaults:	i	0
	x	&null

Errors:	101	i not integer
	205	i < 0
	307	inadequate space in block region

---

log(r1, r2) : r3   compute logarithm

log(r1, r2) produces the logarithm of r1 to the base r2.

Default:	r2	*e*

Errors:	102	r1 or r2 not real
	205	r1 <= 0 or r2 <= 1

See also: exp()

---

many(c, s, i1, i2) : i3   locate many characters

many(c, s ,i1, i2) succeeds and produces the position in s after the longest initial sequence of characters in c within s[i1:i2]. It fails if s[i1] is not in c.

Defaults:	s	&subject
	i1	&pos if s is defaulted, otherwise 1
	i2	0

Errors:	101	i1 or i2 not integer
	103	s not string
	104	c not cset

See also: any() and match()

---

map(s1, s2, s3) : s4   map characters

map(s1, s2, s3) produces a string of size ∗s1 obtained by mapping characters of s1 that occur in s2 into corresponding characters in s3.

Defaults:	s2	string(&ucase)
	s3	string(&lcase)

Errors:	103	s1, s2, or s3 not string
	208	∗s2 ~= ∗s3
	306	inadequate space in string region

whatabout s2 i2 ?

match(s1, s2, i1, i2) : i3

match(s1, s2, i1, i2) produces i1 + *s1 if s1 == s‡

Defaults: s2   &subject
             i1   &pos if s2 is defaulted, other
             i2   0

Errors: 101   i1 or i2 not integer
             103   s1 or s2 not string

See also: =s, any(), and many()

---

member(X, x) : x   test for membership

If X is a set, member(X, x) succeeds x if x is a member of X but fails otherwise. If X is a table, member(X, x) succeeds if x is a key of an element in X but fails otherwise. member(X, x) produces x if it succeeds.

Error: 122   X not set or table

See also: delete() and insert()

---

mmout(s) : n   write text to allocation history

mmout(s) writes s to the allocation history file. s is given no interpretation.

Error: 103   s not string

See also: mmpause() and mmshow()

---

mmpause(s) : n   write pause to allocation history

mmpause(s) writes s to the allocation history file as a pause point with identification s.

Default: s   "programmed pause"

Error: 103   s not string

See also: mmout() and mmshow()

mmshow(x, s) : n   redraw in allocation history

mmshow(x, s) specifies redrawing of x in the allocation history file. The color is defined by s as follows:

"b"	black
"g"	gray
"w"	white
"h"	highlight; blinking black and white if possible
"r"	normal color

If x is not in an allocated data region, mmshow() has no effect.

Default: s   "r"

Error: 103   s not string

See also: mmout() and mmpause()

---

move(i) : s   move scanning position

move(i) produces &subject[&pos:&pos + i] and assigns &pos + i to &pos, but fails if i is out of range. move(i) reverses the assignment to &pos if it is resumed.

Error: 101   i not integer

See also: tab()

---

name(x) : s   produce name

name(x) produces the name of the variable x. If x is an identifier or a keyword that is a variable, the name of the identifier or keyword is produced. If x is a record field reference, the record type and field name are produced with a separating period. If x is a string, the name of the string and the subscript range are shown. If x is a subscripted list or table, the type name followed by the subscripting expression is produced.

Error: 111   x not a variable

See also: variable()

---

numeric(x) : N   convert to numeric

numeric(x) produces an integer or real number resulting from converting x, but fails if the conversion is not possible.

See also: integer() and real()

open(s1, s2) : f   open file

open(s1, s2) produces a file resulting from opening s1 according to options given in s2, but fails if the file cannot be opened. The options are:

character	effect
"r"	open for reading
"w"	open for writing
"a"	open for writing in append mode
"b"	open for reading and writing
"c"	create
"t"	translate line termination sequences to linefeeds
"u"	do not translate line termination sequences to linefeeds

The default mode is to translate line termination sequences to linefeeds on input and conversely on output. The untranslated mode should be used when reading and writing binary files.

Default:	s2	"rt"

Errors:	103	s1 or s2 not string
	209	invalid option

See also: close()

---

ord(s) : i   produce ordinal

ord(s) produces an integer (ordinal) between 0 and 255 that is the internal representation of the one-character string s.

Errors:	103	s not string
	205	*s not 1

See also: char()

---

pop(L) : x   pop from list

pop(L) produces the leftmost element of L and removes it from L, but fails if L is empty. pop is a synonym for get.

Error: 108   L not list

See also: get(), pull(), push(), and put()

pos(i1) : i2   test scanning position

pos(i1) produces &pos if &pos = i1 but fails otherwise.

Error: 101   i1 not integer

See also: &pos and &subject

---

proc(x, i) : p   convert to procedure

proc(x, i) produces a procedure corresponding to the value of x, but fails if x does not correspond to a procedure. If x is the string name of an operator, i specifies the number of arguments: 1 for unary (prefix), 2 for binary (infix), and 3 for ternary.

Default: i   1

Errors: 101   i not integer
                205   i not 1, 2, or 3

See also: args()

---

pull(L) : x   pull from list

pull(L) produces the rightmost element of L and removes it from L, but fails if L is empty.

Error: 108   L not list

See also: get(), pop(), push(), and put()

---

push(L, x) : L   push onto list

push(L, x) adds x to the left end of L and produces L.

Errors: 108   L not list
                307   inadequate space in block region

See also: get(), pop(), pull(), and put()

---

put(L, x) : L   put onto list

put(L, x) adds x to the right end of L and produces L.

Errors: 108   L not list
                307   inadequate space in block region

See also: get(), pop(), pull(), and push()

read(f) : s   read line

read(f) produces the next line from f but fails on an end of file.

Default:	f	&input

Errors:	105	f not file
	212	f not open for reading
	306	inadequate space in string region

See also:	reads()

---

reads(f, i) : s   read string

reads(f, i) produces a string consisting of the next i characters from f, or the remaining characters of f if fewer remain, but fails on an end of file. In reads(), unlike read(), line termination sequences have no special significance. reads() should be used for reading binary data.

Defaults:	f	&input
	i	1

Errors:	101	i not integer
	105	f not file
	205	i <= 0
	212	f not open for reading
	306	inadequate space in string region

See also:	read()

---

real(x) : r   convert to real

real(x) produces a real number resulting from converting x, but fails if the conversion is not possible.

Error:	307	inadequate space in block region

See also:	integer() and numeric()

---

remove(s) : n   remove file

remove(s) removes (deletes) the file named s, but fails if s cannot be removed.

Error:	103	s not string

See also:	rename()

rename(s1, s2) : n   rename file

rename(s1, s2) renames the file named s1 to be s2, but fails if the renaming cannot be done.

Error: 103   s1 or s2 not string

See also: remove()

---

repl(s1, i) : s2   replicate string

repl(s1, i) produces a string consisting of i concatenations of s1.

Errors: 101   i not integer
              103   s1 not string
              205   i < 0
              306   inadequate space in string region

---

reverse(s1) : s2   reverse string

reverse(s1) produces a string consisting of the reversal of s1.

Errors: 103   s1 not string
              306   inadequate space in string region

---

right(s1, i, s2) : s3   position string at right

right(s1, i, s2) produces a string of size i in which s1 is positioned at the right, with s2 used for padding at the left as necessary.

Defaults: i   1
              s2   " " (blank)

Errors: 101   i not integer
              103   s1 or s2 not string
              205   i < 0
              306   inadequate space in string region

See also: center() and left()

---

rtod(r1) : r2   convert radians to degrees

rtod(r1) produces the degree equivalent of r1 given in radians.

Error: 102   r1 not real

See also: dtor()

runerr(i, x)   terminate with run-time error

runerr(i, x) terminates program execution with error i and offending value x.

Default: x   no offending value

---

† **save(s) : i**   save executable image

save(s) saves an executable image of the current running program in the file named s and produces the size of the file, but fails if the file cannot be created.

Error: 103   s not string

---

seek(f, i) : f   seek to position in file

seek(f, i) seeks to position i in f but fails if the seek cannot be performed. The first byte in the file is at position 1. seek(f, 0) seeks to the end of file f.

Errors: 101   i not integer
            105   f not file

See also: where()

---

seq(i1, i2) : i3, i4, ...   generate sequence of integers

seq(i1, i2) generates an endless sequence of integers starting at i1 with increments of i2.

Defaults: i1   1
            i2   1

Errors: 101   i1 or i2 not integer
            211   i2 = 0

See also: i1 to i2 by i3

---

set(L) : S   create set

set(L) produces a set whose members are the distinct values in the list L.

Default: L   [ ]

Errors: 108   L not list
            307   inadequate space in block region

sin(r1) : r2   compute sine

sin(r1) produces the sine of r1 given in radians.

Error: 102   r1 not real

See also: asin()

---

sort(X, i) : L   sort list or table

sort(X, i) produces a list containing values from x. If X is a list or set, sort(X, i) produces the values of X in sorted order. If X is a table, sort(X, i) produces a list obtained by sorting the elements of X, depending on the value of i. For i = 1 or 2, the list elements are two-element lists of key/value pairs. For i = 3 or 4, the list elements are alternative keys and values. Sorting is by keys for i odd, by values for i even.

Default: i   1

Errors: 101   i not integer
                115   X not list, set, or table
                205   i not 1, 2, 3, or 4
                307   inadequate space in block region

---

sqrt(r1) : r2   compute square root

sqrt(r1) produces the square root of r1.

Errors: 102   r1 not real
                205   r1 < 0

See also: N1 ^ N2

---

stop(x1, x2, ..., xn)   stop execution

stop(x1, x2, ..., xn) terminates program execution with an error exit status after writing strings x1, x2, ..., xn. If xi is a file, subsequent output is to xi. Initial output is to standard error output.

Default: xi   "" (empty string)

Errors: 109   xi not string or file
                213   xi file not open for writing

See also: exit() and write()

string(x) : s   convert to string

string(x) produces a string resulting from converting x, but fails if the conversion is not possible.

Error: 306   inadequate space in string region

---

† **system(s) : i**   call system function

system(s) calls the C library function *system* to execute s and produces the resulting integer exit status.

Error: 103   s not string

---

tab(i) : s   set scanning position

tab(i) produces &subject[&pos:i] and assigns i to &pos, but fails if i is out of range. It reverses the assignment to &pos if it is resumed.

Error: 101   i not integer

See also: move()

---

table(x) : T   create table

table(x) produces a table with a default value x.

Default: x   &null

Error: 307   inadequate space in block region

---

tan(r1) : r2   compute tangent

tan(r1) produces the tangent of r1 given in radians.

Errors: 102   r1 not real
                204   r1 a singular point of tangent

See also: atan()

---

trim(s1, c) : s2   trim string

trim(s1, c) produces a string consisting of the characters of s1 up to the trailing characters contained in c.

Default: c   ' ' (blank)

Errors: 103   s1 not string
                104   c not cset
                306   inadequate space in string region

type(x) : s   produce type name

type(x) produces a string corresponding to the type of x.

---

upto(c, s, i1, i2) : i3, i4, ... in   locate characters

upto(c, s ,i1, i2) generates the sequence of integer positions in s preceding a character of c in s[i1:i2]. It fails if there is no such position.

Defaults:	s	&subject
	i1	&pos if s is defaulted, otherwise 1
	i2	0

Errors:	101	i1 or i2 not integer
	103	s not string
	104	c not cset

See also: bal() and find()

---

variable(s) : x   produce variable

Produces the variable for the identifier or keyword named s, but fails if there is no such variable. Local identifiers override global identifiers.

Error: 103   s not string

See also: name()

---

where(f) : i   produce position in file

where(f) produces the current byte position in f. The first byte in the file is at position 1.

Error: 105   f not file

See also: seek()

---

write(x1, x2, ..., xn) : xn   write line

write(x1, x2, ..., xn) writes strings x1, x2, ..., xn with a line termination sequence added at the end. If xi is a file, subsequent output is to xi. Initial output is to standard output.

Default: xi   "" (empty string)

Errors:	109	xi not string or file
	213	xi file not open for writing

See also: writes()

writes(x1, x2, ..., xn) : xn   write string

writes(x1, x2, ..., xn) writes strings x1, x2, ..., xn without a line termination sequence added at the end. If xi is a file, subsequent output is to xi. Initial output is to standard output.

Default: xi   "" (empty string)

Errors: 109   xi not string or file
              213   xi file not open for writing

See also: write()

PREFIX OPERATIONS

In a prefix operation, the operator symbol appears before the argument on which it operates. If evaluation of the argument fails, the operation is not performed. If the argument generates a sequence of results, the operation may be performed several times.

There are comparatively few prefix operations. They are listed in the order of the types of arguments: numeric, cset, string, co-expression, and then those that apply to arguments of several different types.

+N : N   compute positive

+N produces the numeric value of N.

Error: 102   N not integer or real

See also: N1 + N2

–N : N   compute negative

–N produces the negative of N.

Errors: 102   N not integer or real
              203   integer overflow

See also: N1 – N2

~c1 : c2   compute cset complement

~c1 produces the cset complement of c1 with respect to &cset.

Errors: 104   c1 not cset
              307   inadequate space in block region

=s1 : s2   match string in scanning

=s1 is equivalent to tab(match(s1)).

Error: 103   s1 not string

See also: match(), tab(), and N1 = N2

@C : x   activate co-expression

@C produces the outcome of activating C.

Error: 118   C not co-expression

See also: x @ C

---

^C1 : C2   create refreshed co-expression

^C1 produces a refreshed copy of C1.

Errors: 118   C1 not co-expression
             305   inadequate space in static region

See also: N1 ^ N2

---

*x : i   compute size

*x produces the size of x.

Error: 112   x not cset, string, co-expression, or a structure

See also: N1 * N2

?x1 : x2   generate random value

If x1 is an integer, ?x1 produces a number from a pseudo-random sequence. If x1 > 0, it produces an integer in range 1 to x1, inclusive. If x1 = 0, it produces a real number in range 0.0 to 1.0.

If x1 is a string, ?x1 produces a randomly selected one-character substring of x1 that is a variable if x1 is a variable.

If x1 is a list, table, or record, ?x1 produces a randomly selected element, which is a variable, from x1.

If x1 is a set, ?x1 produces a randomly selected member of x1.

Errors: 113   x1 not integer, string, or a structure.
             205   x1 < 0
             306   inadequate space in string region if x1 is string

See also: s ? *expr*

!x1 : x2, x3, ..., xn   generate values

If x1 is a file, !x1 generates the remaining lines of x1.

If x1 is a string, !x1 generates the one-character substrings of x1, and produces variables if x1 is a variable.

If x1 is a list, table, or record, !x1 generates the elements, which are variables, of x1. For lists and records, the order of generation is from the beginning to the end, but for tables it is unpredictable.

If x1 is a set, !x1 generates the members of x1 in no predictable order.

Errors:	103	x1 originally string, but type changed between resumptions
	116	x1 not string, file, or a structure.
	212	x1 is file but not open for reading
	306	inadequate space in string region if x1 is string or file

---

/x : x   check for null value

/x produces x if the value of x is the null value, but fails otherwise. It produces a variable if x is a variable.

See also: N1 / N2

\x : x   check for non-null value

\x produces x if the value of x is not the null value, but fails otherwise. It produces a variable if x is a variable.

See also: *expr* \ i

.x : x   dereference variable

.x produces the value of x.

See also: R. *f*

INFIX OPERATIONS

In an infix operation, an operator symbol stands between the two arguments on which it operates. If evaluation of an argument fails, the operation is not performed. If an argument generates a sequence of results, the operation may be performed several times.

There are many infix operations. They are listed first by those that perform computations (such as N1 + N2) and then by those that perform comparisons (such as N1 < N2). Assignment operations are listed last. See the index, if necessary.

N1 + N2 : N3   compute sum

N1 + N2 produces the sum of N1 and N2.

Errors: 102   N1 or N2 not integer or real
               203   integer overflow
               204   real overflow or underflow

See also: +N

N1 − N2 : N3   compute difference

N1 − N2 produces the difference of N1 and N2.

Errors: 102   N1 or N2 not integer or real
               203   integer overflow
               204   real overflow or underflow

See also: −N

N1 * N2 : N3   compute product

N1 * N2 produces the product of N1 and N2.

Errors: 102   N1 or N2 not integer or real
               203   integer overflow
               204   real overflow or underflow

See also: *x

N1 / N2 : N3   compute quotient

N1 / N2 produces the quotient of N1 and N2.

Errors: 102   N1 or N2 not integer or real
               201   N2 = 0
               204   real overflow or underflow

See also: /x

N1 % N2 : N3   compute remainder

N1 % N2 produces the remainder of N1 divided by N2. The sign of the result is the sign of
N1.

Errors: 102   N1 or N2 not integer or real
               202   N2 = 0
               204   real overflow or underflow

N1 ^ N2 : N3   compute exponential

N1 ^ N2 produces N1 raised to the power N2.

Errors: 102   N1 or N2 not integer or real
             204   real overflow, underflow, or N1 = 0 and N2 <= 0
             206   N1 < 0 and N2 real

See also: ^C, exp(), and sqrt()

---

x1 ++ x2 : x3   compute cset or set union

x1 ++ x2 produces the cset or set union of x1 and x2.

Errors: 120   x1 and x2 not both cset or both set
             307   inadequate space in block region

---

x1 -- x2 : x3   compute cset or set difference

x1 -- x2 produces the cset or set difference of x1 and x2.

Errors: 120   x1 and x2 not both cset or both set
             307   inadequate space in block region

---

x1 ** x2 : x3   cset or set intersection

x1 ** x2 produces the cset or set intersection of x1 and x2.

Errors: 120   x1 and x2 not both cset or both set
             307   inadequate space in block region

---

s1 || s2 : s3   concatenate strings

s1 || s2 produces a string consisting of s1 followed by s2.

Errors: 103   s1 or s2 not string
             306   inadequate space in string region

See also: L1 ||| L2

L1 ||| L2 : L3   concatenate lists

L1 ||| L2 produces a list consisting of the values in L1 followed by the values in L2.

Errors: 108   L1 or L2 not list
             307   inadequate space in block region

See also: s1 || s2

R.*f* : x   get field of record

R.*f* produces a variable for the *f* field of record R.

Errors: 107   R not a record type
                 207   R does not have field *f*

See also: .x

---

x1 @ C : x2   transmit value to co-expression

x1 @ C activates C, transmitting the value of x1 to it; it produces the outcome of activating
C.

Error: 118   C not co-expression

See also: @C

---

x1 & x2 : x2   evaluate in conjunction

x1 & x2 produces x2. It produces a variable if x2 is a variable.

N1 > N2 : N2   compare numerically

N1 > N2 produces N2 if N1 is numerically greater than N2, but fails otherwise.

Error: 102   N1 or N2 not integer or real

See also: N1 >= N2, N1 = N2, N1 <= N2, N1 < N2, and N1 ~= N2

N1 >= N2 : N2   compare numerically

N1 >= N2 produces N2 if N1 is numerically greater than or equal to N2, but fails otherwise.

Error: 102   N1 or N2 not integer or real

See also: N1 > N2, N1 = N2, N1 <= N2, N1 < N2, and N1 ~= N2

N1 = N2 : N2   compare numerically

N1 = N2 produces N2 if N1 is numerically equal to N2, but fails otherwise.

Error: 102   N1 or N2 not integer or real

See also: N1 > N2, N1 >= N2, N1 <= N2, N1 < N2, N1 ~= N2, and =s

N1 <= N2 : N2   compare numerically

N1 <= N2 produces N2 if N1 is numerically less than or equal to N2, but fails otherwise.

Error: 102   N1 or N2 not integer or real

See also: N1 > N2, N1 >= N2, N1 = N2, N1 < N2, and N1 ~= N2

N1 < N2 : N2   compare numerically

N1 < N2 produces N2 if N1 is numerically less than N2, but fails otherwise.

Error: 102   N1 or N2 not integer or real

See also: N1 > N2, N1 >= N2, N1 = N2, N1 <= N2, and N1 ~= N2

N1 ~= N2 : N2   compare numerically

N1 ~= N2 produces N2 if N1 is not numerically equal to N2, but fails otherwise.

Error: 102   N1 or N2 not integer or real

See also: N1 > N2, N1 >= N2, N1 = N2, N1 <= N2, and N1 < N2

---

s1 >> s2 : s2   compare lexically

s1 >> s2 produces s2 if s1 is lexically greater than s2, but fails otherwise.

Errors: 103   s1 or s2 not string
              306   inadequate space in string region

See also: s1 >>= s2, s1 == s2, s1 <<= s2, s1 << s2, and s1 ~== s2

---

s1 >>= s2 : s2   compare lexically

s1 >>= s2 produces s2 if s1 is lexically greater than or equal to s2, but fails otherwise.

Errors: 103   s1 or s2 not string
              306   inadequate space in string region

See also: s1 >> s2, s1 == s2, s1 <<= s2, s1 << s2, and s1 ~== s2

s1 == s2 : s2   compare lexically

s1 == s2 produces s2 if s1 is lexically equal to s2, but fails otherwise.

Errors: 103   s1 or s2 not string
                 306   inadequate space in string region

See also: s1 >> s2, s1 >>= s2, s1 <<= s2, s1 << s2, and s1 ~== s2

---

s1 <<= s2 : s2   compare lexically

s1 <<= s2 produces s2 if s1 is lexically less than or equal to s2, but fails otherwise.

Errors: 103   s1 or s2 not string
                 306   inadequate space in string region

See also: s1 >> s2, s1 >>= s2, s1 == s2, s1 << s2, and s1 ~== s2

---

s1 << s2 : s2   compare lexically

s1 << s2 produces s2 if s1 is lexically less than s2, but fails otherwise.

Errors: 103   s1 or s2 not string
                 306   inadequate space in string region

See also: s1 >> s2, s1 >>= s2, s1 == s2, s1 <<= s2, and s1 ~== s2

---

s1 ~== s2 : s2   compare lexically

s1 ~== s2 produces s2 if s1 is not lexically equal to s2, but fails otherwise.

Errors: 103   s1 or s2 not string
                 306   inadequate space in string region

See also: s1 >> s2, s1 >>= s2, s1 == s2, s1 <<= s2, and s1 << s2

---

x1 === x2 : x2   compare values

x1 === x2 produces the value of x2 if x1 and x2 have the same value, but fails otherwise.

See also: x1 ~=== x2

---

x1 ~=== x2 : x2   compare values

x1 ~=== x2 produces the value of x2 if x1 and x2 do not have the same value, but fails otherwise.

See also: x1 === x2

x1 := x2 : x1   assign value

x1 := x2 assigns the value of x2 to x1 and produces the variable x1.

Errors: 101   x1 requires integer, but x2 not integer
               103   x1 requires string, but x2 not string
               111   x1 not a variable

See also: x1 *op*:= x2, xi :=: x2, x1 <– x2, and x1 <–> x2

---

x1 *op*:= x2   augmented assignment

x1 *op*:= x2 performs the operation x1 *op* x2 and assigns the result to x1; it produces the variable x1. For example, i1 +:= i2 produces the same result as i1 := i1 + i2. There are augmented assignment operators for all infix operations except assignment operations. The error conditions for augmented assignment operations are the same as for the basic operations.

Error: 111   x1 not variable

See also: x1 := x2

---

x1 :=: x2 : x1   exchange values

x1 :=: x2 exchanges the values of x1 and x2 and produces the variable x1.

Errors: 101   x1 or x2 requires integer, but other argument not integer
               103   x1 or x2 requires string, but other argument not string
               111   x1 or x2 not a variable

See also: x1 := x2 and x1 <–> x2

---

x1 <– x2 : x1   assign value reversibly

x1 <–x2 assigns the value of x2 to x1 and produces the variable x1. It reverses the assignment if it is resumed.

Errors: 101   x1 requires integer, but x2 not integer
               103   x1 requires string, but x2 not string
               111   x1 not a variable

See also: x1 := x2 and x1 <–> x2

x1 <-> x2 : x1   exchange values reversibly

x1 <-> x2 exchanges the values of x1 and x2 and produces the variable x1. It reverses the
exchange if it is resumed.

Errors: 101   x1 or x2 requires integer, but other argument not integer
              103   x1 or x2 requires string, but other argument not string
              111   x1 or x2 not a variable

See also: x1 <- x2 and x1 :=: x2

OTHER OPERATIONS

The operations on the following pages have varying types of syntax. Some have more than
two arguments. If evaluation of an argument fails, the operation is not performed. If an
argument generates a sequence of results, the operation may be performed several times.

---

i1 to i2 by i3 : i1, ..., in   generate integers in sequence

i1 to i2 by i3 generates the sequence of integers from i1 to i2 in increments of i3.

Default: i3   1 if by clause is omitted

Errors: 101   i1, i2, or i3 not integer
              211   i3 = 0

See also: seq()

[x1, x2, ..., xn] : L   create list

[x1, x2, ..., xn] produces a list containing the values x1, x2, ..., xn. [ ] produces an empty
list.

Error: 307   inadequate space in block region

See also: list()

x1[x2] : x3   subscript

If x1 is a string, x1[x2] produces a one-character string consisting of character x2 of x1. x1[x2] fails if x2 is out of range. x1[x2] produces a variable if x1 is a variable.

If x1 is a list or record, x1[x2] produces element x2 of x1.

If x1 is a table, x1[x2] produces the element corresponding to key x2 of x1.

In all cases, x2 may be nonpositive.

In all cases, the subscripting operation fails if the subscript is out of range.

Errors: 101   x1 is string, list, or a record, but x2 not integer
            114   x1 not string, list, table, or record.

See also: x[i1:i2], x[i1+i2], and [i1−:i2]

---

x1[i1:i2] : x2   produce substring or list section

If x1 is a string, x1[i1:i2] produces the substring of x1 between i1 and i2. x1[i1:i2] produces a variable if x1 is a variable.

If x1 is a list, x1[i1:i2] produces a list consisting of the values of x1 in the given range.

In either case, i1 and i2 may be nonpositive.

In either case, the subscripting operation fails if a subscript is out of range.

Errors: 101   i1 or i2 not integer
            114   x1 not string or list
            307   inadequate space in block region if x1 is list

See also: x1[x2], x[i1+:i2], and x[i1−:i2]

---

x1[i1+:i2] : x2   produce substring or list section

If x1 is a string, x1[i1+:i2] produces the substring of x1 between i1 and i1 + i2. x1[i1+:i2] produces a variable if x1 is a variable.

If x1 is a list, x1[i1+:i2] produces a list consisting of the values of x1 in the given range.

In either case, i1 and i2 may be nonpositive.

In either case, the subscripting operation fails if a subscript is out of range.

Errors: 101   i1 or i2 not integer
            114   x1 not string or list
            307   inadequate space in block region if x1 is list

See also: x1[x2], x[i1:i2], and x[i1−:i2]

x1[i1–:i2] : x2   produce substring or list section

If x1 is a string, x1[i1–:i2] produces the substring of x1 between i1 and i1 – i2. x1[i1–:i2] produces a variable if x1 is a variable.

If x1 is a list, x1[i1–:i2] produces a list consisting of the values of x1 in the given range.

In either case, i1 and i2 may be nonpositive.

In either case, the subscripting operation fails if a subscript is out of range.

Errors:	101	i1 or i2 not integer
	114	x1 not string or list
	307	inadequate space in block region if x1 is list

See also: x1[x2], x[i1 :i2], and x[i1+:i2]

---

x(x1, x2, ..., xn) : xm   process argument list

If x is a function or procedure, x(x1, x2, ..., xn) produces the outcome of calling x with arguments x1, x2, ..., xn.

If x is an integer, x(x1, x2, ..., xn) produces the outcome of xi, but fails if i is out of the range 1, ..., n. In this case, it produces a variable if xi is a variable; i may be nonpositive.

Default: x   –1

Errors:	106	x not procedure or integer
	117	x is main, but there is no main procedure (during start up)

See also: x!L, x{...}

---

x!L   process argument list

If x is a function or procedure, x!L produces the outcome of calling x with the arguments in the list L. If x is an integer, x!L produces L[x] but fails if x is out of range of L.

Errors:	106	x not procedure or integer
	108	L not list

See also: x(...)

---

x{x1, x2, ..., xn} : xm   process argument list as co-expressions

x{x1, x2, ..., xn} is equivalent to x([create x1, create x2, ..., create xn]).

Error: 106   x not procedure or integer

See also: x(...)

KEYWORDS

Keywords are listed in alphabetical order.

Some keywords are variables; values may be assigned to these. However, the allowable type depends on the keyword. See the assignment operations for error conditions.

&ascii : c   ASCII characters

The value of &ascii is a cset consisting of the 128 ASCII characters.

&clock : s   time of day

The value of &clock is a string consisting of the current time of day, as in "19:21:00".

&collections : i1, i2, i3, i4   garbage collections

&collections generates the total number of garbage collections followed by the number caused by allocation in the static, string, and block regions, respectively.

&cset : c   all characters

The value of &cset is a cset consisting of all 256 characters.

&current : C   current co-expression

The value of &current is the currently active co-expression.

&date : s   date

The value of &date is the current date, as in "1989/10/15".

&dateline : s   date and time of day

The value of &dateline is the current date and time of day, as in "Sunday, October 15, 1989".

&digits : c   digits

The value of &digits is a cset containing the ten digits.

&error : i   errors to convert to failure

If the value of **&error** is nonzero, a run-time error is converted to expression failure and **&error** is decremented. **&error** is zero initially. **&error** is a variable.

&errornumber : i   number of last error

The value of **&errornumber** is the number of the last error converted to failure. **&error-number** fails if no error has occurred.

&errortext : s   description of last error

The value of **&errortext** is the error message corresponding to the last error converted to failure. **&errortext** fails if no error has occurred.

&errorvalue : x   value causing last error

The value of **&errorvalue** is the value that caused the last error converted to failure. **&errorvalue** fails if no error has occurred or no specific value caused the error.

&errout : f   standard error output

The value of **&errout** is the standard error output file.

&fail   failure

&fail produces no result.

&features : s1, s2, ..., sn   implementation features

The value of **&features** generates strings identifying the features of the executing version of Icon.

&file : s   source file

The value of **&file** is the name of the file from which the current program line was compiled.

&host : s   host system

The value of **&host** is a string that identifies the host system on which Icon is running.

&input : f   standard input

The value of &input is the standard input file.

&lcase : c   lowercase letters

The value of &lcase is a cset consisting of the 26 lowercase letters.

&letters : c   letters

The value of &letters is a cset consisting of the 52 upper- and lowercase letters.

&level : i   procedure level

The value of &level is the level of the current procedure call.

&line : i   source line number

The value of &line is the number of the source-program line in which it appears.

&main : C   main co-expression

The value of &main is the co-expression for the main program.

&null : n   null value

The value of &null is the null value.

&output : f   standard output

The value of &output is the standard output file.

&pos : i   scanning position

The value of &pos is the position of scanning in &subject. The scanning position may be changed by assignment to &pos. Such an assignment fails if it would be out of range of &subject. &pos is a variable.

&random : i   random seed

The value of &random is the seed for the pseudo-random sequence. The seed may be changed by assignment to &random. &random is zero initially. &random is a variable.

&regions : i1, i2, i3   storage regions

&region generates the current sizes of the static, string, and block regions, respectively. The size of the static region may not be meaningful.

&source : C   source co-expression

The value of &source is the co-expression for the activator of the current co-expression.

&storage : i1, i2, i3   storage utilization

&storage generates the current amount of space used in the static, string, and block regions, respectively. The space used in the static region may not be meaningful.

&subject : s   subject of scanning

The value of &subject is the string being scanned. The subject of scanning may be changed by assignment to &subject. &subject is a variable.

&time : i   elapsed time

The value of &time is the number of milliseconds since beginning of program execution.

&trace : i   procedure tracing

If the value of &trace is nonzero, a trace message is produced when a co-expression is activated or a procedure is called, returns, suspends, or is resumed. &trace is decremented for each message produced. &trace is zero initially. &trace is a variable.

&ucase : c   uppercase letters

The value of &ucase is a cset consisting of the 26 uppercase letters.

&version : s   Icon version

The value of &version is a string identifying the version of Icon.

CONTROL STRUCTURES

The way that arguments of a control structure are evaluated depends on the control structure; in fact, that is what distinguishes a control structure from a function or operation.

Most control structures are identified by reserved words. They are arranged alphabetically on the following pages, with the few control structures that use operator symbols appearing at the end.

---

break *expr* **: x**   break out of loop

break *expr* exits from the enclosing loop and produces the outcome of *expr*.

Default: *expr*   &null

See also: next

---

case *expr* **of { ... } : x**   select according to value

case *expr* of { ... } produces the outcome of the case clause that is selected by the value of *expr*.

---

create *expr* **: C**   create co-expression

create *expr* produces a co-expression for *expr*.

Error: 305   inadequate space in static region

See also: ^C

---

every *expr1* **do** *expr2*   generate every result

every *expr1* do *expr2* evaluates *expr2* for each result generated by *expr1*; it fails when *expr1* does not produce a result. The do clause is optional.

---

fail   fail from procedure

fail returns from the current procedure, causing the call to fail.

See also: return and suspend

---

if *expr1* **then** *expr2* **else** *expr3* **: x**   select according to outcome

if *expr1* then *expr2* else *expr3* produces the outcome of *expr2* if *expr1* succeeds, otherwise the outcome of *expr3*. The else clause is optional.

next   go to beginning of loop

next transfers control to the beginning of the enclosing loop.

See also: break

---

not *expr* **: n**   invert failure

not *expr* produces the null value if *expr* fails, but fails if *expr* succeeds.

---

repeat *expr*   evaluate repeatedly

repeat *expr* evaluates *expr* repeatedly.

---

return *expr*   return from procedure

return *expr* returns from the current procedure, producing the outcome of *expr*.

Default: *expr*   &null

See also: fail and suspend

---

suspend *expr1* **do** *expr2*   suspend from procedure

suspend *expr1* do *expr2* suspends from the current procedure, producing each result generated by *expr1*. If suspend is resumed, *expr2* is evaluated before resuming *expr1*. The do clause is optional.

Default: *expr1*   &null (only if the do clause is omitted)

See also: fail and return

---

until *expr1* **do** *expr2*   loop until result

until *expr1* do *expr2* evaluates *expr2* each time *expr1* fails; it fails when *expr1* succeeds. The do clause is optional.

See also: while *expr1* do *expr2*

---

while *expr1* **do** *expr2*   loop while result

while *expr1* do *expr2* evaluates *expr2* each time *expr1* succeeds; it fails when *expr1* fails. The do clause is optional.

See also: until *expr1* do *expr2*

expr1 | *expr2* : **x1, x2, ...**   evaluate alternatives

expr1 | *expr2* generates the results for *expr1* followed by the results for *expr2*.

See also: |*expr*

|*expr* : **x1, x2, ...**   evaluate repeatedly

|*expr* generates the results for *expr* repeatedly, terminating if *expr* fails.

See also: *expr1* | *expr2*

---

expr \ **i** : **x1, x2, ..., xi**   limit generator

expr \ i generates at most i results from the outcome for *expr*.

Errors: 101   i not integer
               205   i < 0

See also: \x

---

s ? *expr* : **x**   scan string

s ? *expr* saves the current subject and position and then sets them to the values of **s** and 1, respectively. It then evaluates *expr*. The outcome is the outcome of *expr*. The saved values of the subject and position are restored on exit from *expr*.

Error: 103   s not string

See also: ?x

GENERATORS

The following expressions may produce more than one result if the context in which they are evaluated requires it.

bal(c1, c2, c3, s, i1, i2)	&collections
find(s1, s2, i1, i2)	&features
key(T)	&regions
seq(i1, i 2)	&storage
upto(c, s, i1, i2)	|*expr*
!x	*expr1*	*expr2*

D

Error Messages

Chapter 12 describes the various kinds of errors that may occur when compiling and running Icon programs. The corresponding error messages are designed to be self-explanatory. They are listed here for reference.

SYNTAX ERRORS

There are many possible syntax errors. As mentioned in Chapter 12, the actual source of an error may precede the place where an erroneous construction is detected. The messages for syntax errors are:

```
end of file expected
global, record, or procedure declaration expected
invalid argument list
invalid by clause
invalid case clause
invalid case control expression
invalid create expression
invalid declaration
invalid default clause
invalid do clause
invalid else clause
invalid every control expression
invalid field name
invalid global declaration
```

invalid if control expression
invalid initial expression
invalid keyword construction
invalid local declaration
invalid argument
invalid argument for unary operator
invalid argument in alternation
invalid argument in assignment
invalid argument in augmented assignment
invalid repeat expression
invalid section
invalid then clause
invalid to clause
invalid until control expression
invalid while control expression
link list expected
missing colon
missing colon or ampersand
missing end
missing field list in record declaration
missing identifier
missing left brace
missing link file name
missing of
missing parameter list in procedure declaration
missing procedure name
missing record name
missing right brace
missing right brace or semicolon
missing right bracket
missing right bracket or ampersand
missing right parenthesis
missing semicolon
missing semicolon or operator
missing then
syntax error

If any of these errors occurs in a program, the program is not linked and no icode file is produced.

There is one warning message:

dereferencing operator applied to numeric literal

This message does not prevent linking and the production of an icode file.

RUN-TIME ERRORS

Run-time error messages are numbered and divided into categories, depending on the nature of the error.

Category 1: Invalid Type or Form

```
101  integer expected
102  numeric expected
103  string expected
104  cset expected
105  file expected
106  procedure or integer expected
107  record expected
108  list expected
109  string or file expected
110  string or list expected
111  variable expected
112  invalid type to size operation
113  invalid type to random operation
114  invalid type to subscript operation
115  list, set, or table expected
116  invalid type to element generator
117  missing main procedure
118  co-expression expected
119  set expected
120  cset or set expected
121  function not supported
122  set or table expected
123  invalid type
124  table expected
```

Category 2: Invalid Value or Computation

```
201  division by zero
202  remaindering by zero
203  integer overflow
204  real overflow, underflow, or division by zero
205  value out of range
206  negative first argument to real exponentiation
207  invalid field name
208  second and third arguments to map of unequal length
209  invalid second argument to open
210  non-ascending arguments to detab/entab
211  by value equal to zero
```

212 attempt to read file not open for reading
213 attempt to write file not open for writing
214 input/output error
215 attempt to refresh &main
216 external function not found

Category 3: Capacity Exceeded

301 evaluation stack overflow
302 system stack overflow
303 inadequate space for evaluation stack
304 inadequate space in qualifier list
305 inadequate space for static allocation
306 inadequate space in string region
307 inadequate space in block region

Category 4: Feature Not Implemented

401 co-expressions not implemented

Category 5: Programmer-Specified Error

500 program malfunction

E

Implementation Differences

There are many Icon implementations, ranging from personal computers to mainframes. In some cases, Icon is implemented for different operating systems on the same computer, and in some cases there are several different implementations for the same operating system and computer.

To date, all of these implementations are based on a generic implementation developed at The University of Arizona. Consequently, these implementations are the same in most respects, and most programs written for one implementation can be run on other implementations with little or no change.

Different computer architectures and operating systems, however, vary somewhat in the environments they provide. This may affect some features of Icon. In addition, the generic implementation of Icon is written in C with a small amount of optional assembly-language code. Different C compilers themselves differ in the features they support, and not all implementations include the features that require assembly language. Furthermore, some implementations of Icon contain additional system-dependent features.

While differences in Icon due to different computer architectures, operating systems, and C compilers are relatively minor and only affect portions of Icon, persons who write Icon programs for use on a variety of implementations should be aware of possible problems.

User guides for specific implementations of Icon contain information about features that are not supported or that differ from the standard implementation, as well as information about system-dependent extensions. The keyword &features, described at the end of this appendix, also allows checking of many system-specific features during program execution.

CHARACTER SETS

Most computers use the ASCII character set. The notable exception is the IBM 370 architecture, which uses the EBCDIC character set.

Both ASCII and EBCDIC have 256 characters. The difference between the two character sets lies in the correspondence between character codes (0 to 255) and graphics. See Appendix B for a listing of both character sets.

Since Icon internally operates on characters without regard for their associated graphics, differences in character sets do not affect most programs. For example, although the letter A is assigned to character code 65 in ASCII but character code 193 in EBCDIC, most operations on A do not depend on its specific character code.

The places where differences in character sets are most apparent is in sorting and lexical comparison, which are based on character codes. For example, in ASCII the uppercase letters have smaller codes than the lowercase ones, but the converse is true for EBCDIC. Consequently,

> "A" << "a"

succeeds for ASCII implementations of Icon but fails for EBCDIC implementations of Icon. Sorting produces correspondingly different results in ASCII and EBCDIC implementations.

It is worth noting that different implementations of Icon on EBCDIC systems may take different views of this situation. It is possible, for example, to map EBCDIC to ASCII on input and vice-versa on output, thus obtaining the ASCII correspondence between character codes and graphics internally. Users of Icon on 370 systems should consult user guides regarding this possibility.

The cset &ascii presents a different problem. On ASCII implementations of Icon, it consists of characters with codes 0 through 127 — the first half of the entire character set. Different EBCDIC implementations treat &ascii differently. Some assign the same character codes to it as on ASCII systems, so that the corresponding graphics are different from those on ASCII systems. Other EBCDIC implementations assign character codes to &ascii so that the graphics are the same as on ASCII implementations. Similarly, the interpretation of ASCII control characters given in \^ escape sequences in literals varies on EBCDIC systems. Consult user manuals.

Since most EBCDIC terminals do not support brackets, the combination $< and $> can be used in place of [and] in program text. Similarly, $(and $) are equivalent to { and } . These multi-character equivalents are also available on ASCII implementations of Icon, allowing programs that use them to run on both ASCII and EBCDIC systems.

ENVIRONMENT VARIABLES

Most operating systems support environment variables. (There are different names for environment variables on different systems, but the facilities generally are the same.)

Since environment variables are used by Icon primarily to set run-time parameters such as storage region sizes, the absence of environment variables usually does not, in itself, directly affect Icon programs.

Systems that do not support environment variables usually provide another way of setting implementation parameters. For example, ProIcon for the Macintosh [1] provides menus for setting run-time parameters.

In addition to run-time parameters, the function getenv() requires environment variables. If environment variables are not supported, getenv() simply fails (on the principle that in the absence of environment variables, no environment variable is set).

Since memory monitoring and the production of allocation history files are controlled by an environment variable, these features usually are not supported if environment variables are not available. Some implementations support these features in other ways. Consult user guides.

Some systems also use environment variables in addition to those described in Chapter 12. Again, consult user guides

STORAGE MANAGEMENT

As described in Chapter 12, Icon has two forms of storage management, fixed-region and expandable-region, depending on the implementation. Expandable-region storage management is more flexible than fixed-region storage management, but it is not supported by most C compilers.

The form of storage management has no direct effect on Icon programs, although the environment may require different configurations for running Icon programs in the two cases.

CO-EXPRESSIONS

Not all implementations of Icon support co-expressions. Since co-expressions require changing system stacks, which cannot be done directly in C, assembly language is required. The necessary code is simple on some systems but difficult (or even impractical) on others.

If co-expressions are not implemented, features related to them are not available, but the rest of Icon is unaffected.

Since co-expressions are not available on all implementations of Icon, they should not be used in Icon programs that are intended to be used on a wide range of systems.

LARGE-INTEGER ARITHMETIC

Large-integer arithmetic may not be supported on a computer a with small amount of memory. If large-integer arithmetic is not supported, integer overflow results in error termination.

INPUT AND OUTPUT

The keyboard functions kbhit(), getch(), and getche() are particularly useful on personal-computer systems where program operation can be controlled by user-typed characters, independently of standard input. Not all operating systems support these keyboard functions. Consult the user guides.

Icon's input and output functions are comparatively simple and are supported on most systems.

As noted in Chapter 11, random-access input and output may behave strangely on text files in translated mode for systems that use multi-character line terminators.

Pipes and the "p" option for the open() function generally are supported only on UNIX systems. Some other options for open() are system-dependent also. Consult user guides.

Some systems support special file names for input and output to devices, such as the console, printer, and auxiliary ports. Consult user guides.

Some systems, noticeably those running on IBM 370 computers, use a different notion of file naming than is used in examples in this book. Consult user guides.

EXIT CODES

On most operating systems, the exit code for the normal termination of a program is 0 and the exit code for error termination is 1. However, some operating systems use other values.

The function exit() terminates program execution, indicating normal completion if its argument is omitted. Similarly, normal termination of execution by returning from the initial call of the main procedure indicates normal completion, while termination due to a run-time error indicates an error. The function stop() terminates program execution, indicating an error.

EXECUTING COMMANDS

The system() function is supported on most, but not all, implementations of Icon that run in command-line environments. It is not supported (and has no meaning) for implementations of Icon that run in visual-interface environments unless those environments also provide command-line facilities. In any event, the use of **system()** is highly specific to the implementation on which Icon runs.

COMMAND-LINE OPTIONS

The –x option to icont for running an icode file is not supported on some systems and may malfunction on other systems if the amount of available memory is inadequate. Since this option is only a shortcut, the lack of support for –x only constitutes an inconvenience. It also is easy to provide a script that accomplishes the same thing on most systems.

The –e option to iconx is provided as a method of redirecting standard error output on systems that do not support this facility directly. However, some implementations do not support the –e option. Consult user guides.

ICON SUBSETS

The implementation of Icon is organized so that some features can be omitted by individual implementors. The primary reason for such subsetting is to reduce the size of the Icon run-time system in environments where the amount of memory is limited.

The most likely candidates for omission are large-integer arithmetic and the mathematical functions. Other possibilities are string invocation, error trace back, memory monitoring, external functions, and calling Icon. In all cases, the remainder of Icon operates properly, independent of the omitted features.

LANGUAGE FEATURES

The presence or absence of many features can be checked during program execution. The keyword &features generates strings listing the features available in an implementation. The first value is the operating system for the implementation, and the second value is the character set, followed by specific features. The possible values that can be generated by &features are:

       Amiga or Atari ST or …
       ASCII or EBCDIC
       calling to Icon
       co–expressions
       direct execution
       environment variables
       error trace back
       executable images
       expandable regions or fixed regions
       external functions

> large integers
> math functions
> memory monitoring
> pipes
> string invocation
> system function

Some implementations support additional features.

Ordinarily, implementation features are of interest only for writing programs that are to be run on systems different from those on which they are developed. For example, a program that uses co-expressions can check for their presence as follows:

```
if not(&features = = "co-expressions") then
    stop("co-expressions not supported")
```

F

Sample Programs

This appendix contains several sample programs that illustrate Icon programming techniques in the context of somewhat larger problems than those given in the body of the book.

These programs were written by several different programmers. Consequently, they show somewhat different programming styles and layout than those used elsewhere in this book.

The programs here are from a library that is available in machine-readable form [12]. See the ordering information at the end of this book.

COMMAND-LINE OPTIONS

Most Icon programs are run in a command-line environment in which program options and parameters can be given on the command line when the Icon program is run. Command-line arguments are passed to the main procedure as a list of strings as described in Chapter 12.

The conventions for specifying options vary somewhat from system to system. The UNIX convention is used by programs in the Icon program library [12] and is applicable to operating systems other than UNIX. Following UNIX conventions, an option is indicated by a dash followed by a letter that identifies the option. For example,

    iconx filter −u

runs the icode file filter and passes the option −u to it. It is, of course, up to the program filter to interpret and use the option.

An option may have an argument, which follows the letter with an optional intervening blank. For example,

    iconx filter −o log

might be used to specify that the output file for filter is log.

The procedure that follows interprets command-line arguments. It is called as

    options(arg, optstring)

where arg is the argument list (such as the one passed to the main procedure) and optstring is a specification for allowable options. For example, options(arg,"ou") specifies o and u as allowable options. The expected type of an argument also can be specified. If the option letter is followed by a colon (:), the argument is interpreted as a string. If the option letter is followed by a plus (+), the argument should be an integer, while if it is followed by a period (.), the argument should be a real number. For example, options(arg,"uo:n+") specifies that the o option should be followed by a string argument and that the n option should be followed by an integer argument.

The value returned by options() is a table of specified options. The keys in this table are the option letters and the corresponding values are the arguments for the options (or 1 if there is no argument for a key). The remaining arguments on the command line are left in the list arg. Processing terminates with the first non-option argument. A dash (−) not followed by a letter is interpreted as an argument rather than an option; it is often interpreted as a designation for standard input or standard output. The special argument − −terminates option processing.

If an error is detected, options() terminates program execution with an appropriate error message.

Several programs in this appendix link options() and provide examples of its usage.

```
# options.icn
#
# authors: Bob Alexander and Gregg Townsend

procedure options(arg, optstring)
  local x, i, c, otab, flist, o, p

  /optstring := string(&letters)
  otab := table()
  flist := [ ]
  while x := get(arg) do
    x ? {
      if ="−" & not pos(0) then {
        if ="−" & pos(0) then break
        while c := move(1) do
          if i := find(c, optstring) + 1 then
            otab[c] :=
              if any(':+.', o := optstring[i]) then {
                p := "" ~== tab(0) | get(arg) |
                  stop("No parameter following −", c)
                case o of {
                  ":" :   p
                  "+" :   integer(p) |
                      stop("−", c, " needs integer parameter")
                  "." :   real(p) |
                      stop("−", c, " needs real parameter")
                }
              }
            else 1
          else stop("Unrecognized option: −", c)
      }
      else put(flist, x)
    }

  while push(arg, pull(flist))
  return otab
end
```

BRIDGE HANDS

The following program shuffles, deals, and displays hands in the game of bridge. See Chapter 16 for a discussion of the programming techniques used.

An example of the output is:

```
            S:  KQ987
            H:  52
            D:  T94
            C:  T82

S:  3                    S:  JT4
H:  T7                   H:  J9863
D:  AKQ762               D:  J85
C:  QJ94                 C:  K7

            S:  A652
            H:  AKQ4
            D:  3
            C:  A653
```

There are two command-line options: −h *n* instructs the program to produce *n* hands (the default is 1) and −s *n* sets the random seed to *n*, which alters the hands produced. The default seed is 0. Notice how **options()** is used to process these options.

```
# deal.icn
#
# author: Ralph Griswold

link options

global deck, deckimage, handsize, suitsize, denom, rank, blanker

procedure main(args)
  local hands, opts

  deck := deckimage := string(&letters)
  handsize := suitsize := *deck / 4
  rank := "AKQJT98765432"
  blanker := repl(" ", suitsize)
  denom := &lcase[1+:suitsize]

  opts := options(args, "h+s+")
  hands := \opts["h"] | 1
  &random := \opts["s"]
```

```
        every 1 to hands do show()

end

#  Display the hands
#
procedure show()
   local layout, i
   static bar, offset

   initial {
     bar := "\n" || repl("–", 33)
     offset := repl(" ", 10)
     }

   deck := shuffle(deck)
   layout := [ ]
   every push(layout, disp(deck[(0 to 3) * handsize + 1 +: handsize]))

   every write(offset, !layout[1])
   write()
   every i := 1 to 4 do
     write(left(layout[4][i], 20), layout[2][i])
   write()
   every write(offset, !layout[3])
   write(bar)
end

#  Put the hands in a form to display
#
procedure disp(hand)
   static clubmap, diamondmap, heartmap, spademap

   initial {
     clubmap := denom || repl(blanker, 3)
     diamondmap := blanker || denom || repl(blanker, 2)
     heartmap := repl(blanker, 2) || denom || blanker
     spademap := repl(blanker, 3) || denom
     }

   return [
     "S: "  || arrange(hand,spademap),
     "H: "  || arrange(hand,heartmap),
     "D: "  || arrange(hand,diamondmap),
     "C: "  || arrange(hand,clubmap)
     ]
end
```

```
# Arrange hands for presentation
#
procedure arrange(hand, suit)
   return map(map(hand, deckimage, suit) – – ' ', denom, rank)
end

# Shuffle deck
#
procedure shuffle(deck)
   local i

   every i := *deck to 2 by –1 do
      deck[?i] :=: deck[i]
   return deck
end
```

MAILING LABELS

This program produces labels by using coded information taken from the input file. In the input file, a line beginning with a # is a label header. Subsequent lines up to the next header or end of file are accumulated and output so that they are centered horizontally and vertically on label forms. Lines beginning with * are treated as comments and are ignored.

The following options are available:

−c *n*   Print *n* copies of each label.

−s *s*   Select only those labels whose headers contain a character in *s*.

−t   Format for curved tape labels (the default is to format
          for rectangular mailing labels).

−w *n*   Limit line width to *n* characters. The default width is 40.

−l *n*   Limit the number of printed lines per label to *n*. The default is 8.

−d *n*   Limit the depth of the label to *n*. The default is 9 for rectangular labels
          and 12 for tape labels (−t).

−f   Print the first line of each selected entry instead of labels.

Options are processed from left to right. If the number of printed lines is set to a value that exceeds the depth of the label, the depth is set to the number of lines. If the depth is set to a value that is less than the number of printed lines, the number of printed lines is set to the depth.

```
# labels.icn
#
# author: Ralph Griswold

link options

global line, lsize, repet, llength, ldepth, first, opts

procedure main(args)
  local selectors, y, i

   line := ""
   selectors := '#'
   lsize := 9
   ldepth := 8
   llength := 40
   repet := 1
   i := 0
   opts := options(args, "c+fd+l+s:tw+")
   if \opts["f"] then first := 1
   selectors := cset(\opts["s"])
   if \opts["t"] then {
      lsize := 12
      if ldepth > lsize then ldepth := lsize
      }
   llength := nonneg("w")
   if ldepth := nonneg("l") then {
      if lsize < ldepth then lsize := ldepth
      }
   if lsize := nonneg("d") then {
      if ldepth > lsize then ldepth := lsize
      }
   repet := nonneg("c")

   repeat {                                          # processing loop
      if line[1] == "#" & upto(selectors, line)
         then obtain() else {
            line := read() | break
            }
         }
end

#  Obtain next label
#
procedure obtain()
  local label, max
```

```
      label := [ ]
      max := 0
      line := ""

   while line := read() do {
      if line[1] == "*" then next
      if line[1] == "#" then break
      if \first then {
         write(line)
         return
         }
      else put(label, line)
      max <:= *line
      if *label > ldepth then {
         error(label[1], 1)
         return
         }
      if max > llength then {
         error(label[1], 2)
         return
         }
      }
   every 1 to repet do format(label, max)
end

#  Format a label
#
procedure format(label, width)
   local j, indent

   indent := repl(" ", (llength − width) / 2)
   j := lsize − *label

   every 1 to j / 2 do write()
   every write(indent, !label)
   every 1 to (j + 1) / 2 do write()
end

#  Issue label for an error
#
procedure error(name, type)
   static badform
   initial badform := list(lsize)
   case type of {
      1:  badform[3] := "   **** too many lines"
      2:  badform[3] := "   **** line too long"
      }
```

```
            badform[1] := name
            every write(&errout, !badform)
         end

         procedure nonneg(s)
            s := \opts[s] | fail
            return 0 < integer(s) | stop("–", s, " needs positive numeric parameter")
         end
```

FILE DUMPS

This program reads an ASCII file and writes out a representation of each character in several forms: hexadecimal, octal, decimal, symbolic, and ANSI code. The name of the file is given as a command-line argument so that it can be opened in the untranslated mode.

```
         # fileprnt.icn
         #
         # author: Ralph Griswold

         procedure main(arg)
            local width, chars, nonprint, prntc, asc, hex, sym, dec
            local oct, ascgen, hexgen, octgen, chrgen, prtgen, c
            local cnt, line, length, bar

            input := open(arg[1], "u") | stop("***cannot open input file")
            width := 16
            chars := string(&cset)
            nonprint := chars[1:33] || chars[128:0]
            prntc := map(chars, nonprint, repl(" ", *nonprint))

            asc := table("  |")
            hex := table()
            sym := table()
            dec := table()
            oct := table()
            ascgen := create "NUL" | "SOH" | "STX" | "ETX" | "EOT" | "ENQ" |
               "ACK" | "BEL" | " BS" | " HT" | " LF" | " VT" | " FF" | " CR" | " SO" |
               " SI" | "DLE" | "DC1" | "DC2" | "DC3" | "DC4" | "NAK" | "SYN" |
               "ETB" | "CAN" | " EM" | "SUB" | "ESC" | " FS" | " GS" | " RS" | " US" |
               " SP"
```

```
        " SP"
      hexgen := create !"0123456789ABCDEF" || !"0123456789ABCDEF"
      octgen := create (0 to 3) || (0 to 7) || (0 to 7)
      chrgen := create !chars
      prtgen := create !prntc
      every c := !&cset do {
        asc[c] := @ascgen || "|"
        oct[c] := @octgen || "|"
        hex[c] := " " || @hexgen || "|"
        sym[c] := " " || @prtgen || " |"
        }
      asc[char(127)] := "DEL|"                   # special case

      cnt := -1                                  # to handle 0-indexing of bytes

      while line := reads(input, width) do {     # read enough for one line
        length := *line                          # maybe not that many bytes
        bar := "\n" || repl("-", 5 + length * 4)
        write()
        writes("BYTE|")
        every writes(right(cnt + (1 to length), 3), "|")
        write(bar)
        writes(" HEX|")
        every writes(hex[!line])
        write(bar)
        writes(" OCT|")
        every writes(oct[!line])
        write(bar)
        writes(" DEC|")
        every writes(right(ord(!line), 3), "|")
        write(bar)
        writes(" SYM|")
        every writes(sym[!line])
        write(bar)
        writes(" ASC|")
        every writes(asc[!line])
        write(bar)
        cnt +:= length
        }

   end
```

CONCORDANCES

This program produces a simple concordance consisting of a list of all words in the input and the numbers of the lines in which they appear. Words less than three characters long are ignored. If a word occurs more than once on a line, the number of occurrences is given in parentheses after the line number.

There are two options:

–l *n*	set maximum line length to *n* (default 72); wraps
–w *n*	set maximum width for word to *n* (default 15); truncates

Note that the program is organized to make it easy, via item(), to handle other kinds of tabulations.

```
# concord.icn
#
# author: Ralph Griswold

link options

global uses, colmax, namewidth, lineno

procedure main(args)
   local opts, uselist, name, line

   opts := options(args, "l+w+")          # process options
   colmax := \opts["l"] | 72
   namewidth := \opts["w"] | 15

   uses := table("")
   lineno := 0

   every tabulate(item(), lineno)           # tabulate all the citations

   uselist := sort(uses, 3)               # sort by uses
   while name := get(uselist) do
      format(left(name, namewidth) || get(uselist))
end

# Add line number to citations for name. If it already has been cited,
#  add (or increment) the number of citations.
#
procedure tabulate(name, lineno)
   local new, count, number

   lineno := string(lineno)
   new := ""
```

```
      uses[name] ? {
        while new ||:= tab(upto(&digits)) do {
          number := tab(many(&digits))
          new ||:= number
          }
        if /number | (number ~== lineno)
          then uses[name] ||:= lineno || ", "          # new line number
        else {
          if ="(" then count := tab(upto(')')) else count := 1
          uses[name] := new || "(" || count + 1 || "), "
          }
        }
end

#  Format the output, breaking long lines as necessary.
#
procedure format(line)
  local i

  while *line > colmax + 2 do {
    i := colmax + 2
    until line[i −:= 1] == " "                      # back off to break point
    write(line[1 :i])
    line := repl(" ", namewidth) || line[i + 1:0]
    }
  write(line[1 :−2])
end

#  Get an item. Different kinds of concordances can be obtained by
#  modifying this procedure.
#
procedure item()
  local i, word, line

  while line := read() do {
    lineno +:= 1
    write(right(lineno, 6), " ", line)
    line := map(line)                               # fold to lowercase
    i := 1
    line ? {
      while tab(upto(&letters)) do {
        word := tab(many(&letters))
        if *word >= 3 then suspend word             # skip short words
        }
      }
    }
end
```

N QUEENS

This program uses co-expressions to display solutions to the *n*-queens problem on an ANSI-standard terminal. The number of queens is given by a command-line argument. The default is 8. The −s option causes the display to stop after each solution and wait for the user to enter a return to continue. The −a option causes the placement of each queen to be shown during the search for a solution. The −h option provides a help message.

The solutions are printed showing the positions of the queens on the chessboard. The following output is typical:

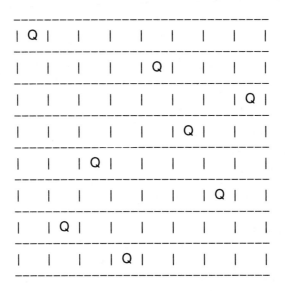

```
# vnq.icn
#
# author: Steve Wampler

link options

global n, nthq, solution, goslow, showall, line, border

procedure main(args)
   local i, opts

   opts := options(args, "ahs")
```

```
      n := integer(get(args)) | 8      # default is 8 queens
      if \opts["s"] then goslow := "yes"
      if \opts["a"] then showall := "yes"
      if \opts["h"] then helpmesg()

      line := repl("|   ", n) || "|"
      border := repl("– – – –", n) || "–"
      clearscreen()
      movexy(1, 1)
      write()
      write(" ", border)
      every 1 to n do {
         write(" ", line)
         write(" ", border)
         }

      nthq := list(n+2)                 # need list of queen placement routines
      solution := list(n)               # ... and a list of column solutions

      nthq[1] := &main                  # 1st queen is main routine.
      every i := 1 to n do              # 2 to n+1 are real queen placement
         nthq[i+1] := create q(i)       #    routines, one per column.
      nthq[n+2] := create show()        # n+2nd queen is display routine.

      write(n, "–Queens:")
      @nthq[2]                          # start by placing queen in first colm.

      movexy(1, 2 * n + 5)
   end

   # q(c) – place a queen in column c (this is c+1st routine).
   procedure q(c)
      local r
      static up, down, rows

      initial {
         up := list(2 * n –1, 0)
         down := list(2 * n –1, 0)
         rows := list(n, 0)
         }

      repeat {
         every (0 = rows[r := 1 to n] = up[n + r – c] = down[r + c –1] &
            rows[r] <– up[n + r – c] <– down[r + c –1] <– 1) do {
```

```
      solution[c] := r            # record placement.
      if \showall then {
        movexy(4 * (r − 1) + 5, 2 * c + 1)
        writes("@")
        }
      @nthq[c + 2]               # try to place next queen.
      if \showall then {
        movexy(4  * (r − 1) + 5, 2 * c + 1)
        writes(" ")
        }
      }
    @nthq[c]                     # tell last queen placer 'try again'
    }
end

# show the solution on a chess board.

procedure show()
  local c
  static count, lastsol

  initial count := 0

  repeat {
    if /showall & \lastsol then {
      every c := 1 to n do {
        movexy(4 * (lastsol[c] − 1) + 5, 2 * c + 1)
        writes(" ")
        }
      }
    movexy(1, 1)
    write("solution: ", right(count +: = 1, 10))
    if /showall then {
      every c := 1 to n do {
        movexy(4 * (solution[c] − 1) + 5, 2 * c + 1)
        writes("Q")
        }
      lastsol := copy(solution)
      }
    if \goslow then {
      movexy(1, 2 * n + 4)
      writes("Press return to see next solution:")
```

```
            read() | {
               movexy(1, 2 * n + 5)
               stop("Aborted.")
               }
            movexy(1, 2 * n + 4)
            clearline()
            }

         @nthq[n+1]                        # tell last queen placer to try again
         }
   end

   procedure helpmesg()
      write(&errout, "Usage: vnq [–s] [–a] [n]")
      write(&errout, "\twhere –s means to stop after each solution, ")
      write(&errout, "\t    –a means to show placement of every queen")
      write(&errout, "\t         while trying to find a solution")
      write(&errout, "\t  and  n is the size of the board (defaults to 8)")
      stop()
   end

   # Move cursor to x, y
   #
   procedure movexy (x, y)
      writes("\^[[", y, ";", x, "H")
      return
   end

   #
   # Clear the text screen
   #
   procedure clearscreen()
      writes("\^[[2J")
      return
   end

   #
   # Clear the rest of the line
   #
   procedure clearline()
      writes("\^[[2K")
      return
   end
```

PRINTING IN COLUMNS

This program arranges a number of data items from standard input, one per line, into multiple columns. Items are arranged in column-wise order, that is, the sequence runs down the first column, then down the second, and so forth.

If a null line appears in the input stream, it signifies a break in the list and the following line is taken as a title for subsequent data items. No title precedes the initial sequence of items.

The options are:

[–w line_width] [–s space_between] [–m min_width] [–t tab_width] [–x] [–h]

The parameters are:

line_width: the maximum width allowed for output lines (default: 80)

space_between: minimum number of blanks between items (default: 2)

min_width: minimum width for each entry (default: no minimum)

tab_width: tab width used to entab output lines; if zero is specified, no
                          tabs are used (default: no tabs)

The option –x causes items to be printed in row-wise order rather than column-wise order. The option –h produces help text.

```
# colm.icn
#
# author: Bob Alexander

link options

procedure main(arg)
  local usage, help, opt, rowwise, maxcols, space, minwidth, tabwidth
  local f, entries, entry

  #
  #  Define usage and help strings.
  #
  usage := "_
    Usage:\tcolm [–w line_width] [–s space_between] [–m min_width]\n_
      \t\t[–t tab_width] [–x] [file ...]\n_
        \tcolm –h  for help"
  help := "_
    \tline_width:\tthe maximum width allowed for output lines\n_
      \t\t\t(default: 80).\n_
```

```
            \tspace_between:\tminimum number of blanks between items\n_
              \t\t\t(default: 2).\n_
            \tmin_width:\tminimum width to be printed for each entry\n_
              \t\t\t(default: no minimum).\n_
            \ttab_width:\ttab width used to print output lines.\n_
              \t\t\t(default: no tabs).\n_
            \t-x\t\tprint items in row-wise order rather than\n_
              \t\t\tcolumn-wise."
    #
    # Process command line options.
    #
    opt := options(arg, "hxw+s+m+t+")
    if \opt["h"] then write(usage, "\n\n", help) & exit()
    rowwise := opt["x"]
    maxcols := \opt["w"] | 80
    space := \opt["s"] | 2
    minwidth := \opt["m"] | 0
    tabwidth := (\opt["t"] | 0) + 1
    if tabwidth = 1 then entab := 1
    if *arg = 0 then arg := [&input]
    #
    # Loop to process input files.
    #
    while f := get(arg) do {
      f := (&input === f) | open(f) | stop("Can't open ", f)
      #
      # Loop to process input groups (separated by empty lines).
      #
      repeat {
        entries := [ ]
        #
        # Loop to build a list of non-empty lines of an input file.
        #
        while entry := "" ~== read(f) do
          put(entries, entry)
        #
        # Now write the data in columns.
        #
        every write(entab(columnize(entries, maxcols, space,
          minwidth, rowwise), tabwidth))
        write("\n", read(f)) | break        # print the title line, if any
        }
      close(f)
      write()
      }
  end
```

```
procedure columnize(entries, maxcols, space, minwidth, rowwise)
  local mean, cols, lines, width, i, x, wid, extra, t, j
    #
    #  Process arguments — provide defaults.
    #
    /maxcols := 80              # max width of output lines
    /space := 2                 # min no. of blanks between columns
    /minwidth := 0              # min column width
    # rowwise: if nonnull, entries are listed in row–wise order rather than
    # columnwise
    #
    #  Starting with a trial number–of–columns that is guaranteed
    #  to be too wide, successively reduce the number until the
    #  items can be packed into the allotted width.
    #
    mean := 0
    every mean +:= *!entries
    mean := mean / (0 ~= *entries) | 1
    every cols := (maxcols + space) * 2 / (mean + space) to 1 by –1 do {
      lines := (*entries + cols – 1) / cols
      width := list(cols, minwidth)
      i := 0
      if /rowwise then {                  # if column–wise
        every x := !entries do {
          width[i / lines + 1] <:= *x + space
          i +:= 1
          }
        }
      else {                              # else row–wise
        every x := !entries do {
          width[i % cols + 1] <:= *x + space
          i +:= 1
          }
        }
      wid := 0
      every x := !width do wid +:= x
      if wid <= maxcols + space then break
      }
    #
    #  Now output the data in columns.
    #
    extra := (maxcols – wid) / (0 < cols – 1) | 0
    if /rowwise then {                          # if column–wise
      every i := 1 to lines do {
        t := ""
```

```
            every j := 0 to cols − 1 do
              t ||:= left(entries[i + j * lines], width[j + 1] + extra)
            suspend trim(t)
            }
        }
      else {                                      # else row–wise
        every i := 0 to lines − 1 do {
          t := ""
          every j := 1 to cols do
            t ||:= left(entries[j + i * cols], width[j] + extra)
          suspend trim(t)
          }
        }
      end
```

DIFFERENCE ENGINE

The procedure dif(stream, compare, eof, group) is a generator that produces a sequence of differences between an arbitrary number of input streams. Each result is returned as a list of diff_recs, one for each input stream, with each diff_rec containing a list of items that differ and their position in the input stream. The diff_rec type is declared as:

```
record diff_rec(pos, diffs)
```

For example, if two input streams are:

```
a b c d e f g h
a b d e f i j
```

the output sequence is:

```
[diff_rec(3, [c]), diff_rec(3, [ ])]
[diff_rec(7, [g, h]), diff_rec(6, [i, j])]
```

The procedure fails if there are no differences.

The first argument, stream, is a list of data objects that represent input streams from which dif() extracts its input "elements". Different types of objects produce different actions, as follows:

Type	Action
file	file is read to get records
co–expression	co-expression is activated to get records
list	records are obtained from the list using get()

diff_proc   a record type defined in dif() to allow a procedure (or procedures) supplied by the caller of dif() to be called to get records. diff_proc has two fields, the procedure to call and the argument with which to call it. Its declaration is:

record diff_proc(proc, arg)

The remaining arguments of dif() are optional. If compare is supplied, it is an item comparison procedure, which succeeds if "equal" but otherwise fails. The default is the identity comparison, === . The comparison must allow for the fact that the eof object (see next) might be an argument, and a pair of eofs must compare equally. If eof is supplied, it must be a value that is distinguishable from other values in the stream. The default is &null. If group is supplied, it is a procedure that is called with the current number of unmatched items as its argument. It must return the number of matching items required for file synchronization to occur. The default is the formula $trunc((2.0 * log(m)) + 2.0)$ where m is the number of unmatched items.

```
# dif.icn
#
# author: Bob Alexander

record diff_rec(pos, diffs)
record diff_proc(proc, arg)
record diff_file(stream, queue)

procedure dif(stream, compare, eof, group)
   local f, linenbr, line, difflist, gf, i, j, k, l, m, n, x, test, result, synclist
   local nsyncs, syncpoint
   #
   # Provide default arguments and initialize data.
   #
   /compare := proc("===", 2)
   /group := groupfactor
   f := [ ]
   every put(f, diff_file(!stream, [ ]))
   linenbr := list(*stream, 0)
   line := list(*stream)
   test := list(*stream)
   difflist := list(*stream)
   every !difflist := [ ]
   #
   # Loop to process all records of all input streams.
```

```
#
repeat {
  #
  # This is the "idle loop" where we spin until we find a discrepancy
  # among the data streams. A line is read from each stream, with a
  # check for eof on all streams. Then the line from the first
  # stream is compared to the lines from all the others.
  #
  repeat {
    every i := 1 to *stream do line[i] := diffread(f[i]) | eof
    if not (every x := !line do (x === eof) | break) then break break
    every !linenbr +:= 1
    if (every x := !line[2:0] do compare(x, line[1]) | break) then break
  }
  #
  # Aha! We have found a difference. Create a difference list,
  # one entry per stream, primed with the differing line we just found.
  #
  every i := 1 to *stream do difflist[i] := [line[i]]
  repeat {
    #
    # Add a new input line from each stream to the difference list.
    # Then build lists of the subset of different lines we need to
    # actually compare.
    #
    every i := 1 to *stream do
      put(difflist[i], diffread(f[i]) | eof)
    gf := group(*difflist[1])
    every i := 1 to *stream do
      test[i] := difflist[i][-gf:0]
    #
    # Create a "synchronization matrix", with a row and column for
    # each input stream. The entries will be initially &null, then
    # will be set to the synchronization position if sync is
    # achieved between the two streams. Another list is created to
    # keep track of how many syncs have been achieved for each
    # stream.
    #
    j := *difflist[1] - gf + 1
    synclist := list(*stream)
    every !synclist := list(*stream)
    every k := 1 to *stream do
      synclist[k][k] := j
    nsyncs := list(*stream, 1)
```

```
#
# Loop through positions to start comparing lines. This set of
# nested loops will be exited when a stream achieves sync with
# all other streams.
#
every i := 1 to j do {
  #
  # Loop through all streams.
  #
  every k := 1 to *stream do {
    #
    # Loop through all streams.
    #
    every l := 1 to *stream do {
      if /synclist[k][l] then {      # avoid unnecessary comparisons
        #
        # Compare items of the test list to the differences list
        # at all possible positions. If they compare, store the
        # current position in the sync matrix and bump the count
        # of streams sync'd to this stream. If all streams are in
        # sync, exit all loops but the outer one.
        #
        m := i − 1
        if not every n := 1 to gf do {
          if not compare(test[k][n], difflist[l][m +:= 1]) then break
          }
        then {
          synclist[k][l] := i      # store current position
          if (nsyncs[k] +:= 1) = *stream
          then break break break break
          }
        }
      }
    }
  }
#
# Prepare an output set. Since we have read the input streams past
# the point of synchronization, we must queue those lines before
# their  input streams.
#
synclist := synclist[k]
result := list(*stream)
every i := 1 to *stream do {
  j := synclist[i]
  while difflist[i][j −:= 1] === eof  # trim past eof
```

```
                    result[i] := diff_rec(linenbr[i], difflist[i][1:j + 1])
                    f[i].queue := difflist[i][synclist[i] + gf:0] ||| f[i].queue
                    linenbr[i] +:= synclist[i] + gf – 2
                    difflist[i] := [ ]
                    }
                suspend result
                }
        end


        #
        #  diffread() – – Read a line from an input stream.
        #
        procedure diffread(f)
            local x

            return get(f.queue) | case type(x := f.stream) of {
                "file"              : read(x)
                "co–expression"     : @x
                "diff_proc"         : x.proc(x.arg)
                "list"              : get(x)
                }
        end


        #
        #  groupfactor() – – Determine how many like lines we need to close
        #  off a group of differences. This is the default routine – – the
        #  caller may provide another.
        #
        procedure groupfactor(m)
            return integer(2.0 * log(m, 10) + 2.0)
        end
```

FILE DIFFERENCES

This program, which uses the difference engine from the preceding section, shows the differences between *n* files. It is invoked as

```
diffn file1 file2 ... filen
```

```
# diff.icn
#
# author: Bob Alexander

link dif
global f1, f2
```

```
record dfile(file, linenbr)
procedure main(arg)
  local f, i, files, drec, status

  #
  # Analyze command-lne arguments, open the files, and output some
  # initial display lines.
  #
  if *arg < 2 then stop("usage: diffn file file ...")
  f := list(*arg)
  every i := 1 to *arg do
    f[i] := dfile(open(arg[i]) | stop("Can't open ", arg[i]), 0)
  files := list(*arg)
  every i := 1 to *arg do {
    write("File ", i, ": ", arg[i])
    files[i] := diff_proc(myread, f[i])
    }
  #
  # Invoke dif() and display its generated results.
  #
  every drec := dif(files) do {
    status := "diffs"
    write("=================================")
    every i := 1 to *drec do {
      write("– – – – File ", i, ", ",
        (drec[i].pos > f[i].linenbr & "end of file") | "line " || drec[i].pos,
          " – – – – (", arg[i], ")")
      listrange(drec[i].diffs, drec[i].pos)
      }
    }
  if /status then write("==== Files match ====")
  return
end

# List a range of differing lines, each preceded by its line number.
#
procedure listrange(dlist, linenbr)
  local x

  every x := !dlist do {
    write(x)
    linenbr +:= 1
    }
  return
end
```

```
# Line-reading procedure to pass to dif().
#
procedure myread(x)
    return x.linenbr <- x.linenbr + 1 & read(x.file)
end
```

PARSING

This program illustrates the use of co-expressions to perform parsing. It converts programs containing expressions in infix form to prefix form. The grammar for programs is:

```
<prog>    ::=  <stmt> | <prog> ; <stmt>
<stmt>    ::=  <id> := <expr>
<expr>    ::=  <term> | <expr> <add_op> <term>
<term>    ::=  <factor> | <term> <mult_op> <factor>
<factor>  ::=  <id> | <integer> | ( <expr> )
```

There is a procedure that implements each of the productions. For example, <prog> is handled by **prog()**. The classes <id>, <integer>, <add_op>, and <mult_op> are recognized by the lexical analyzer. Tabs, blanks, and line terminators are treated as white space. Comments start with **#** and continue to the next line terminator.

For example, the input

```
x := (2 + 3) * 4;
y := x;
```

produces the output

```
x
2
3
+
4
*
:=
y
x
:=
```

The results of the co-expression **lex** come from two sequences of results joined by alternation. The first is the sequence of tokens from the input. The second is an endless sequence of end-of-file tokens. The tokens from the input are produced by a scanning expression. The subject of the scanning expression is the sequence of input lines. For each input line, **get_tok()** generates the tokens from the line. On an end of line, **get_tok()** fails and the next input line is generated for the subject.

```
# parse.icn
#
# author: Ken Walker

global lex                        # co-expression for lexical analyzer
global next_tok                   # next token from input

record token(type, string)

procedure main()
  lex := create (((!&input ? get_tok()) | |token("eof", "eof"))
  prog()
end


#
# get_tok is the main body of lexical analyzer
#
procedure get_tok()
  local tok

  repeat {                        # skip white space and comments
    tab(many(' \t'))
    if ="#" | pos(0) then fail

    if any(&letters) then         # determine token type
      tok := token("id", tab(many(&letters ++ '_')))
    else if any(&digits) then
      tok := token("integer", tab(many(&digits)))
    else case move(1) of {
      ";"        : tok := token("semi", ";")
      "("        : tok := token("lparen", "(")
      ")"        : tok := token("rparen", ")")
      ":"        : if ="=" then tok := token("assign", ":=")
                     else tok := token("colon", ":")
      "+"        : tok := token("add_op", "+")
      "-"        : tok := token("add_op", "-")
      "*"        : tok := token("mult_op", "*")
      "/"        : tok := token("mult_op", "/")
      default  : err("invalid character in input")
      }
    suspend tok
    }
end


#
# The procedures that follow make up the parser
#
```

main [(hand-annotation bracketing the main procedure)

→ (hand-annotation arrow pointing at procedure get_tok())

```
—→    procedure prog()
        next_tok := @lex
        stmt()
        while next_tok.type == "semi" do {
          next_tok := @lex
          stmt()
          }
        if next_tok.type ~== "eof" then
          err("eof expected")
      end

—→    procedure stmt()
        if next_tok.type ~== "id" then
          err("id expected")
        write(next_tok.string)
        if (@lex).type ~== "assign" then
          err(":= expected")
        next_tok := @lex
        expr()
        write(":=")
      end

=→    procedure expr()
        local op

        term()
        while next_tok.type == "add_op" do {
          op := next_tok.string
          next_tok := @lex
          term()
          write(op)
          }
      end

=→    procedure term()
        local op

        factor()
        while next_tok.type == "mult_op" do {
          op := next_tok.string
          next_tok := @lex
          factor()
          write(op)
          }
      end
```

```
procedure factor()
  case next_tok.type of {
    "id" | "integer": {
      write(next_tok.string)
      next_tok := @lex
      }
    "lparen": {
      next_tok := @lex
      expr()
      if next_tok.type ~== "rparen" then
        err(") expected")
      else
        next_tok := @lex
      }
    default:
      err("id or integer expected")
    }
end

procedure err(s)
  stop(" ** error ** ", s)
end
```

STRING REPRESENTATIONS OF OBJECTS

These procedures provide a way of storing any Icon value as a string and retrieving it. The procedure encode(x) converts x to a string s that can be converted back to x by decode(s). These procedures handle all kinds of values, including structures of arbitrary complexity and even loops. For "scalar" types — null, integer, real, cset, and string — decode(encode(x)) is identical to x except for possible precision loss for real numbers.

For structure types — lists, records, sets, and tables — decode(encode(x)) is, of course, not identical to x, but it has the same "shape" and its elements bear the same relationship to the original that they would if they were encoded and decoded individually. Not much can be done with files, procedures, and co-expressions except to preserve type and identification.

The encoding of strings and csets handles all characters in such a way that it is safe to write the encoding to a file and read it back. No particular effort was made to use an encoding of values that minimizes the length of the resulting string. Note, however, that there are no limits on the length of strings that Icon can read and write.

The encoding of a value consists of four parts: a tag, a length, a type code, and a string of the specified length that encodes the value itself.

The tag is omitted for scalar values that are self-defining. For other values, the tag serves as a unique identification. If such a value appears more than once, only its tag appears after the first encoding. Therefore, there is a type code that distinguishes a label for a previously encoded value from other encodings. Tags are strings of lowercase letters. Since the tag is followed by a digit that starts the length, the two can be distinguished.

The type code consists of a single letter taken from the first character of the type name, with lower- and uppercase letters used to avoid ambiguities.

Where a structure contains several elements, the encodings of the elements are concatenated. Note that the form of the encoding contains the information needed to separate consecutive elements.

Here are some examples of values and their encodings:

x	encode(x)
1	"1i1"
2.0	"3r2.0"
&null	"0n"
"\377"	"4s\\377"
'\376\377'	"8c\\376\\377"
procedure main	"a4pmain"
&main	"b0C"
[ ]	"c0L"
set()	"d0S"
table("a")	"e3T1sa"
L1 := ["hi", "there"]	"f11L2shi5sthere"

A loop is illustrated by

```
L2 := [ ]
put(L2, L2)
```

for which

x	encode(x)
L2	"g3L1lg"

```
# codeobj.icn
#
# author: Ralph Griswold

global outlab, inlab

record triple(type, value, tag)
```

```
# Encode an arbitrary value as a string.
#
procedure encode(x, level)
   local str, tag, Type
   static label

   initial label := create star(string(&lcase))

   if /level then outlab := table()            # table is global, but reset at
                                               # each root call.
   tag := ""
   Type := typecode(x)
   if Type == !"ri" then str := string(x)      # first the scalars
   else if Type == !"cs" then str := image(string(x))[2:-1]
   else if Type == "n" then str := ""
   else if Type == !"LSRTfpC" then             # next the structures and others
      if str := \outlab[x] then Type := "l"    # if the object has been
                                               # processed, use its label

      else {
         tag := outlab[x] := @label            # else make a label for it.
         str := ""
         if Type == !"LSRT" then {             # structures
            every str ||:= encode(             # generate and recurse
               case Type of {
                  !"LS" : !x                    # elements
                  "T"   : x[[ ]] | !sort(x, 3)  # default, then elements
                  "R"   : type(x) | !x          # type then elements
                  }
               , 1)                            # indicate internal call
            }
         else str ||:= case Type of {          # other things
            "f"  :  image(x)
            "C"  :  ""
            "p"  :  image(x) ? {               # might be record constructor
               tab(find("record constructor ") + *"record constructor ") |
                  tab(upto(' ') + 1)
               tab(0)
               }
            }
         }
      }
   else stop("unsupported type in encode: ", image(x))
   return tag || *str || Type || str
end
```

```
# Produce a one-letter code for the type.
#
procedure typecode(x)
   local code

   # Be careful of records and their constructors.

   image(x) ? {
      if ="record constructor " then return "p"
      else if ="record" then return "R"
      }
   code := type(x)
   if code == ("list" | "set" | "table" | "co-expression") then
      code := map(code, &lcase, &ucase)
   return code[1]

end


# Generate decoded results. At the top level, there is only one,
# but for structures the procedure is called recursively and generates
# the decoded elements.
#
procedure decode(s, level)
   local p

   if /level then inlab := table()   # global but reset
   every p := separ(s) do {
      suspend case p.type of {
         "l"     : inlab[p.value]        # label for an object
         "i"     : integer(p.value)
         "s"     : escape(p.value)
         "c"     : cset(escape(p.value))
         "r"     : real(p.value)
         "n"     : &null
         "L"     : delist(p.value, p.tag)
         "R"     : derecord(p.value, p.tag)
         "S"     : deset(p.value, p.tag)
         "T"     : detable(p.value, p.tag)
         "f"     : defile(p.value)
         "C"     : create &fail         # can't hurt much to fail
         "p"     : (proc(p.value) | stop("encoded procedure not found")) \ 1
         default: stop("unexpected type in decode: ", p.type)
         }
      }
end
```

```
#  Generate triples for the encoded values in concatenation.
#
procedure separ(s)
   local p, size

   while *s ~= 0 do {
     p := triple()
     s ?:= {
       p.tag := tab(many(&lcase))
       size := tab(many(&digits)) | break
       p.type := move(1)
       p.value := move(size)
       tab(0)
       }
     suspend p
     }
end


#  Decode a list. The newly constructed list is added to the table that
#  relates tags to structure values.
#
procedure delist(s, tag)
   local L

   inlab[tag] := L := [ ]                    # insert object for label
   every put(L, decode(s, 1))
   return L
end


#  Decode a set. Compare to delist() above.
#
procedure deset(s, tag)
   local S

   inlab[tag] := S := set()
   every insert(S, decode(s, 1))
   return S
end


#  Decode a record.
#
procedure derecord(s, tag)
   local R, C

   # A co–expression is used to control generation, since the record must
   # constructed before the fields are produced.

   C := create decode(s, 1)
```

```
        inlab[tag] := R := proc(@C)() | stop("error in decoding record")
        every !R := @C
        return R
      end


      #  Decode a table.
      #
      procedure detable(s, tag)
        local t, C
        # See derecord() above; it's the default value that motivates the use of
        # a co-expression here.

        C := create decode(s, 1)
        inlab[tag] := t := table(@C)
        while t[@C] := @C
        return t
      end


      #  Decode a file.
      #
      procedure defile(s)

        s := decode(s, 1)                      # result is an image of original file.
        return case s of {                     # files aren't so simple ...
          "&input"   : &input
          "&output"  : &output
          "&errout"  : &errout
          default    : s ? {
             ="file("                          # open for reading to play it safe
             open(tab(upto(')'))) | stop("cannot open encoded file")
             }
          }
      end


      #  Interpret escapes in string produced by image(s). There will be no
      #  octal or control escapes.
      procedure escape(s)
        local ns, c

        ns := ""
        s ? {
          while ns ||:= tab(upto('\\')) do {
            move(1)
            ns ||:= case c := move(1 | 0) of {
              "b"            :  "\b"
```

```
                    "d"          :  "\d"
                    "e"          :  "\e"
                    "f"          :  "\f"
                    "l"          :  "\n"
                    "n"          :  "\n"
                    "r"          :  "\r"
                    "t"          :  "\t"
                    "v"          :  "\v"
                    ""           .  ""
                    "\""         :  "\""
                    "\'"         :  "\'"
                    "x"          :  hexcode()
                    default      :  c
                    }
                }
            ns ||:= tab(0)
            }
        return ns
    end

    procedure hexcode()
        local i, s
        static cdigs
        initial cdigs := ~'0123456789ABCDEFabcdef'

        move(i := 2 | 1) ? s := tab(upto(cdigs) | 0)
        move(*s – i)

        return char("16r" || s)
    end

    procedure star(s)
        suspend "" | (star(s) || !s)
    end
```

RANDOMLY GENERATED SENTENCES

This program generates randomly selected strings ("sentences") from a grammar specified by the user. Grammars are basically context-free and resemble BNF in form, although there are a number of extensions.

The program works interactively, allowing the user to build, test, modify, and save grammars. Input to the program consists of various kinds of specifications, which can be intermixed. The two main kinds of specifications are:

- Productions that define nonterminal symbols in a syntax similar to the rewriting rules of BNF, with various alternatives consisting of the concatenation of nonterminal and terminal symbols.

- Generation specifications that cause the generation of a specified number of sentences from the language defined by a given nonterminal symbol. Grammar output specifications cause the definition of a specified nonterminal or the entire current grammar to be written to a given file. Source specifications cause subsequent input to be read from a specified file.

In addition, any line beginning with # is considered to be a comment, while any line beginning with = causes the rest of that line to be used subsequently as a prompt to the user whenever rsg is ready for input (there normally is no prompt). A line consisting of a single = stops prompting. A backslash at the end of a line causes the next line to be appended to form a longer line and the backslash is discarded.

Examples of productions are:

```
<expr>::=<term>|<term>+<expr>
<term>::=<elem>|<elem>*<term>
<elem>::=x|y|z|(<expr>)
```

Productions may occur in any order. The definition for a nonterminal symbol can be changed by specifying a new production for it.

There are a number of special devices to facilitate the definition of grammars, including eight predefined, built-in nonterminal symbols:

symbol	definition
<lb>	<
<rb>	>
<vb>	|
<nl>	line terminator
<>	empty string
<&lower>	any single lowercase letter
<&upper>	any single uppercase letter
<&letter>	any single letter
<&digit>	any single digit

In addition, if the string between a < and a > begins and ends with a single quotation mark, it stands for any single character between the quotation marks. For example,

```
<'xyz'>
```

is equivalent to

```
x|y|z
```

A generation specification consists of a nonterminal symbol followed by a nonnegative integer. An example is

```
<expr>10
```

which specifies the generation of 10 <expr>s. If the integer is omitted, it is assumed to be 1. Generated sentences are written to standard output.

A grammar output specification consists of a nonterminal symbol, followed by –>, followed by a file name. Such a specification causes the current definition of the nonterminal symbol to be written to the given file. If the file is omitted, standard output is assumed. If the nonterminal symbol is omitted, the entire grammar is written out. Thus,

```
–>
```

causes the entire grammar to be written to standard output.

A source specification consists of @ followed by a file name. Subsequent input is read from that file.

When an end of file is encountered, input reverts to the previous file. Input files can be nested.

The following options are available:

–s *n* Set the seed for random generation to n. The default seed is 0.

–l *n* Terminate generation if the number of symbols remaining to be processed exceeds n. The default limit is 1,000.

–t   Trace the generation of sentences. Trace output goes to standard error output.

Syntactically erroneous input lines are noted but are otherwise ignored. Specifications for a file that cannot be opened are noted and treated as erroneous.

If an undefined nonterminal symbol is encountered during generation, an error message that identifies the undefined symbol is produced, followed by the partial sentence generated up to that point. Exceeding the limit of symbols remaining to be generated as specified by the –l option is handled similarly.

Generation may fail to terminate because of a loop in the rewriting rules or, more seriously, because of the progressive accumulation of nonterminal symbols. The latter problem can be identified by using the –t option and controlled by using the –l option. The problem often can be circumvented by duplicating alternatives that lead to fewer rather than more nonterminal symbols. For example, changing

        `<term>::=<elem>|<elem>*<term>`

to

        `<term>::=<elem>|<elem>|<elem>*<term>`

increases the probability of selecting `<elem>` from 1/2 to 2/3.

```
# rsg.icn
#
# author: Ralph Griswold

link options

global defs, ifile, in, limit, prompt, tswitch

record nonterm(name)
record charset(chars)

procedure main(arg)
  local line, plist, s, opts
                                        # procedures to try
  plist := [define, generate, grammar, source, comment, prompter, error]
  defs := table()                       # table of definitions
  defs["lb"] := [["<"]]                 # built-in definitions
  defs["rb"] := [[">"]]
  defs["vb"] := [["|"]]
  defs["nl"] := [["\n"]]
  defs[""] := [[""]]
  defs["&lower"] := [[charset(&lcase)]]
  defs["&upper"] := [[charset(&ucase)]]
  defs["&letter"] := [[charset(&letters)]]
  defs["&digit"] := [[charset(&digits)]]

  opts := options(arg, "tl+s+")
  limit := \opts["l"] | 1000
  tswitch := \opts["t"]
  &random := \opts["s"]
  ifile := [&input]                     # stack of input files
  prompt := ""
  while in := pop(ifile) do {           # process all files
    repeat {
      if *prompt ~= 0 then writes(prompt)
      line := read(in) | break
```

```
            while line[-1] == "\\" do line := line[1:-1] || read(in) | break
            (!plist)(line)
            }
         close(in)
         }
end

#  process alternatives
#
procedure alts(defn)
   local alist

   alist := [ ]
   defn ? repeat {
      put(alist, syms(tab(upto('|') | 0)))
      move(1) | break
      }
   return alist
end

#  look for comment
#
procedure comment(line)
   if line[1] == "#" then return
end

#  look for definition
#
procedure define(line)
   return line ?
      defs[(="<", tab(find(">::=")))] := (move(4), alts(tab(0)))
end

#  define nonterminal
#
procedure defnon(sym)
   local chars, name

   if sym ? {
      ="\"" &
      chars := cset(tab(-1)) &
      ="\""
      }
   then return charset(chars)
   else return nonterm(sym)
end
```

```
# note erroneous input line
#
procedure error(line)
  write("*** erroneous line: ", line)
  return
end


# generate sentences
#
procedure gener(goal)
  local pending, symbol

  pending := [nonterm(goal)]
  while symbol := get(pending) do {
    if \tswitch then
      write(&errout, symimage(symbol), listimage(pending))
    case type(symbol) of {
      "string"  :   writes(symbol)
      "charset" :   writes(?symbol.chars)
      "nonterm" :   {
        pending := ?\defs[symbol.name] ||| pending | {
          write(&errout, "*** undefined nonterminal: <",
            symbol.name, ">")
          break
          }
        if *pending > \limit then {
          write(&errout, "*** excessive symbols remaining")
          break
          }
        }
      }
    }
  write()
end

# look for generation specification
#
procedure generate(line)
  local goal, count

  if line ? {
    ="<" &
    goal := tab(upto('>')) \ 1 &
    move(1) &
    count := (pos(0) & 1) | integer(tab(0))
    }
```

```
      then {
        every 1 to count do
          gener(goal)
        return
        }
      else fail
end

#  get right hand side of production
#
procedure getrhs(L)
  local rhs

  rhs := ""
  every rhs ||:= listimage(!L) || "|"
  return rhs[1:-1]
end

#  look for request to write out grammar
#
procedure grammar(line)
  local file, out, name

  if line ? {
    name := tab(find("->")) &
    move(2) &
    file := tab(0) &
    out := if *file = 0 then &output else {
      open(file, "w") | {
        write(&errout, "*** cannot open ", file)
        fail
        }
      }
    }
  then {
    (*name = 0) | (name[1] == "<" & name[-1] == ">") | fail
    pwrite(name, out)
    if *file ~= 0 then close(out)
    return
    }
  else fail
end

#  produce image of list of grammar symbols
#
procedure listimage(L)
  local s, x
```

```
      s := ""
      every x := !L do
        s ||:= symimage(x)
      return s
   end
   #  look for new prompt symbol
   #
   procedure prompter(line)
      if line[1] == "=" then {
         prompt := line[2:0]
         return
         }
   end

   #  write out grammar
   #
   procedure pwrite(name, ofile)
      local nt, L
      static builtin

      initial builtin := ["lb", "rb", "vb", "nl", "", "&lcase", "&ucase", "&digit"]

      if *name = 0 then {
         L := sort(defs, 3)
         while nt := get(L) do {
            if nt == !builtin then {
               get(L)
               next
               }
            write(ofile, "<", nt, ">::=", getrhs(get(L)))
            }
         }
      else write(ofile, name, "::=", getrhs(\defs[name[2:-1]])) |
         write("*** undefined nonterminal: ", name)
   end

   #  look for file with input
   #

   procedure source(line)
      local file, new

      return line ? {
         if ="@" then {
            new := open(file := tab(0)) | {
               write(&errout, "*** cannot open ", file)
               fail
               }
```

```
            push(ifile, in) &
            in := new
            return
            }
         }
    end

    #  produce string image of grammar symbol
    #
    procedure symimage(x)
      return case type(x) of {
        "string"      : x
        "nonterm"     : "<" || x.name || ">"
        "charset"     : "<' " || x.chars || " '>"
        }
    end

    #  process the symbols in an alternative
    #
    procedure syms(alt)
      local slist
      static nonbrack

      initial nonbrack := ~'<'

      slist := [ ]
      alt ? {
        while put(slist, tab(many(nonbrack)) |
          defnon(2(="<", tab(upto('>')), move(1))))
          }
      return slist
    end
```

G

Solutions to Selected Exercises

The following solutions use only those features of Icon that are described up to the point of the corresponding exercise. Better solutions can be formulated in some cases by using additional features.

Exercise 1.1

```
procedure locate(s)
   count := 0
   lineno := 0
   while line := read() do {
      lineno := lineno + 1
      if find(s, line) then {
         write(lineno, ": ", line)
         count := count + 1
         }
      }
   if count > 0 then return count else fail
end
```

Exercise 2.1

```
procedure main()
  while line := read()
  write(line)                    # assumes input not empty
end
```

Exercise 2.2

```
procedure main()
  while write(read()) do
    read() | break
end
```

Exercise 2.3

```
procedure first(i)
  every 1 to i do
    write(read()) | break
end
```

Exercise 2.7

```
procedure exor(s1, s2)
  while line := read() do
    if find(s1, line) then {
      if not find(s2, line) then suspend line
      }
    else if find(s2, line) then suspend line
end
```

The braces around the inner if-then expression are needed to prevent the subsequent else clause from grouping incorrectly.

Exercise 3.2

```
procedure swords(s)
  while line := read() do
    line ? {
      while tab(upto(&letters)) do {
        word := tab(many(&letters))
        if word ? find(s) then suspend word
      }
    }
end
```

Exercise 3.5

```
procedure pre(s, c)
  suspend (s ? tab(upto(c)))
end
```

Exercise 3.6

```
procedure strip(s)
  while s ? {
    ="(" &
    t := tab(bal(')')) &
    pos(-1) &
    s := t
    }
  return s
end
```

Exercise 4.1

```
procedure main()
  chars := ''                   # start with empty cset
  while chars ++:= read()
  write(*chars)
end
```

Exercise 4.3

```
procedure space(s)
  s1 := ""
  s ? {
    while s1 ||:= move(1) || " "
    }
  return s1[1:-1]
end
```

Exercise 4.4

```
procedure rotate(s, i)
  if i <= 0 then i +:= *s
  return s[i + 1:0] || s[1:i + 1]
end
```

Exercise 4.8

```
procedure delete(s, c)
  result := ""                    # start with an empty string
  s ? {
    while result ||:= tab(upto(c)) do
      tab(many(c))
    result ||:= tab(0)            # append the rest of the string
    }
  return result
end
```

Exercise 4.14

```
procedure enrepl(s)
  s1 := ""
  s ? while c := move(1) do {
    i := 1 + (*tab(many(c)) | 0)
    if i > 4 then s1 ||:= c || "(" || i || ")"
    else s1 ||:= repl(c, i)
    }
  return s1
end
```

Exercise 4.15

```
procedure derepl(s)
  s1 := ""
  s ? {
    while s1 ||:= tab(upto('(') − 1) do {
      c := move(1)
      move(1)
      s1 ||:= repl(c, tab(upto(')')))
      move(1)
      }
    s1 ||:= tab(0)
    }
  return s1
end
```

Exercise 4.16

```
procedure allbal(s, c)
  s ? repeat {
    suspend "" ~== tab(bal(c))
    move(1) | break
    }
end
```

Exercise 5.1b

```
procedure main()
  sum := 0.0
  count := 0
  while sum +:= read() do
    count +:= 1
  write(sum / count)
end
```

Exercise 5.3

```
procedure fact(i)
  j := 1
  every  j *:= (i to 2 by −1)
  return j
end
```

Exercise 6.2

```
procedure main()
  lines := [ ]
  while push(lines, read())
  while write(get(lines))
end
```

This method is impractical for a large file, since the entire file must be stored in memory before any line is written.

Exercise 6.6

```
procedure Default(T)
  return T[ [ ] ]
end
```

Since [ ] is a newly created list, it cannot be a key that already is in the table.

Exercise 6.8

```
record complex(rpart, ipart)

# Assume complex numbers are represented by strings such as
# "2.0+3.5i" and "-3.7-1.3i".

procedure strcpx(s)          # convert string to complex number
  i := upto('+-', s, 2)
  return complex(+s[1:i], +s[i:-1])
end

procedure cpxstr(x)          # convert complex number to string
  if x.ipart < 0 then return x.rpart || x.ipart || "i"
  else return x.rpart || "+" || x.ipart || "i"
end

procedure cpxadd(x1, x2)     # add two complex numbers
  return complex(x1.rpart + x2.rpart,x1.ipart + x2.ipart)
end

procedure cpxsub(x1, x2)     # subtract two complex numbers
  return complex(x1.rpart - x2.rpart, x1.ipart - x2.ipart)
end

procedure cpxmul(x1, x2)     # multiply two complex numbers
  return complex(x1.rpart * x2.rpart - x1.ipart * x2.ipart,
    x1.rpart * x2.ipart + x1.ipart * x2.rpart)
end

procedure cpxdiv(x1, x2)     # divide two complex numbers
  denom := x2.rpart ^ 2 + x2.ipart ^ 2
  return complex((x1.rpart * x2.rpart + x1.ipart * x2.ipart) /
    denom, (x1.ipart * x2.rpart - x1.rpart * x2.ipart) / denom)
end
```

Exercise 7.4

```
procedure genpos(L, x)
  every i := 1 to *L do
  if L[i] === x then suspend i
end
```

Exercise 7.5

```
procedure geneq(L1, L2)
  suspend !L1 === !L2
end
```

Exercise 8.4

```
procedure acker(i, j)
  if i = 0 then return j + 1
  if j = 0 then return acker(i − 1, 1)
  return acker(i − 1, acker(i, j − 1))
end
```

Exercise 8.7

In order to tabulate Ackermann's function, the pair of arguments must be saved. This is accomplished in the following procedure by forming a string for the argument pair.

```
procedure acker(i, j)
  local args, k
  static ackermem

  initial ackermem := table(0)

  args := i || "," || j
  if (k := ackermem[args]) > 0 then return k
  if i = 0 then return ackermem[args] := j + 1
  if j = 0 then return ackermem[args] := acker(i − 1, 1)
  return ackermem[args] := acker(i − 1, acker(i, j − 1))
end
```

Exercise 8.8

```
procedure qseq()
  local i, qmem
  qmem := table()

  suspend qmem[1 | 2] := 1
  i := 2
  repeat suspend qmem[i +:= 1] :=
    qmem[i − qmem[i − 1]] + qmem[i − qmem[i − 2]]
end
```

Exercise 9.3

```
procedure Odd(L)            # called as Odd{expr}
  local C

  C := L[1]
  suspend |@C do @C
end
```

Exercise 9.4

```
procedure Repalt(L)         # called as Repalt{expr}
  local x

  repeat {
    while x := @L[1] do suspend x
    if *L[1] = 0 then fail       # termination condition
    L[1] := ^L[1]
    }
end
```

Exercise 9.5

```
procedure Limit(L)          # called as Limit{expr1, expr2}
  local i, x

  while i := @L[2] do {          # expr2 can generate results!
    every 1 to i do
      if x := @L[1] then suspend x
      else break
    L[1] := ^L[1]
    }
end
```

Exercise 10.2

```
procedure hexcvt(s)
  return integer("16r" || s)
end
```

Exercise 12.3

In order to keep track of the depth of recursion in Ackermann's function, some method is needed to differentiate between recursive calls of Ackermann's function and other calls. It is not safe to use &level, since Ackermann's function might be called from any level. The identifier level is used here to keep the computation of the level local to the function.

```
procedure ackertrace(i, j)
   static level
   local result

   initial level := 0

   write(repl("x", level +:= 1))
   if i = 0 then result := j + 1
   else if j = 0 then result := ackertrace(i – 1, 1)
   else result := ackertrace(i – 1, ackertrace(i, j – 1))
   level –:= 1
   return result
end
```

Exercise 12.5

```
procedure pause(i)
   local j

   j := &time
   while (&time – j) < i
   return
end
```

Exercise 13.7

```
procedure gensubstr(s)
   local i

   suspend s[(i := 1 to *s):((i + 1) to (*s + 1))]
end
```

Exercise 14.5

```
procedure limit(p, i)
  local j

  j := &pos
  suspend p() \ i
  &pos := j
end
```

Exercise 14.7

```
procedure arbno(L[ ])
  suspend "" | (L[1]!L[2:0] || arbno!L)
end
```

Exercise 14.10

```
procedure main()
  while writes(line := read()) do
    if line ? (ABCD("", "", "", "") & pos(0))
    then write(" accepted") else write(" rejected")
end

procedure ABCD(A, B, C, D)
  suspend (=A || =B || =C || =D) |
    (="a" || ABCD(A, "b" || B, C || "c", D) || ="d")
end
```

Exercise 15.3

```
procedure depth(rtree)
  local count

  count := 0
  every count <:= 1 + depth(\(rtree.lptr | \rtree.rptr))
  return count
end
```

Exercise 15.5

```
procedure rcopy(rtree)
  local R

  R := node(rtree.value)
  R.lptr := rcopy(\rtree.lptr)
  R.rptr := rcopy(\rtree.rptr)
  return R
end
```

Exercise 15.17

```
procedure nodecount(R, counted)
  /counted := set()
  insert(counted, R)
  every nodecount(\(R.lptr | R.rptr), counted)
  return *counted
end
```

Exercise 16.4

```
procedure uscore(s)
  static labels, trans, max

  initial {
    labels := "1"
    trans := "_\b1"
    max := *labels
    trans := uscore(string(&cset - - '\b_'))
    labels := string(&cset - - '\b_')
    max := *labels
    }

  if *s <= max then
    return map(left(trans, 3 * *s), left(labels, *s), s)
  else return uscore(left(s, *s - max)) ||
    map(trans, labels, right(s, max))
end
```

Exercise 16.5

```
procedure boldface(s)
  local c
  static labels, trans, max

  initial {
    labels := "1"
    trans := "1\b1\b1\b1\b1"
    max := *labels
    trans := boldface(string(&cset − − '\b'))
    labels := string(&cset − − '\b')
    max := *labels
    }

  if *s <= max then
    return map(left(trans,9 * *s), left(labels, *s), s)
  else return boldface(left(s, *s − max)) ||
    map(trans, labels, right(s, max))
end
```

Exercise 17.2

```
procedure large(s)
  s ? {
    tab(any('+ −'))
    if tab(many(&digits)) & pos(0) then return s
    else fail
    }
end
```

Exercise 17.3

```
procedure cdigit(s)
  local s1

  s1 := ""
  s ? {
    tab(0)
    while s1 := "," || move(-3) || s1
    if pos(1) then s1 := s1[2:0]
    else s1 := tab(1) || s1
    }
  return s1
end
```

An interesting alternative solution can be formulated using mapping techniques.

Exercise 17.9

```
procedure palseq(i)
  while i ~== reverse(i) do {
    suspend i
    i := add(i, reverse(i))
    }
  return i
end
```

If built-in large-integer arithmetic is available,

```
i := add(i, reverse(i))
```

can be replaced by

```
i +:= reverse(i)
```

References

1. The Bright Forest Company, *The ProIcon Programming Language for Apple Macintosh Computers*. Tucson, Arizona, 1989.

2. Manna, Zohar, *Mathematical Theory of Computation*. New York: McGraw-Hill Book Company, 1974.

3. Bird, R. S., "Tabulation Techniques for Recursive Programs", *Computer Surveys*, 12, no. 4 (1980), 403-417.

4. Hofstadter, D. R., *Gödel, Escher, Bach: An Eternal Golden Braid*. New York: Basic Books, 1979.

5. Knuth, Donald E., *The Art of Computer Programming, Volume I*. Reading, Massachusetts: Addison-Wesley Publishing Company, Inc., 1968.

6. Marlin, Christopher D., *Coroutines: A Programming Methodology, a Language Design, and an Implementation*, New York: Springer-Verlag, 1980.

7. Griswold, Ralph E. and Griswold, Madge T. , *The Implementation of the Icon Programming Language*, Princeton, New Jersey: Princeton University Press, 1986.

8. Griswold, Ralph E., *Icon-C Interfaces*. Technical Report TR90-8, Department of Computer Science, The University of Arizona, Tucson, Arizona, 1990.

9. Dahl, O.-J., E. W. Dijkstra and C. A. R. Hoare, *Structured Programming*. New York: Academic Press, 1972.

10. Gimpel, J. F., *Algorithms in SNOBOL4*. New York: John Wiley & Sons, 1976.

11. Wetherell, C. S., "Probabilistic Languages: A Review and Some Open Questions", *Computer Surveys*, 12, no. 4 (1980), pp. 361-379.

12. Griswold, Ralph E., *The Icon Program Library*. Technical Report TR90-7, Department of Computer Science, The University of Arizona, Tucson, Arizona, 1990.

Index

Program Material for the Icon Programming Language

The Icon Project at The University of Arizona distributes public-domain implementations of the Icon programming language for many computers and operating systems, including the Amiga, the Atari ST, the Macintosh, MS-DOS, MVS, OS/2, UNIX, VAX/VMS, and VM/CMS. The Icon Project also distributes a library of Icon programs.

The cost of this program material for Icon varies from $15 to $50, depending on the system and distribution media. For information, contact:

> The Icon Project
> Department of Computer Science
> Gould-Simpson Building
> The University of Arizona
> Tucson, AZ   85721
>
> (602) 621-4049

An enhanced version of Icon for the Macintosh, called ProIcon, is marketed by:

> Catspaw, Inc.
> P.O. Box 1123
> Salida, CO   81201-1123
>
> (719) 539-3884